"Highfield locates atonement theology in the broad Christus Victor tradition but more fully explores the patristic and biblical ideas of recapitulation through representation (the second Adam motif). He attends to the biblical and patristic themes that are more characteristic of Eastern Orthodoxy. In this way, Highfield offers a path forward that blends both Western and Eastern theologies, and by this retains the best of the Western tradition while reorienting atonement theology toward the main thing: *theosis* through recapitulation. Thus, it is, at once, eminently biblical, fresh, and integrative. This is a compelling theological account of atonement in the context of historic Christian tradition."

—**John Mark Hicks**, Lipscomb University

"Another book on the atonement? This one, we certainly need! Ron Highfield weaves theological arguments and biblical sensibilities into a message of salvation in Jesus that is faithful to the scriptural gospel and aimed at engaging our contemporaries as good news. *The New Adam* sets the question of the Christian doctrine of salvation fully in conversation with the human condition, in its misery and hope, with the long history of Christian sense-making of Jesus's death, and with the biblical narrative. The result is a bold and welcome proposal that depicts Jesus's story as the true human story, Israel's story reworked, and our story remade."

—**Joel B. Green**, Fuller Theological Seminary

"This compelling book is Christian theology at its best: a work that both helps the church clarify its message and encourages the church to share this message as the good news it is. Highfield offers a sweeping primer for understanding the meaning of God's work in Jesus Christ—working carefully with biblical texts and church history. If I could place a copy in the hands of every Christian leader, I would!"

—**Mike Cope**, Pepperdine University

"I have read countless books and articles on the atonement over the years and I can say without hesitation that *A New Adam* is far and away the best I've seen. Understanding Christ's atoning work can be very confusing, but Highfield brings light into our gloom, pointing a way forward to a viable ancient-future faith. If I had to suggest one book for thinking people to read on the atonement, it would be this one. Highly recommended!"

—**Robin A. Parry**, Anglican priest and author of *The Evangelical Universalist*

The New Adam

The New Adam

What the Early Church Can Teach Evangelicals
(and Liberals) about the Atonement

Ron Highfield

FOREWORD BY
Thomas H. Olbricht

 CASCADE *Books* · Eugene, Oregon

THE NEW ADAM
What the Early Church Can Teach Evangelicals (and Liberals)
about the Atonement

Cascade Books
An Imprint of Wipf and Stock Publishers
199 W. 8th Ave., Suite 3
Eugene, OR 97401

www.wipfandstock.com

PAPERBACK ISBN: 978-1-7252-7432-7
HARDCOVER ISBN: 978-1-7252-7433-4
EBOOK ISBN: 978-1-7252-7434-1

Cataloguing-in-Publication data:

Names: Highfield, Ron, author. | Olbricht, Thomas H., foreword.

Title: The new Adam : what the early church can teach evangelicals
(and liberals) about the atonement / by Ron Highfield ; foreword by Thomas H.
Olbricht.

Description: Eugene, OR: Cascade Books, 2021 | Includes bibliographical refer-
ences and index.

Identifiers: ISBN 978-1-7252-7432-7 (paperback) | ISBN 978-1-7252-7433-4
(hardcover) | ISBN 978-1-7252-7434-1 (ebook)

Subjects: LCSH: Atonement—History of doctrines—Early church, ca. 30–600
| Atonement | Atonement—History of doctrines | Salvation—History of doc-
trines—Early church, ca. 30–600 | Salvation

Classification: BT263 H54 2021 (print) | BT263 (ebook)

04/21/21

With appreciation to

Jim Howard

Harold Hazelip

Thomas H. Olbricht

for introducing me to biblical, historical,
and systematic theology.

Therefore, if anyone is in Christ, the new creation has come. The old has gone, the new is here! All this is from God, who reconciled us to himself through Christ and gave us the ministry of reconciliation: that God was reconciling the world to himself in Christ, not counting people's sins against them.

—2 CORINTHIANS 5:17–19

. . . but following the only true and steadfast Teacher, the Word of God, our Lord Jesus Christ, who did, through His transcendent love, become what we are, that He might bring us to be even what He is Himself.

—IRENAEUS OF LYON[1]

Death used to be strong and terrible, but now, since the sojourn of the Savior and the death and resurrection of His body, it is despised; and obviously it is by the very Christ Who mounted on the cross that it has been destroyed and vanquished finally. When the sun rises after the night and the whole world is lit up by it, nobody doubts that it is the sun which has thus shed its light everywhere and driven away the dark.

—ATHANASIUS[2]

1. *AH* 5 (*ANF* 1:526).
2. *St. Athanasius On the Incarnation*, 59.

Contents

Foreword

Ron Highfield, author of *The New Adam,* is one of the foremost theologians of the Stone-Campbell Restoration Movement over its more than two-hundred-year history. His wide-ranging theological reflection in this volume demonstrates that he is conversant in the theology of the early church (patristics) as well as medieval, Reformation (especially the Calvinistic Reformed), continental, and North American liberalism, and neo-orthodoxy. His explorations include classical and recent Calvinistic and Neo-evangelical North American theological polemicists. His reflections demonstrate grounds for the confidence that he has left no stone unturned in his probing of this weighty topic.

Not only has Highfield digested the theological deliberations of the major Christian thinkers through the ages, he demonstrates familiarity with recent New Testament studies, especially the contributions of N. T. Wright, the world-renowned British scholar.

Highfield has taught theology at Pepperdine University for more than thirty years and has published other major theological volumes, including *Barth and Rahner in Dialogue* (Peter Lang, 1989), *Great is the Lord* (Eerdmans, 2008), *God, Freedom and Human Dignity* (Intervarsity, 2013), and *The Faithful Creator* (Intervarsity, 2015). He also contributed to *Four Views on Providence* (Zondervan, 2011). Highfield believes that while theology has an imperative explanatory function, it should in addition achieve a practical, existential impact. In his exemplary book *Great is the Lord*, Highfield declared that it is not enough to establish a consummate intellectual concept of God. To do so is to characterize God as an object, such as the breathtaking Mount Everest. Rather, God is the ultimate personal reality who is to be praised and not simply comprehended as a cosmic It. In *The*

ix

New Adam, Highfield aspires to introduce a noteworthy rationale in respect to the atonement so as to challenge postmodernists to an existential appreciation and acceptance of a fundamental biblical perspective regarding what Jesus accomplished by his death and resurrection. His committed purpose is much more than simply to enlighten the intellectually curious. To achieve these ends, he begins this book with reflections on the human condition, especially explicating the views of the French intellectual Blaise Pascal and the Danish author Søren Kierkegaard. He continues with an examination of believers within the Scriptures. As a final outcome, Highfield hopes the perspective he advances will motivate contemporary readers to embrace this account of God's amazing grace. Highfield's aim is apologetic, not so much for non-believers, but as a platform for those who are involved in telling the old, old story of Jesus and his love.

Highfield through the years has maintained a nuanced commitment to historical Christianity. He overflows the boundaries of evangelical or neo-evangelical theology. On occasion he recognizes common predilections with the evangelicals, but he also often finds himself compelled to critique some of their entrenched views. Ron can best be located as a restorationist in theology. The restorationist outlook, propounded by the early Alexander Campbell, has attained a new footing in a coterie of philosophers assembled by Caleb Clanton.[1] As to his own approach, Highfield commenced under the influence especially of Karl Barth and therefore his methodology had affinity with dialectical theology. When Highfield dissects major theological conundrums, however, one concludes that his method is analytical theology. This in part reflects, I think, Highfield's early academic training in math and natural science.[2]

Finally, I want to comment on Highfield's conclusion regarding the biblical doctrine of the atonement with which I heartily agree. He has done far more than I to place the doctrine in the context of the history of Christian theology and concluded with a much more nuanced argument, so I will present only a cursory version of how I arrived at the same understanding. When I taught the atonement in theology classes, I utilized Gustaf Aulèn's three major claims on the atonement. I told my students that metaphors are endemic in all these perspectives and the question to be raised is whether

1. J. Caleb Clanton, ed., *Restoration Philosophy: New Philosophical Engagements with the Stone-Campbell Tradition* (Knoxville: The University of Tennessee Press, 2019).

2. Nicholas Wolterstorff, "How Philosophical Theology Became Possible within the Analytic Tradition of Philosophy," in A*nalytic Theology: New Essays in the Philosophy of Theology*, edited by Oliver Crisp and Michael C. Rea (New York: Oxford University Press, 2009).

the metaphor puts the focus of Christ's death and resurrection at the same point as does the biblical account.

The first Aulén perspective was designated the classical approach. According to the classical argument, Christ approached Satan, the jailor for humankind. He bartered an arrangement to release humankind and he would himself submit to Satan's incarceration. The dominance of Satan, however, was not adequate to restrain Christ. He broke the bonds of prison and set the captives free. The downside of this metaphor is that Satan is assigned a more central role than he ever achieved in the biblical texts.

The second approach was that of John Calvin (1509–64), who argued that God's justice was at stake. Christ by his death satisfied the justice of God. The basic metaphor is a courtroom event. Humans are declared guilty by a prosecuting attorney. A bailiff prevents their release. Humans are judged guilty as charged. As the sentence is being administered Christ steps forward and volunteers to plead guilty in their stead. God could not be just and clear the guilty based on any grounds within himself. Without the death of Christ human guilt was unforgiveable. The penal satisfaction view has had a long lasting life and, as Highfield documents, is argued vociferously by current Calvinists. It is true that some sections in Scripture reflect a court case metaphor of God against humans, but that is only a minor metaphor. For these reasons this position also fails as a biblical doctrine of the atonement.

The third perspective is that of Peter Abelard of France (1079–1142). His metaphor was drawn from human experience and love relationships. The significance of the death and resurrection of Christ was that it provided a moral example of God's great love. The death and resurrection of Jesus, however, made no ontological—that is, fundamental—change in reality. The focus was on love as an attractive model; as an experience apart from an impact upon the cosmos through the action of the Father, Son, and Holy Spirit. So the moral metaphor too is weighed in the balance and found wanting.

I therefore appreciate the deep theological insight in Highfield's presentation and defense of a biblical vision of the atonement. His declaration cuts to the heart of the matter. It is based upon the overarching covenant love analogy (metaphor) that is manifest as a cohesive cord from Genesis to Revelation.

> Christ embodies and manifests the love, justice, mercy, grace, and forgiveness of God in a way that makes them effective in the human sphere. The death of Christ does not evoke, merit, or purchase God's forgiveness. God needs no cause, motive, or justification to love. Nor does Christ's death satisfy God's retributive justice. To the contrary, it manifests unambiguously

God's eternal, essential, and reliable love. Christ reveals for us in
time what God is in himself in eternity: creative, self-bestowing
love. Jesus's love, forgiveness, humiliation, and suffering in his
humanity in time correspond to God's eternal love. Not only
is the heart of God revealed in the event of Jesus's death; it is
revealed in the manner of his death (Phil 2:8)

How does Highfield arrive at this challenging conclusion? That is what
this book is all about. Everyone involved in sharing the biblical faith needs
to put this tome on their books-to-read list and pass it on to readers hungry
for an authentic gospel message respecting the atonement.

Thomas H. Olbricht
Distinguished Professor Emeritus of Religion
Pepperdine University

Acknowledgements

I WOULD LIKE TO express my gratitude to Seaver College, Pepperdine University, for granting me a sabbatical leave in 2017 to work on this project. I want also to acknowledge Jim Gash, President, Rick Marrs, Provost, Michael Feltner, Dean of Seaver College, and Dan Rodriguez, Chair of the Religion and Philosophy Division for supporting and encouraging my work in teaching and research.

Abbreviations

AH	*Against Heresies*
ANET	*Ancient Near Eastern Texts Relating to the Old Testament*
ANF	*Ante-Nicene Fathers*
CC	*Creeds of Christendom*
CV	*Communio Viatorum*
EQ	*Evangelical Quarterly*
IET	*Institutes of Elenctic Theology*
JSNT	*Journal for the Study of the New Testament*
JTI	*Journal of Theological Interpretation*
JTS	*Journal of Theological Studies*
JVG	*Jesus and the Victory of God*
NIDNT	*New International Dictionary of New Testament Theology*
NPNF1	*Nicene-Post Nicene Fathers, Series 1*
NPNF2	*Nicene-Post Nicene Fathers, Series 2*
NTPG	*The New Testament and the People of God*
OCD	*Oxford Classical Dictionary*
ODCC	*Oxford Dictionary of the Christian Church*
PFG	*Paul and the Faithfulness of God*

PQ	*Philosophical Quarterly*
PSA	*Penal Substitutionary Atonement*
RSG	*Resurrection of the Son of God*
TDNT	*Theological Dictionary of the New Testament*
TI	*Theological Investigations*
TS	*Theological Studies*
WTJ	*Westminster Theological Journal*
WW	*Word & World*

Introduction

FRIENDS SOMETIMES ASK HOW long it takes to write a book. "A lifetime!" I reply without hesitation. We bring everything we have learned to each project we take up. In writing this book I have been acutely conscious of this truth. I have been listening to the Christian message of sin, salvation, and atonement my whole life. I heard it explained in church services and college classes. I read about it in the Bible and in books of theology. All along I thought I understood what my teachers were saying. A few years ago, however, after having taught theology for over a decade, I realized I did not understand at all. Whenever I taught about the atonement, I found myself repeating phrases taken from Scripture and describing textbook theories of atonement apart from a lively sense of their truth. Nor was I able to help my students understand. I began to pay closer attention to the ways contemporary preachers, teachers, and popular authors explained the message of salvation. I concluded that they understood it no better than I. At that point, I determined that I had to write this book. It has been a long journey, and there were times when I thought I would never achieve the breakthrough I was seeking. But the moment came when I saw a little light, a glow that grew brighter as I moved toward it. Now when I contemplate the salvation that has come into the world through Jesus Christ I rejoice with my mind as well as my heart. I hope this book can help others understand the Christian message of salvation in a way that resonates with their experience and strikes them as good news. I offer it as a guide for professors, students, pastors, teachers, and church leaders in their ministries. The book aims to help readers gain a sense of rapport and continuity with the community created by the original gospel events and discover new ways of presenting this good news to those outside. In working toward these ends, I desire to be faithful to Scripture, respectful of tradition, and consistent with reason. Of course, many other writers care about these matters and hold dear these values. I engage with their ideas to affirm or criticize, accept or reject. However, two theological viewpoints on salvation require extensive examination because of their outsized influence and largely negative impact on contemporary Christianity. I consider them soteriological dead ends, and we must move passed them if the light is to grow brighter.

Soteriological Dead Ends

Two options dominate the field for making sense of sin and salvation in contemporary Protestant Christianity, the evangelical penal substitution and the liberal moral influence theories of atonement.[1] Each theory proposes its own analysis of the problem to which Jesus Christ is the answer. Evangelical soteriology argues that sin offends God deeply and that to be true to his perfect justice God cannot merely forgive but must punish sin as it deserves. However in his great mercy, God sent Jesus into the world to endure in our place the punishment sin deserves and earn our forgiveness. In this way, Jesus Christ embodies God's love and satisfies his justice in his one act of dying on the cross. In contrast to this evangelical perspective, liberal atonement theory views sin as individual imperfection, ignorance, and sensuality or as unjust social structures that foster racism, sexism, economic disparities, and other evils. God is not an angry judge but a loving Father. Jesus helps us overcome sin by teaching about the love of God and living in a way that inspires us to live the way he lived. Jesus died on a Roman cross not to divert God's wrath away from us and onto himself but to witness to God's justice and love. God did not kill Jesus. The Romans killed him because he would not compromise his message. The way he died demonstrates his unwavering faith in the love of God and inspires the same confidence in us.

In my view, neither evangelical PSA nor liberal moral influence theory can meet the challenge we face today, that is, how may contemporary theology help the church to restate its soteriology in a way both true to the apostolic faith and comprehensible to people living now? Since the evangelical theory pervades not only evangelical theology but also evangelical sermons, song lyrics, and personal piety, I devote two full chapters to documenting, analyzing, and criticizing this viewpoint. Despite its claims of biblical faithfulness, traditional rootedness, and theological soundness, I argue that evangelical PSA falls short in all three areas. Nor can it be made

---

1. I will use the abbreviation PSA instead of "penal substitutionary atonement" frequently but not exclusively from this point on.

understandable to people inside or outside the contemporary church. Since liberal theology and mainline churches are the default religious options for those looking for alternatives to evangelicalism, I devote a chapter to liberal soteriology. Liberalism rightly senses that traditional soteriology makes no sense to modern people, so it attempts to translate Christianity into present-day terms. However, in my view, it evacuates the substance of the apostolic faith in the process. Nor does its simplistic diagnosis of the human condition take seriously the human capacity for evil. Consequently, its solutions strike me as superficial.

A Way Forward

This book moves toward its goal in a three-part argument. First, since the Christian message of sin and salvation speaks to the human condition, we need to describe this condition from within. In what modern philosophers might call an "existential phenomenology,"[2] I want to explore the wretchedness and greatness of humanity in a way that can be recognized by our contemporaries, whether they consider themselves religious or not. I realize that there is no neutral place from which to examine ourselves. Nevertheless, we can describe what we see as the human lot in ways that can be understood and evaluated by those who do not share our context completely. Clearly, this is possible to some degree because when we read such ancient philosophers as Plato, Aristotle, and Epictetus, we recognize our experience in theirs. We can agree on much of the physical, psychological, and social phenomena, even if we disagree about the solution to our problems and the way to human fulfillment. In conducting this examination, I sought help from mythmakers, philosophers, poets, and novelists. But Blaise Pascal and Søren Kierkegaard were my constant companions in writing these two chapters.

In the second part of the book, comprised of two chapters, we will look again at the human condition, this time from within a Christian theological framework. The Christian faith also speaks of the human condition, but not in the way of science, philosophy, or psychology. It speaks about humanity in relation to God and hence uses a theological vocabulary. It speaks about human beings as creatures made in the "image and likeness of God" (Gen 1:26–27). Human beings are called, commissioned,

---

2. By using the term "existential phenomenology" I am not asserting that I have used the phenomenological methods of Kierkegaard, Husserl, Heidegger, or Sartre in a consistent way. My approach is eclectic. I draw on any writer that helps me describe how our own existence appears to us.

and made responsible to God. But we have failed to live up to our calling and have become sinners and slaves. We are lost, dead, blind, and alienated from God. Despite such wretchedness, we are loved by God, who in Jesus Christ forgives, heals, reconciles, and gives new life. We are given hope of sharing in divine glory in union with God through Christ and the Spirit in the resurrection of the dead.

In part three, we will examine the Christian understanding of salvation in relation to the two previous parts. I hope to breathe new life into the Christian vocabulary of the means and nature of salvation. This salvation has two parts. It includes the way in which God blesses us with forgiveness, spiritual power, illumination, and resurrection for human wretchedness and with glorification, eternal life, and union with God in a final realization of human greatness. All of this occurs through Jesus Christ in the power of the Spirit. In this part, I give a chapter each to the biblical theology of the cross and resurrection of Jesus. I devote two chapters to analysis and critique of evangelical PSA and one chapter to analysis and critique of the liberal moral influence theory of atonement. In two chapters, I restate the heart of Christian soteriology in a way I believe avoids the theological defects of PSA and liberal moral influence theories and makes sense to our contemporaries. In terms of textbook categories used for organizing atonement theories, my overarching understanding of soteriology most resembles those of Irenaeus of Lyon (ca. 130–ca. 202) and Athanasius (296–373), that is, recapitulation[3] and *theōsis*.[4] In my understanding, these two ideas need to be combined so that we are speaking of *theōsis* through recapitulation. The eternal Son of God joined himself to our fallen, mortal humanity and lived faithfully as the true "image and likeness of God" through every stage of life even to the point of death on a cross. Therefore, God raised him from the dead so that he has become a new Adam that gives humanity a new beginning. He bore our humanity through life and death into glory, immortality, and incorruptibility, that is, into sharing in divine life. Many of the church fathers after Irenaeus called this transformation *theōsis* or *theopoiēsis*, that is, the process of becoming or being made like God through union with Christ and the transforming work of the Spirit. As Irenaeus himself said, by "following the only true and steadfast Teacher, the Word of God, our Lord Jesus

---

3. The word "recapitulation" translates the Greek word *anakephalaiōsis*, forms of which are used in Eph 1:10 and Rom 13:9. It means *to sum up* or *bring together*. The recapitulation theme permeates Irenaeus's works.

4. I agree with Blackwell, *Christosis*, that studying the patristic tradition of salvation as *theōsis* can heighten our awareness of themes often neglected in the study of Paul's soteriology and free us from the narrow juridical interpretation of Paul. In doing this, we must, of course, guard against reading later meanings of *theōsis* back into Paul.

Christ, who did, through His transcendent love, become what we are, that He might bring us to be even what He is Himself."[5] And in what theologians now call the "exchange formula," Athanasius writes, "He, indeed, assumed humanity that we might become God."[6]

The concluding chapter draws the whole argument together in a concise statement that addresses the concern at the origin of this book, that is, that the traditional biblical and theological language the church uses to present its message of salvation to our contemporaries makes little sense in terms of their experience. It does not resonate with their understanding of the wretchedness or the great possibilities of human existence. How, they ask, can the death of Jesus heal our broken world and bring humanity's great potential to fulfillment? The book answers that in Christ, God sums up in one person what all humans should have become. In his life and death, Jesus faithfully imaged the Father in the world, and through his resurrection into glory brought one of us into the divine life. One of us! He left behind the futile history that Paul called "Adam" and established a new beginning for all who trust in him. He is the Savior, and he is one of us! He has the power, wisdom, and will to make us like him. If this message is true, it is the best news possible, a firm foundation for a life of faith, hope, and love, a life filled with joy, peace, and goodness. It is a life of meaning and fruitful work, marked by courage and confidence. If God raised Jesus from the dead, this message is indeed true and this quality of life is indeed possible here and now. Paul voices the conviction of the first generation of Christians and all who believe their witness when he says,

> But Christ has indeed been raised from the dead, the firstfruits of those who have fallen asleep. . . . "Death has been swallowed up in victory." "Where, O death, is your victory? Where, O death, is your sting?" The sting of death is sin, and the power of sin is the law. But thanks be to God! He gives us the victory through our Lord Jesus Christ. (1 Cor 15:20, 54–57)

---

5. *AH* 5 (*ANF* 1:526). As Minns points out, Christ secured our salvation, not merely as an automatic result of the incarnation. Rather "it was necessary that he should pass through every stage of life, from infancy to mature years . . . offering to each age an appropriate example of holiness, justice, obedience and authority" (*Irenaeus: An Introduction*, 107).

6. Athanasius, *St. Athanasius On the Incarnation*, 54.

Part One

The Human Condition

A View from Within

1

The Paradox of Human Existence

HUMAN BEINGS ARE CURIOUS animals. We look up at the stars and gaze at waterfalls. We travel half way around the earth to see an eclipse of the sun. We marvel at huge mountains, tall trees, and powerful animals. And yet, as Augustine observes, "in ourselves we are uninterested."[1] We expend great energy to find answers to our questions about nature and are curious about the affairs of others. But we do not question ourselves *about ourselves*. Every other thing we study is external to us. We take it apart to unlock its secrets, but find ourselves looking at external surfaces and disconnected parts only. We never experience external things from inside in their unity and wholeness. There is only one thing we can experience as a whole from inside and that is ourselves. In the words of Lucien Laberthonnière (1860–1932), "There is only one problem, the problem of ourselves, from which all others derive."[2] This "problem" is what I intend to pursue in this chapter and in Part One of this book.

Mythmakers, philosophers, poets, and theologians in all ages ask questions about the human condition: What are the different types of experience possible for us? What are the kinds of human emotions and what is the range of those emotions? What are the structures of human existence common to all human beings? What makes us different from other animals? Different thinkers describe human existence in different ways and offer different explanations for why we are constructed as we are. Yet they all notice that human beings possess a dual nature unlike any other creature. We are body and mind, finite and infinite, large and small,

1. Augustine, *Confessions* 10.16, trans. Chadwick, *Saint Augustine*, 187.

2. Laberthonnière, *Études de philosophie cartésienne*, 1, quoted in Copleston, SJ, *History of Philosophy* 9:238.

of heaven and of earth, one thing and all things,[3] located and omnipresent, and temporal and eternal. We are not just one but *both* sides of these paradoxes. If we were simply finite, we could not experience existence as we do. Nor would we be human if we were simply infinite. The combination of both dimensions makes human beings capable of that unique state Augustine called "the human condition."[4]

The greatness and wretchedness of humanity is a persistent theme of Western literature. Sometimes wretchedness, at other times greatness, is emphasized, but usually both are acknowledged. Gregory of Nazianzus (329–390) probes the paradox of the human condition in a way that anticipates Pascal:

> What is man that thou art mindful of him? What is this new mystery concerning me? I am small and great, lowly and exalted, mortal and immortal, earthly and heavenly. I share one condition with the lower world and another with God; one with the flesh, the other with the Spirit. I must be buried with Christ, rise with Christ, be joint heir with Christ, become a son of God, a god myself.[5]

Such church fathers as Lactantius (ca. 250–ca. 325), Gregory of Nyssa (ca. 330–ca. 395), Nemesius of Emesa (fl ca. 390), and Augustine of Hippo (354–430) extolled the greatness of humanity, especially the gift of reason.[6] But they were clear that our dignity is a divine gift that demands our grateful response. In the pre-scholastic Middle Ages, theologians in the Latin West drew on Augustine for their views of human dignity and misery. Pope Innocent III (pope from 1198–1206) before he became pope had written a treatise entitled *On Contempt for the World: On the Misery of the Human Condition*. Acknowledging that misery of condition does not disprove dignity of nature, Lotario dei Conti di Segni (Innocent's birth name) promised a complementary treatise on the dignity of human nature. But Lotario was unable to keep his pledge, and his unfulfilled promise provided an excuse

---

3. Aristotle said, "The soul is in a way all existing things" (Aristotle, *On the Soul* 3.8, McKeon, *Basic Writings*, 595).

4. Augustine, *Confessions* 4.12, trans. Chadwick, *Saint Augustine*, 59.

5. Gregory of Nazianzus, *Oration* 7.23, quoted in Russell, *The Doctrine of Deification*, 217.

6. Lactantius, *On the Workmanship of God or the Formation of Man*; Gregory of Nyssa, *On the Creation of Man*; Nemesius of Emesa, *On Human Nature*; Augustine of Hippo, *Confessions; Two Books on Genesis Against the Manichees; On the Literal Interpretation of Genesis*; and *On the Holy Trinity*.

for the composition of many humanist essays on the dignity of humanity in the following three centuries.[7]

Petrarch (1304–74) wrote the first of these, *The Remedies of Both Kinds of Fortune,* thereby initiating the literary genre "The Dignity of Man."[8] Many such treatises followed in the next 150 years. Some retained the earlier emphasis on such theological themes as the image of God and the incarnation of the Son of God in human flesh. Others moved in a secular direction. Lorenzo Valla (1407–57) in his *Dialogue on the True Good,* defended the Epicurean view on the goodness of pleasure against the Stoic rejection of pleasure. Pico Mirandola (1463–94) in his *Oration on the Dignity of Man* (1486), emphasized humanity's created openness to self-realization according to its own will.

Blaise Pascal (1623–62)

Though I will draw on some of this earlier literature, I will give center stage to Blaise Pascal because he brings special notice to the paradoxical relationship between greatness and wretchedness in a way I want to emphasize in this chapter. Pascal lived at the dawn of the modern era, in the age of Galileo, Bacon, and Descartes. His thoughts on the greatness and wretchedness of humanity were found among the notes he made in preparation for an apologetic work designed to address the issues of his age in a way that could reach the nascent modern mind. These notes were collected and published as *Pensées,* which is French for "thoughts." Below are some of his thoughts on the paradoxical relationship between human greatness and human misery.

> Man's greatness comes from knowing he is wretched: a tree does not know that it is wretched. Thus it is wretched to know that one is wretched but there is greatness in knowing one is wretched.[9]

> Man must not be allowed to believe either that he is equal to animals or to angels, nor to be unaware of either, but he must know both.[10]

---

7. Trinkaus, *In Our Image and Likeness* 1:179–99. In these pages, Trinkaus surveys patristic and medieval thinkers' views on human dignity.

8. Trinkaus, *In Our Image and Likeness* 1:192.

9. Pascal, *Pensées,* 59.

10. Pascal, *Pensées,* 60.

> Man's greatness is so obvious that it can even be deduced from
> his wretchedness, for what is nature in animals we call wretch-
> edness in man.[11]

Had Pascal spoken only about human wretchedness we might consider him a gloomy pessimist. Had he spoken only about human greatness
we would think him an untethered optimist. But he holds them in such
careful tension that Peter Kreeft designates him a "paradoxicalist."[12] Human beings are not part wretched and part great or sometimes wretched
and sometimes great. They are wretched in their greatness and great in
their wretchedness. Pascal understands human wretchedness and greatness in much the same way as thinkers before him did. We exist in bodies
that are mortal, fragile, and weak. We are a speck of dust in an infinite
universe, a reed battered by the storm. We live at a particular place and
time and are far more ignorant than knowing. We are subject to such violent passions as fear, anger, and lust. We are happy, anxious, hopeful, and
despairing all in one day, depending on changes in external circumstance.
And in our fear, anger, lust, and despair, we can sink lower and become
more violent that any species of animal. Carnivorous animals are raven-
ous, but human beings alone can be vicious.

Our weaknesses would not seem wretched, however, if we could not
think and choose. As Pascal says so eloquently, a tree may be wretched,
but it does not know that it is wretched. Only human beings can be truly
wretched because, unlike trees, they know they are missing good things
they could enjoy and suffer needless disabilities. Pascal knows that trees
are not literally wretched. It is not in their nature to want more than they
have or to imagine being what they are not. Human beings experience life
as trees would if trees possessed reason and self-awareness. With reason,
trees could imagine walking, flying, and swimming. They could feel shame
or pride in comparing themselves to other trees and would realize that one
day they will die. It is our greatness that transforms our objective limits
into subjective wretchedness.

For Pascal, this paradoxical structure explains so much of human
experience and raises so many haunting questions. The tension in this du-
ality is so great that we are tempted to relieve it by denying one aspect or
another. Despairing of realizing our greatness, we seek escape by plunging
into animal sensuality, giving free reign to the passions. After describing
the violent behavior of one of the characters in his novel *The House of*

---

11. Pascal, *Pensées*, 59.

12. Kreeft, *Christianity for Modern Pagans*, 47. Other paradoxicalists, according to
Kreeft, are the apostle Paul, Augustine, Kierkegaard, and Dostoevsky (ibid., 51).

the Dead, Dostoevsky concludes, "I declare that the noblest creature can become so hardened and bestial that nothing distinguishes it from that of a wild animal."[13] But we cannot escape our greatness in this way, for it revenges our abandonment by making us even more aware of our wretchedness. If only we could become dumb and blind trees! Of course, we cannot really want to become a tree, dog, or sheep, because we would lose all awareness of what we are. We could gain no pleasure or relief from this transformation. Perhaps we might wish to be a dog for one night, but even then, we would want to know what we are, what we are doing, and what we had been. But with such knowledge we would again become aware of our wretchedness and greatness!

On the other hand, we may be tempted to flee our wretchedness by denying our limits and focusing only on our reason, imagination, and freedom. We put our trust in science, hoping that it will eventually place immortality within our reach. Some people wish to live in an imaginary world where they transcend the limits of time and space and all physical laws. Some dream of a utopia able to transform individual selfish acts into social goods. Others mistake their own wills for the creative power that rules the world. The character Krillov in Dostoevsky's novel *The Possessed* announces, "Three years I have sought the attribute of my divinity, and I have found it. It is my will. It is everything by which I can show, to its capital point, my insubordination, and my terrible freedom."[14] This way out of the paradox of greatness and wretchedness is also closed. No matter how much we learn, how boldly we dream, how organized we become, or how violently we assert our wills, we cannot transcend our limits. As Pascal reminds us, it takes only a teaspoon of water or a whiff of infected air to bring us down.[15] No matter how fast we fly the shadow of disease and death, of chance and fate, moves ever before us.

Søren Kierkegaard

Sources for Pascal's views on the paradox of wretchedness and greatness consist of a few notes made in preparation for a longer work. Søren Kierkegaard (1813–55) develops this paradox in detail and with profound psychological and spiritual insight. He begins his book *The Sickness unto Death* with a dense statement, which he unfolds in the rest of the book:

13. Dostoevsky, *The House of the Dead*, 194, quoted in Walsh, *After Ideology*, 47.
14. Dostoevsky, *The Possessed*, quoted in Emonet, *The Greatest Marvel of Nature*, 79.
15. Pascal, *Pensées*, 95.

> A human being is spirit. But what is spirit? Spirit is the self. But
> what is the self? The self is a relation that relates itself to itself
> or is the relation's relating itself to itself in the relation; the self
> is not the relation but is the relation's relating itself to itself. A
> human being is a synthesis of the infinite and the finite, of the
> temporal and the eternal, of freedom and necessity, in short, a
> synthesis. A synthesis is a relation between two. Considered in
> this way, a human being is still not a self.[16]

Like Pascal, Kierkegaard sees the quality of human existence as determined by the tension between two opposing dimensions. Kierkegaard
states explicitly what Pascal merely assumes, that is, the human self is of a
higher relational order than the first relation. The specific form of human
existence comes into being only as the first relation "relates itself to itself."
That is to say, I who am this relation between greatness and wretchedness,
infinite and finite, eternity and time, freedom and necessity, become aware
of myself, relate to myself, enact myself, become myself, and judge myself.
In this active relating of themselves to themselves human beings exist as
spirit. For Kierkegaard, the individual human person is the most precious
thing in all of creation. In the individual self's relation to itself, the most
decisive issue in history will be settled: how do I stand in relation to the
eternal, to God? Accordingly, Kierkegaard next demonstrates that the self
in relating to itself must also relate to God:

> Such a relation that relates itself to itself, a self, must either have
> established itself or have been established by another. If the rela-
> tion that relates itself to itself has been established by another,
> then the relation is indeed a third, but this relation, the third, is
> yet again a relation and relates itself to that which established
> the entire relation. The human self is such a derived, established
> relation, a relation that relates itself to itself and in relating itself
> to itself it relates itself to another.[17]

In becoming aware of myself, enacting myself, becoming myself, and
judging myself, unavoidably I relate to the one who makes me what I am.
Either I accept and affirm what God made me or I reject it. But if I reject the
existence God gives me, simultaneously I refuse to trust in God's goodness,
grace, and love. Kierkegaard calls this refusal "despair." Despair can drive
us either to plunge into the finite without remembering our infiniteness or
embrace infinity without consciousness of our finiteness. In a way similar to
Pascal, rejecting the paradox in either direction sickens the self. In the direction of exclusive finitude lie sensuality, thoughtlessness, and narrowness.

---

16. Kierkegaard, *Sickness unto Death*, 13.

17. Kierkegaard, *Sickness unto Death*, 13–14.

Embracing the infinite to the exclusion of the finite translates us into an imaginary world of unreal, abstract, impossible, and fantastic things.[18] Despair comes in two forms: (1) "in despair not to will to be oneself"[19] and (2) "in despair to will to be oneself."[20] In the first form, I do not want to be the imperfect and suffering self I think I am. I wish to rid myself of myself. In despairing of myself, I also relate negatively to the one who established the self, that is, God. In the second form of despair—"in despair to will to be oneself"—the self asserts its worth arbitrarily and aspires to greatness by its own power. As you can see, even though the first is passive and the second active, both forms of despair affirm what God does not will and deny what God wills. The first type sinks into sloth, sadness, and sensuality while the second expresses itself as pride, defiance, and violence.[21]

Kierkegaard pictures human existence as caught in a spiritual/psychic dilemma with only one way out. Human beings cannot simply accept themselves as they are by their own judgment because, not being their own creators, they cannot grasp their whole existence to evaluate it. We cannot look at ourselves and see that "it is very good" (Gen 1:31). We bounce back and forth between pride and shame, neither of which is based on truth. Our spiritual/psychic existence is unstable and restless. We hope to get away from a self we cannot accept and establish a self that we can accept, lured by the prospect of expanding the self to infinity or narrowing the self to mere bodily life. But we cannot achieve our objective whichever direction we move, and we find no rest. Only by relating rightly to the one who established the self can we will wholeheartedly to be the self we truly are:

> The opposite of being in despair is to have faith. Therefore, the formula set forth above, which describes a state in which there is no despair at all, is entirely correct, and this formula is also the formula for faith: in relating itself to itself, and in willing to be itself, the self rests transparently in the power that established it.[22]

The antidote to spiritual/psychical instability and restlessness is to rest in God, that is, to trust God's decisions about what we are and who we become. The task of the self, Kierkegaard suggests, is to become itself. God alone has the power to create us and bring us to our destiny. Our task is to accept, validate, and repeat God's determination of ourselves by relating to ourselves only through our God-relation.

18. Kierkegaard, *Sickness unto Death*, 30–33.

19. Kierkegaard, *Sickness unto Death*, 47–66.

20. Kierkegaard, *Sickness unto Death*, 67–74.

21. In a way similar to Kierkegaard and Dostoevsky, Albert Camus in *The Rebel* examines two extreme reactions to the absurdity of the human condition: suicide and murder. One can see the resemblance to Kierkegaard's two forms of despair.

22. Kierkegaard, *Sickness unto Death*, 49.

2

The Human Condition

Greatness and Wretchedness

WE LIVE IN THE tension between greatness and wretchedness, and to escape the strain we move back and forth between its two extremes. Forgetting our wretchedness we imagine a world without limits, a life of power, wealth, and fame. What we do not have, we will acquire. What we are not, we will become. The recognition we now lack, the future will bring. Since we cannot leave behind our limits, we use our imaginations to construct a self that better conforms to our wishes. It is to this sickness of the self that this chapter is dedicated.

Human Greatness

Paradoxically, our greatness makes possible our wretchedness. Writers from Plato to Augustine to Pascal locate human greatness in the power of our minds to perceive, judge, think, understand, imagine, analyze, synthesize, and create. Reason can perceive and name relationships and qualities. It can see likenesses, identities, and differences among objects of thought. We have power to differentiate among temporal, causal, spatial, logical, quantitative, and qualitative relationships. We employ such concepts as good, perfect, infinite, part and whole, limit, time, space, eternity, causality, truth, being, existence, nothing, inference, and many others. Perhaps one could argue that the human body excels the bodies of animals in many ways. But the power of the human mind so far surpasses the mental power of animals that it is virtually infinite in comparison. The capacities of the mind exceed the excellence of the human body to such an extent that we must create microscopes, telescopes, lasers, computers, and a million other tools to facilitate its reach into the physical world. Even with all our machines, the mind's power to understand, transcend, and imagine far outstrips our physical ability to perceive and manipulate the physical world.

We can allow Italian Marsilo Ficino (1433–99), an admirer of Plato and Augustine of Hippo, to speak for the humanist tradition on the theme of human greatness:

> The force of man is almost similar to the divine nature since man by himself, that is through his intelligence and skill, governs himself without being in the least limited by this physical nature and imitates the individual works of the higher nature. ... With supercelestial intelligence he transcends the heaven. ... [W]ho will deny that he is endowed with a genius, as I would put it, that is almost the same as that of the Author of the heavens, and that man would be able to make the heavens in some way if he only possessed the instruments and the celestial material, since he does make them now, although out of other material, yet similar in structure.[1]

The human mind itself participates in the paradox of wretchedness and greatness. It is always finite in its actual accomplishments, in what it perceives and understands. Darkness and ignorance command much of its space. Yet the greatness of the mind should not be measured by its actual accomplishments but by its power to surround and move incessantly beyond every finite object it encounters. The mind, then, is *virtually* infinite so that we cannot conceive how any finite object could prove inconceivable. The incessant drive of the mind to go beyond whatever finite object we encounter does not derive from a conscious decision but is intrinsic to its nature. It is an inner urge to know not this or that object but simply to know. As long as the objects within our scope of experience are finite, as long as there is anything not yet known, the mind will continue its transcending motion.

The mind comprehends and surpasses the quality of every actual object by virtue of its unquenchable thirst for the perfect, and in its incessant movement toward infinity, it can number and surpass any finite quantity. We can speak of perfection in a relative sense or an absolute sense. A relatively perfect object is the complete realization of its idea, a perfect circle, a perfectly virtuous life, and so on. The idea of absolute perfection entails

1. Ficino, *Theologica Platonica*, quoted in Trinkaus, *In Our Image and Likeness* 2:485–86. Ficino wrote in refutation of Larenzo Valla (1407–57), who defended Epicurus's contention that animals are just as intelligent as humans and that only their lack of speech and hands prevented them from demonstrating their cleverness (Trinkaus, *In Our Image and Likeness* 2:485).

the complete realization of the idea of being itself, which includes all pos-sibilities. As the mind encounters finite things, it perceives their goodness *and* their imperfection, their being *and* nonbeing. It is driven by desire for something better and greater until it arrives at perfection and infinity. Noth-ing less can satisfy the insatiable mind.

Our virtually infinite minds declare everything within our experience finite, render every good attained disappointing, and pronounce every truth comprehended unsatisfying. Paradoxically, because we are great we are doomed to perpetual disappointment, to inescapable wretchedness. Even worse, our minds transcend our present selves in memory and self-reflection, pronouncing us finite and imperfect in every dimension of our existence. Our minds measure our actual accomplishments by the ideals of relative and absolute perfection and infinity. We are ashamed of our flawed bodies. We feel guilty for our ignoble passions, thoughts, and actions. Our ignorance embarrasses us and renders us vulnerable. Our lack of self-knowledge dis-turbs us. Even if we were perfect human beings, we would still not be perfect realizations of all it means to *be*. For even a perfect human being would still be limited. We could imagine being better and more than we are. A perfect human body is still a body, mortal and limited by time and space. We could still be ashamed in the presence of nobler beings.

Though our virtually infinite minds rank as our most precious pos-session, grounding our hope for glory, at the same time they generate our subjective wretchedness. Apart from our self-transcendence we would not be aware of our imperfection and could not experience wretchedness. The mind seeks the highest good, absolute perfection, ultimate unity and harmony, and infinite knowledge. It cannot rest in undisturbed happiness until it finds these unlimited goods, not as projected ideals but as realized possessions. However, we find no basis for hope within the human condition that we will attain this rest. It must come—if it comes at all—from *beyond*.

Six Forms of Wretchedness

The word "wretched" designates a subjective feeling of being deprived of something we want or of a disagreeable presence. Wretchedness, then, has an objective and a subjective aspect. The possibility for subjective wretchedness is grounded in the tension between the objective limits of existence and our ability to transcend these limits in imagination. Human beings are limited in every aspect of their existence: physical, intellectual, spiritual, and social. We become aware of our limits as we relate to a huge world we did not create, do not control, and on which we depend. It confronts us with possibilities for joy and threats of danger. In relation to the world, we experience ourselves as circumscribed in space and time, as poor and small in a world of abundance. Different forms of subjective wretchedness correspond to different objective limitations. In the following study of wretchedness I will examine six pairs of wretchedness, objective and subjective.

Contingency and Anxiety

Whatever comes into being can cease to be and can never control its existence completely. However, since we cannot remember a time we did not exist, we find it difficult to take our contingency seriously. The problems and allurements of the present and the possibilities and threats of the future distract us from this thought. Our contingency confronts us openly when the spell of the ordinary is broken by crises, failure, betrayal, sickness, danger, injury, or death. It seizes us by the throat, demanding our attention. Yet, even in ordinary life our "ontological insecurity" touches every corner of our existence and constitutes anxiety as a permanent existential mood.[2] Existentialist writers sometimes refer to this condition as "facticity."[3] The shock of discovering our contingency confronts us with questions about the origin and end of our existence. Is it a brute fact, an accidental product of mindless forces? Or, is it a gift, and if so, what is the purpose of the gift and who is the giver? Even if we do not consciously voice these questions, they are always just below our surface awareness.

To exist at all, something must exist as a certain kind of thing and a particular instance of that kind.[4] We exist as individual human beings living at specific times and places in particular family trees. We received a huge part of ourselves from whatever caused our coming into being, not through our choices and labor. Whether I experience my existence as positive or negative, whether it exemplifies my wretchedness or greatness, much of what I am is simply given. The existential anxiety that accompanies our contingency reveals itself even in thinkers who attempt to escape its grasp. Karl Marx and Jean Paul Sartre, though acknowledging that we find ourselves in a world we did not create, argue that we really do create our own existence. According to Marx, "the *entire so-called history of the world* is nothing but the begetting of man through human labor, nothing but the coming-to-be of nature for man."[5] As a species, we create everything about

2. Van Deurzen, *Paradox and Passion,* 5.

3. Macquarrie, *Existentialism,* 147–50.

4. In traditional terms, a thing is essence, existence, and subsistence.

5. Marx, "Economic and Philosophic Manuscripts of 1844," 91–92. For an in-depth

ourselves that is distinctively human: language, culture, economies, art, and architecture. For Sartre, "consciousness is in fact a project of founding itself; that is, of attaining to the dignity of the in-itself-for-itself or in-itself-as-self-cause."[6] We are not given our essence by God or any other power. We exist in the futile attempt to establish the stability of our existence by abolishing the distinction between our self and the other so that we become the cause of everything. In McLachan's judgment, "If this is the case then absurdity is the best word to characterize the philosophical anthropology found in *Being and Nothingness*; the for-itself, by nature, possesses an ideal that cannot possibly be fulfilled."[7]

In contrast to Marx and Sartre, most of us cannot escape a sense that we are not the cause of our existence. Everything human beings create presumes a foundation already in existence, given by a source outside and beyond us. The character of that source interests us intensely, because in that source lie the secrets of our identity and destiny. Those who look exclusively for our origin in nature may discover mechanisms by which we evolved, but they cannot fathom the depths of our being. However, if we look for our origin in God, new vistas open before us. Our existence extends its roots into the mysterious depths of a being infinite in love and power. The mystery and depth of the creator becomes an aspect of our own identity and sets us on a never-ending journey into God.

Embodiment and Confinement

Martin Heidegger and other existentialist thinkers propose a number of factors that always accompany human existence: space, time, embodiment, mortality, mood, and others.[8] In this section, I will focus on embodiment and its accompanying mood of confinement. John Macquarrie reminds us of something we all know but rarely consider: "It is only through existing in bodily form that I can be in the world."[9] Our bodies make possible our openness to the world by which we relate to nature, other people, and ourselves. Through the body we enjoy the good the world has to offer. But to be embodied is also to be confined and vulnerable.[10] Consider again Pascal's

---

discussion of these ideas, see Tucker, *Philosophy and Myth in Karl Marx*, 123–35. See also Walsh, *After Ideology*, 122.

6 Sartre, *Being and Nothingness*, 538.

7. McLachlan, *The Desire to Be God*, 28–29.

8. Cohn, *Existential Thought*, 13–15.

9. Macquarrie, *Existentialism*, 67.

10. Embodiment entails the "finitude of existence" (Macquarrie, *Existentialism*, 70).

observation: "Man's greatness is so obvious that it can even be deduced from his wretchedness, for what is nature in animals we call wretchedness in man."[11] We do not feel sorry for animals when they eat grass, smell feces, or copulate in the open, for such behavior is natural for them. They feel no shame or pride. Unlike animals, we can imagine the human condition from outside to see its wretchedness. Imagine that one morning you woke up in the body of a cow. Your sense of wretchedness would be overwhelming. You would find yourself imprisoned in a body not fitted to the powers of your mind. What joy to return to your human body after this confining experience! Now imagine that you were by nature not human but an ethereal being. Your "body" lives on energy drawn from space and can be fully present in one location without losing peripheral awareness of what is happening everywhere else. It is so versatile that you can separate two atoms or move a star, and your ability to communicate with other minds far surpasses the power of a physical brain. Imagine your dismay were you to fall from this glorious status into a human body, an animal frame that must be fed and clothed, that is slow and limited to one place, whose capacity for pleasure is matched by its vulnerability to pain. Your sense of confinement would engulf you. Though we have never experienced these imaginary transitions, we have known sickness, injury, and threat of death. The body's immune system is amazing in its capacity to combat invasive microbes. Its capacity to heal itself from punctures, cuts, and scratches, were we not so used to it, would seem miraculous. Yet, a little water, a sharp stick, or a small stone can injure the body beyond repair.

Our bodies enable us to experience good things, but they also limit how much pleasure and enjoyment we can take in. We can eat only so much food before we become sated. We cannot enjoy constant sex, not only because we achieve temporary satisfaction but also because we would have no time for other pleasures, food, solitude, and conversation. The imagination, which can contain the ocean, must drink through the straw of the body. The mind is our glory and greatness, but the narrow entryway of the five senses limits the information to which the mind has access. The power of the brain is amazing, but it cannot calculate, construct, interpret, or judge at infinite speed. We can conceive the infinite, imagine transcending space and time, and envision perfection, but we cannot attain them through the body. The rationality and freedom that characterize humanity is amazing when compared to the animals. Animals seem to be driven wholly by instinct and passions. But we, too, are animals with instincts and passions. Though we have power to subject the passions to the direction of reason, the relentless

11. Pascal, *Pensées*, 59.

drive and alien rationality of passion insure that reason will not always succeed in directing passion toward the best end.

Desire and Discontent

Just as we do not call ourselves into being, we do not sustain our lives. We
continue to depend on the source that gave us existence. Everything we accomplish makes use of the world in which we live and on which we depend.
We exist only because the physical world exists and possesses the properties it does. Our bodies are made of atoms generated in the hearts of stars,
and we are subject to the same physical forces to which stars must submit.
We are part of the biosphere on which we depend for air, food, and water.
Deprived of these life-sustaining resources, we die. Genetically, we are part
of the human species and depend on an unbroken line of reproduction back
to our earliest ancestors. Psychically, we are individuals only as we relate
to others. Life would be unbearable apart from the care and love found in
human community. What spiritual poverty we would endure were we not
heirs of the cultural heritage of the human family.

Desire to maintain life-giving connections to the world drives us to
act. In his analysis of human action, Blondel describes the end that drives
human life as the project of equalizing the "willing will" with the "willed
will." That is to say, at the foundation of our existence lies an eccentric drive
that wills the infinite—the "willing will"—whereas each particular good desired and attained—the "willed will"—is finite and cannot halt the dynamic
force that moves on beyond each finite good. A human being "can never
come up to his own exigencies. He can never succeed by his own strength,
in putting into his willed activity everything that is at the root of his voluntary activity."[12] Lacroix summarizes Blondel's thesis in these words:

> The study of action reveals that man never acts except to stabilize
> himself, and that he cannot finally achieve this by himself alone.
> I am too great for myself! Between myself and myself there is an
> infinite distance that action ceaselessly strives to bridge without
> ever completely succeeding. The indispensable condition for the
> fulfillment of human action is inaccessible to that action.[13]

Consider all the places to visit, sights to see, and things to do if we had
time and money. However, if we pursue one experience we exclude pursuit
of others. Our capacities enable us to acquire many goods, but lack of time

12. Blondel, *L'Action*, 338, quoted in Lacroix, *Maurice Blondel*, 34.
13. Lacroix, *Maurice Blondel*, 34.

and means forces us to leave many more untried. We can even imagine doing things physically impossible: traveling backward in time, becoming another person, entering a micro world, exploring the surface of the sun, and many more. To some extent we can choose who we become. If we possess the native intelligence we can become a financial planner, lawyer, doctor, or physicist. Given the requisite abilities, a person with the determination can become a great musician, athlete, or writer. However, every decision we make determines us for one and not another possibility. Suppose we received a vision of all the people we could become and were forced to choose which one to let be and which ones to leave uncreated. The burden would be unbearable! We are able to let go of such possibilities only because we are not aware of doing so. Dare we hope that our vast potential will be realized?

If we dwelt on our limits we would become perpetually unhappy. How can we attain happiness when we possess more capacity for joy than we can realize? It seems that unhappiness can be overcome only by achieving our infinite desires or eradicating them. We aspire to become like God or immerse ourselves in pure, thoughtless feeling. Many people seek to escape reflection by immersing themselves in a hedonist life. Or, by bold action and hard work they try to escape all limits. Both are impossible. No matter how much we try to forget, we will remain conscious of unfulfilled desire. We can neither erase nor fill up our imaginations.

Ignorance and Vulnerability

Desire for life entails desire for truth. Finding good things and avoiding dangers requires knowledge, but we lack knowledge enough to succeed always. Nature is highly consistent and reliable at the medium scale and in relatively isolated events. But we cannot always anticipate a flash flood or lightning strike or the formation of a tornado. When we add to nature our own and other peoples' actions, it becomes impossible to predict the exact outcomes of our choices. An accident occurs when two different lines of causality intersect at a point unpredictable from within either line or when a process of nature intersects with a human action. Traffic, home, and industrial accidents injure and kill thousands of people each year. If we knew the causes of such ills as cancer and Alzheimer's disease, perhaps we could prevent or cure them. *If knowledge is power, ignorance is weakness.* Perhaps ignorance of ourselves is the most disturbing blindness from which we suffer. We find nothing surprising in our ignorance of nature, to which we have only external access. However, we are disturbed to learn how little we know about ourselves, since to make good decisions we need self-knowledge.

Sometimes, we desire things we think will make us happy when acquiring them would produce unhappiness. Moreover, since we cannot foresee every consequence of our actions, we cannot be sure that the good we imagine will turn out as we thought. Our objective lack of self-knowledge manifests itself in subjective wretchedness. If, like trees, we had no awareness of ourselves, we would not experience our wretchedness as wretched. However, because we can imagine perfect happiness, we are fixed in despair. We desperately seek happiness against all hope of finding it.

Guilt and Shame

Moral guilt can be considered objectively or subjectively. Objectively considered, moral guilt concerns a person's status in relation to a moral law. Subjectively, it is a feeling of displeasure with ourselves and remorse over our morally deficient actions. According to Kant's analysis, the universal moral law confronts us as a law of reason unquestionably binding on us: we ought never to will for ourselves something we cannot also will to be a universal law.[14] As reasoning beings we are able to make moral judgments, that is, to deliberate about whether or not specific moral laws follow from the universal moral law. Conscience applies our moral judgments to our actions. When conscience makes us aware of our guilt in relation to our moral judgments this awareness is accompanied by a feeling of displeasure and remorse. Feelings of shame usually accompany guilt feelings. Shame is a painful feeling of unworthiness and can be induced by any vicious comparison between us and others. In the context of moral behavior, shame results when we infer our personal unworthiness from our objective guilt. According to Kant, to feel guilty is to feel that our actions deserve punishment.[15] To feel shame is to feel self-loathing because we did the act for which we deserve punishment.

We can apply Kant's analysis to the question of how feelings of guilt make the human condition wretched. Everyone has ideas about how they want to be treated, and implicit in those ideas is the principle that we ought to treat others the same way. We make moral judgments about others' actions, and we make them about our own. Everyone entertains an ideal

14. The following ideas are scattered within Kant's works on moral philosophy, the most significant of which are *The Groundwork of the Metaphysics of Morals*, *The Critique of Practical Reason*, and *The Metaphysics of Morals*. For a helpful and readily accessible article on Kant's moral philosophy, see Johnson and Cureton, "Kant's Moral Philosophy."

15. Kant, *Critique of Practical Reason*, 39–40.

image of themselves, and none of us lives up to that image. Everyone would be condemned if their judgments of other peoples' actions were applied to them. In normal states, where our consciences are quiet, we experience a naïve unity of consciousness. But in our experience of guilt we find ourselves at odds with ourselves in an inner contradiction. Kant imagined the dynamics of conscience as a court room in which there are three voices, judge, defender, and prosecutor.[16] The prosecutor accuses us of breaking the law, the defender attempts to rebut the accusation, but the judge pronounces the verdict. All three voices speak within the individual's consciousness. Hence, a division opens in the human soul between what we know we ought to do and what we have done and between our moral aspirations and the persons we actually are. We experience this state of self-condemnation as greatly distressing, and desire to escape it is overwhelming. Our strategies for return to unity of consciousness are well-known: confess and accept deserved punishment, suppress and deny our guilt, or attempt to make up for the fault by doing meritorious acts.

Death and Meaninglessness

Whether soon or late, in the din of battle or the hush of sleep, death comes to all. Whatever we were given, whatever we have created, whatever we have become will be lost. Human life is animated not only by the drive for gratification of sensual desire but also by desire to create and become. Even the short-term search for gratification is goal-directed, that is, human beings imagine a goal and use their intelligence to achieve it. The value we see in a goal moves us to spend our time and energy attaining it. The joy we find in our labor depends on believing that we can succeed. Each end we achieve becomes a means to another end. A college education attained becomes a means to a higher quality of life. A skill acquired can be used to earn a living. Accumulated wealth can free us from want. However, the end-means-end dynamic of life makes sense only as long as there is a goal ahead, a future before us. Death looms as the negation of all striving. Most human beings have hoped for survival or significance beyond death. This is not what we see from within the human condition. We see an end coming, extinction and oblivion. Hence, the prospect of death casts its shadow backwards over all of life. If we come to believe that life ends in annihilation, the end-means-end driver of life will lose much of its power to move us. If everything we do makes sense only as a means to another end and the chain of meaning terminates in death, the chain must fall back on itself. The end is retroactive, so that the whole

16. Kant, *The Metaphysics of Morals*, 233–35.

participates in the quality of the end. If the end is *nothing* then the beginning is nothing but the commencement of the end.

Since the beginning of human history the specter of death has disturbed the peace of kings and slaves and hunters and poets. The Akkadian Gilgamesh Epic, composed around 2000 BC, tells the story of king Gilgamesh of Uruk and his friend Enkidu. Side-by-side they fought horrible monsters, forging a deep friendship. Enkidu died, not in battle as he wished but on a bed of an illness. Gilgamesh is distraught and utters a lament before the elders of Uruk:

> Hear me, O elders [and give ear] unto me!
>
> It is for Enkidu, my friend, that I weep,
>
> Moaning bitterly like a wailing woman . . . .
>
> What now, is this sleep that has laid hold on thee?
>
> Thou are benighted and canst not hear [me]![17]

Restless and agitated, Gilgamesh wanders in the wild saying,

> When I die, shall I not be like Enkidu?
>
> Woe has entered my belly,
>
> Fearing death I roam over the steppe.[18]

Gilgamesh travels to Mount Mashu where dwells the immortal Utnapishtim, the only human survivor of the great flood. Gilgamesh wishes to ask Utnapishtim about the secret of immortality. Along the way he meets various actors who attempt to dissuade him from his quest:

> Gilgamesh, whither rovest thou?
>
> The life thou pursuest thou shalt not find.
>
> When the gods created mankind,
>
> Death for mankind they set aside,
>
> Life in their own hands retaining.[19]

At the end of his journey Gilgamesh comes face to face with Utnapishtim. The immortal hero tells Gilgamesh the story of the great flood and how he and his wife survived and were made immortal. He informs Gilgamesh about a plant that can make him young again. Gilgamesh finds the plant and begins his return journey to Uruk. On the way he stops at a well for a cool

17. *ANET,* 87.

18. *ANET,* 88.

19. *ANET,* 90.

bath and a drink. As Gilgamesh bathed, a serpent, smelling the fragrance of the plant, steals it. Gilgamesh lost his chance for immortality.

In his spiritual autobiography *A Confession,* nineteenth-century Russian novelist Leo Tolstoy writes of his fall into atheism as a young boy and of his return to faith and tradition in midlife. For a period of about two years he experience an existential crisis in which he considered suicide. At the height of his powers and peak of his career he realized that without God death rendered life utterly meaningless. He describes the impact of this realization:

> The truth was that life is meaningless. I had as it were lived, lived, and walked, walked, till I had come to a precipice and saw clearly that there was nothing ahead of me but destruction . . . I could give no reasonable meaning to any single action or to my whole life. . . . Sooner or later my affairs, whatever they may be, will be forgotten, and I shall not exist. Then why go on making any effort? . . . How can man fail to see this?[20]

Tolstoy likens his predicament to a traveler who jumps into a well to avoid a ferocious animal only to find a dragon at the bottom of the well. The traveler holds on to a bush growing out of a crack in the well. He knows that soon he must resign himself to being eaten by the beast above or the one below, but he hangs on. He sees some drops of honey on the leaves of the bush and licks them with his tongue, but the taste gives him no pleasure. He cannot take his eyes off the dragon. Then he notices two mice, a white one and a black one, gnawing at the branch. Soon the branch will break and he will fall into the dragon's jaws. Applying the story to himself, Tolstoy laments, "I cannot now help seeing day and night going round and bringing me to death. That is all I see, for that alone is true. All else is false."[21] Tolstoy frames well the question posed by death:

> My question—that which at the age of fifty brought me to the verge of suicide—was the simplest of questions. . . . It was: "What will come of what I am doing today or shall do tomorrow? What will come of my whole life?" Differently expressed, the question is: "Why should I live, why wish for anything, or do anything?" It can also be expressed thus: "Is there any meaning in my life that the inevitable death awaiting me does not destroy?"[22]

20. Tolstoy, *A Confession,* 15–17.
21. Tolstoy, *A Confession,* 18.
22. Tolstoy, *A Confession,* 21.

Conclusions

Our analysis of the human condition in the previous two chapters raises questions that cannot be answered from within the human sphere. As far as we can know from self-examination, the paradox of humanity's simultaneous wretchedness and greatness will be resolved only in death. Nevertheless, we have established a vocabulary common to those inside and outside of Christian faith that we can use to describe human greatness and wretchedness. This common understanding can help our contemporaries grasp in a provisional way the meaning of the biblical vocabulary of soteriology: the image of God, sin, death, the devil, slavery, blindness, salvation, forgiveness, and all the rest. In the second part of this book we will see that the Christian diagnosis of the human condition embraces but widens and deepens the analysis of the previous chapters by relating it to the story of God and creation told in the Bible. With this expanded understanding of human wretchedness and greatness clearly in view, our minds will be prepared to hear the biblical message of salvation as good news.

Part Two

The Human Condition

The Biblical Point of View

3

Destined for Glory

The Biblical View of Human Greatness

IN PART ONE, WE explored the human condition from within, basing our assessment on collective and individual experience of ourselves. In myth, philosophical reflection, and science, we can imagine looking at ourselves from an objective point of view. However, when limited to what we can learn from our powers of perception and understanding, nature is the widest context for understanding the human phenomenon. Coming to understand ourselves is then identical to learning how nature brought us into being, how we exemplify its laws, and how the natural environment affects us. As individuals, we exist only in the time between birth and death. Though we may cherish hope for the future of humanity and feel sympathy for other creatures, the two horizons birth and death determine the framework for setting goals, directing action, and measuring success. Such a "phenomenology of human existence," though providing genuine insights, cannot escape the sphere of the self and provide knowledge of the human condition as it really is, that is, as a whole, in its unity, and in relation to all reality and God.[1]

Revelation and Scripture

In contrast, Christianity claims access to a divine point of view. In prophetic inspirations, historical events, and in Jesus Christ, God has provided a divine perspective that transcends the powers of human discovery and

---

1. Prenter, *Creation and Redemption*, 245–50. Barth speaks of self-knowledge apart from divine revelation as "the phenomena of the human" (*CD* 3/2:132).

pulls us beyond ourselves. Unless God really has revealed himself, Christianity's talk about God, creation, the human condition, sin, and salvation possesses no better warrant to truth than mythology or philosophical reflection. Though there is much to say about the nature of revelation, it is enough for my purpose to assert that Christianity's description of the human condition presupposes the reality of divine revelation as the warrant for its claims.[2] The Bible shows little interest in the human phenomenon isolated from its relationship to God. It does not speak directly about the "human condition" or humanity's "greatness and wretchedness." It reserves all "greatness" language for God, and instead of "wretchedness" speaks of sin, death, and the devil. Patristic-era Christian thinkers in dialogue with Greek humanism became interested in the qualities that set human beings apart from the rest of creation.[3] The Middle Ages emphasized the wretchedness of humanity. The Renaissance highlighted humanity's greatness, but the Reformation returned to an even more radical pessimism about humanity's spiritual capacities. Pascal sounded a modern theme when he wrote about the paradox of humanity's greatness and wretchedness. In all three parts of this book I am following Pascal, looking at the human condition of greatness and wretchedness from three different perspectives. Even though the Bible does not speak in Pascal's language, it addresses both themes and keeps them in paradoxical tension. This chapter focuses on Christianity's understanding of human greatness.

The Image of God

The Bible does not call human beings "great," extol the power of the human mind, or speak of humanity's great accomplishments and vast potential. Nonetheless, it speaks about human beings in ways that imply humanity's greatness. Each of them is worthy of consideration, but I will limit my examination to the assertion that God created human beings "in the image and likeness" of God. This idea, first stated in Genesis 1:26, has become an all-encompassing category that includes everything said in the Scriptures and Christian theology about humanity's greatness, special relationship to God, God-given responsibilities, powers, dignity, and destiny.[4] Many tradi-

---

2. My thoughts on the ground and nature of revelation can be found in Highfield, *Great Is the Lord*, 3–19.

3. Pelikan, *Christianity and Classical Culture*, 280–95.

4. Pannenberg claims that traditional Christian theological anthropology centered on two themes: human beings as the image of God and as sinners (*Anthropology*, 20). This division clearly corresponds to Pascal's paradox of human greatness and

tional and modern theological discussions of humanity give a central role to the biblical affirmation that God created humankind in the "image of God" (Gen 1:26–27).[5] In the patristic era, theologians treated Genesis 1:26 "as though it were a rich mine from which one could unearth invaluable nuggets of theological and anthropological truths . . . [yet] they offered widely divergent views as to how humans image God and where actually this image can be said to reside within themselves."[6] Perhaps such intense interest and diversity of opinion about the meaning of this verse arise because the Bible uses the expressions "image of God" or "likeness of God" only four times to refer to the common humanity shared by all human beings (Gen 1:26, 27; 5:1, 9:6; Jas 3:9; cf. 1 Cor 11:7).[7] In addition, the New Testament uses the expression to refer to Christ as the image of God (2 Cor 4:4; Col 1:15; Heb 1:3). The Bible does not explain why humanity is called the image of God or what this designation means, perhaps because in its ancient context its meaning was clear. A near consensus of Old Testament scholarship understands the image of God against the background of ancient Near Eastern theology of kingship.[8] Human beings are royal images placed on earth as "God's representatives and agents in the world, granted authorized power to share in God's rule or administration of earth's resources and creatures."[9] Middelton designates the royal view of the image "functional" as opposed to "substantial" or "relational."[10] Westermann, in contrast to the "consensus," emphasizes the relational aspect of the image in Genesis 1:27. He argues that this statement is not about the nature of humanity as such, the human substance, but about God's act of creation: "The meaning is that mankind is created so that something can happen between God and man. Mankind

---

wretchedness.

5. Westermann challenges this tradition. If the "image of God" were the central concept revealing the essential Old Testament message about humanity, we would expect the Old Testament to say much more about it. "The fact is that it does not . . . " (*Genesis 1–11: A Commentary*, 155).

6. McLeod, SJ, *The Image of God*, 43. In view of this history, Berkhof's words ring too true: "By studying how systematic theologies have poured meaning into Gen 1:26, one could write a piece of Europe's cultural history" (*Christian Faith*, 184).

7. Van Kooten documents the debate between the minimalists and maximalists with reference to how deeply the image of God theme permeates the Old Testament (*Paul's Anthropology in Context*, 6).

8. Jonsson, *The Image of God*.

9. Middleton, *The Liberating Image*, 27.

10. Middleton, *The Liberating Image*, 19–28. Barth in the long fine-print section in *CD* 3/1:194–200, argues for a relational instead of an "ontological" understanding of the image. Barth has been highly influential on contemporary systematic theologians. Old Testament scholars have been less impressed.

is created to stand before God."[11] Westermann and the "consensus" agree in their criticism of the substantialist view, which sees the image as the highest aspect of the human substance, namely the rational soul. While I am inclined to the consensus interpretation of Genesis 1:26—2:3, I do not think we must view the three categories—substantial, functional, and relational—as mutually exclusive. There must be something in human beings (substance) that qualifies them to rule over creation (function) according to God's command and by his power (relation).[12]

The image idea often occurs in ethical contexts, though not as often as modern usage leads us to expect. Genesis 1:27 and 5:1 give the impression that being created in God's image confers a special blessing on humankind, differentiating them from other creatures. Genesis 9:1–3 gives human beings permission to kill animals for food, but forbids killing human beings, and Genesis 9:6 grounds this prohibition in humanity's status as the image of God.[13] In 1 Corinthians 11:7, Paul appeals to the image of God idea to support his understanding of the proper relationship between men and women and between both and God in worship. Laying aside its obscure and controversial aspects, we can agree with Kelsey's modest assessment of Paul's ethical use of the image idea in this text. "The phrase is invoked as a recognized authoritative claim about the basis in human beings of the respect and honor with which they ought to be treated—namely, that in some way, by imaging God, and referring beyond themselves to God, dishonor of them amounts to dishonor of God."[14] James laments that we use the mouth to "praise our Lord and Father, and with it we curse human beings, who have been made in God's likeness" (Jas 3:9). For James, to disrespect human beings shows the hypocrisy of words that supposedly honor God. Even though there are many unanswered questions about the image of God, the ethical and religious imperatives are unambiguous. Human beings remain God's direct and personal possessions and are not like other creatures placed under direct human control.

11. Westermann, *Creation*.

12. Anderson asserts that in contemporary theology the relational view of the image has replaced the "static attribute or rational/spiritual capacity" view ("On Being Human," 180). Horton, develops his doctrine of the image as "a covenantal relationship." What distinguishes human beings from other creatures is that we have been created "with a special commission, for a special relationship with God" (*The Christian Faith*, 381).

13. Given the Decalogue's prohibition of images and the prophetic polemic against images, it is hard to resist the idea that within the doctrine of humanity as the image of God lies an argument against inanimate images. See Van Kooten, *Paul's Anthropology*, 2–5, 46.

14. Kelsey, *Eccentric Existence* 2:945.

Paul's thought about Christ as the image of God includes ethical, substantial, and revelatory aspects of the image. Despite his use of the image theme in 1 Corinthians 11:7 to make a point about the order of creation, Paul focuses on the Son as the image of God. In 2 Corinthians 4:4, Christ is the image of God in which we can see God's glory. In Colossians 1:15, the Son is the "image of the invisible God" and "the firstborn over all creation." In both of these texts, the "image" means a visible expression that truly mirrors the being and character of the invisible God. And in the latter text (Col 1:15), the image signifies priority and rule. The way we relate to the Son, who is the image of God, constitutes our relation to God. In relating to the Son, we become like him, an image of the Image. The first Adam was earthly and we bear the "image of the earthly man," but our destiny is to "bear the image of the man from heaven" (1 Cor 15:49). God predestined us to be "conformed to the image of his Son" (Rom 8:27), and by looking at the Lord's glory we are "being transformed into his image with ever-increasing glory" (2 Cor 3:18). In Colossians 3:10, we are told to put on "the new self, which is being renewed in knowledge in the image of its Creator." In Paul, then, the image of God retains its connection with dignity and rule but is placed within christological and eschatological frameworks. We see in the Bible a triple meaning of the image: the created human being, the eternal Son of God incarnate, and the human being transformed by the Spirit of God into the image of the Son of God.

The Extraordinary Creature

Christianity understands human beings as those God created, equipped, and commissioned to care for the world, for whose salvation God send his Son into the world, and whom God has determined to make like his Son in the resurrection to eternal life. If we read the history of Christian thought about the image of God closely we will see that a certain divine/human relationship is presupposed or stated explicitly in almost every author. To bring this theme into sharper focus we now give our attention to two seminal quotes from this history, one from Psalm 8:3–5 and the other from John Chrysostom (ca. 350–407).

Why Does God Care about Us?

How valuable are human beings, and what is the basis of their worth? Psalm 8 asks these questions in a memorable way:

> When I consider thy heavens, the work of thy fingers, the moon
> and the stars, which thou hast ordained; What is man, that thou
> art mindful of him? and the son of man, that thou visitest him?
> For thou hast made him a little lower than the angels, and hast
> crowned him with glory and honour. Thou madest him to have
> dominion over the works of thy hands; thou hast put all things
> under his feet.[15]

The psalmist asks the question of human greatness in its most basic form. Why does *God* value human beings? The heavens seem so much more glorious and God-like than earth with its tiny human inhabitants. Yet God has given human beings "glory and honor." Why? It cannot be a reward for something we have done. Do we deserve such honor because of the divinely given properties and powers that distinguish us from other earthly creatures? Perhaps this explains why we think so highly of ourselves, but how does it explain why *God* values us? Clearly, the writer has in mind a scale of dignity among creatures, for he speaks of human beings as made "a little lower" than more glorious beings and having "dominion" over the others. Why would the creator, who is the top of the scale of dignity, pay attention to those somewhere in the middle? And why put human beings in charge of the rest of creation? The rhetorical form of the question shows that the author is not expecting an answer but is expressing wonder at the unexplained and undeserved grace and glory that God gives to us.

The psalmist's question voices the central issue to be decided in developing a theology of human dignity (or greatness)[16] and, indeed, to theological anthropology as a whole. The nature and ground of human dignity cannot be known apart from discovering why God treats human beings as worthy of glory and honor. Many fruitless disputes can be bypassed if we keep our focus on this question. We cannot discover the basis of our dignity by comparing ourselves with lower creatures and isolating the excellences and powers of human nature that distinguish us from them or by enumerating our impressive individual and collective achievements. Only in our God-relation can we understand who and what we truly are and how much we are worth.

---

15. Ps 8:3–5 (KJV).

16. Though the ideas of "greatness" and "dignity" are not completely synonymous, their meaning overlaps in ways significant to this study. As they are used most often, greatness emphasizes the *quantitative* difference between the good characteristics among beings whereas dignity puts the focus on the *qualitative* difference between the good characteristics among beings.

The Most Marvelous Thing!

Consider also this statement from John Chrysostom (ca. 350–407):

> And this is, indeed, the most marvelous thing, that He gave us
> not such a world as this in payment for services done; or as a
> recompense for good works; but at the very time He formed us,
> He honoured our race with this kingdom. For He said, "Let us
> make man after our image, and after our likeness." What is the
> sense of this, "after our image, and after our likeness"? The im-
> age of government is that which is meant; and as there is no
> one in heaven superior to God, so let there be none upon earth
> superior to man. This then is one, and the first respect, in which
> He did him honour; by making him after His own image; and
> secondly, by providing us with this principality, not as a payment
> for services, but *making it entirely the gift of His own love toward
> man;* and thirdly, in that He conferred it upon us as a thing of
> nature. For of governments there are some natural, and others
> which are elective;—natural as of the lion over the quadrupeds,
> or as that of the eagle over the birds; elective, as that of an Em-
> peror over us; for he doth not reign over his fellow-servants by
> any natural authority. Therefore it is that he oftentimes loses his
> sovereignty. For such are things which are not naturally inher-
> ent; they readily admit of change and transposition. But not so
> with the lion; he rules by nature over the quadrupeds, as the
> eagle doth over birds. The character of sovereignty is, therefore,
> constantly allotted to his race; and no lion hath ever been seen
> deprived of it. Such a kind of sovereignty God bestowed upon
> us from the beginning, and set us over all things. And not only
> in this respect did He confer honour upon our nature, but also,
> by the very eminence of the spot in which we were placed, fixing
> upon Paradise as our choice dwelling, and bestowing the gift of
> reason, and an immortal soul.[17]

Chrysostom understands the "image" as the authority and capacity to
rule over the earth as God rules over all things. It is noteworthy, however,
that he sees this role as an honor bestowed by divine love and grace. The
dignity inherent in humanity exists *only in relation to God;* it is "entirely the
gift of His own love toward man." In this way, Chrysostom preserves the priority of the God-human relation for human dignity. But he also states that
God gives us this status "as a thing of nature," that is, as a capacity inherent

---

17. Chrysostom, *Homilies Concerning Statues* (*NPNF*1 9:391–92). Emphasis added.

in the definition of humanity.[18] Chrysostom is undoubtedly correct to make this distinction. Humankind's power of reason is a gracious gift from God, it sets us above other creatures, and makes our rule over them unavoidable. But something more needs to be said.

Speaking of a "thing of nature," or of the "dignity," "worthiness," and "greatness" of humankind may lead us to think of dignity as a "thing" that people possess independent of their relationships. But Chrysostom and Psalm 8 tie our greatness to our relation of being loved by God. The "thing of nature" (reason) comes from God, opens us to God, and determines our end as God. Our God-relation, which is our being loved by God, is what makes us what we are and determines what we shall become. It is not merely an external relation but, so to speak, an aspect of our substance. God's love for us is creative, constant, and transformative. It defines us. Human beings just *are* those loved by God in the way he loves us and calls us into a history in which we are given the capacity to love him in return. The true greatness of humanity even in the present life is determined by the end toward which this history aims.[19] What is that end?

The Greatness of Human Dignity

As Psalm 8 reminds us, God does not love us because of something love-able in us. On the other hand, it is not quite correct to say God loves us for no reason. Even as creator, God loves us *for the sake of his Son*.[20] For all eternity the Father has loved his Son in the Spirit and the Son has returned that love in the Spirit. The Son is by nature the "exact representation" of God's being (Heb 1:3) and he is the "image of the invisible God" (Col 1:15) in his appearing as a human being. Our destiny is to be "like him" (1 John 3:2) and to be united with him in his death and resurrection (Rom 6:5). Irenaeus continues this New Testament theme into the postapostolic era when he urges us to follow "the only true and stedfast Teacher, the Word of God, our Lord Jesus Christ, who did, through His transcendent love, become what we are, that He might bring us to be even what He is Himself."[21] The Son identifies with us that we may identify with him and become like

18. Chrysostom, *Homilies Concerning Statues* (*NPNF1* 9:391–92).

19. Webster concludes, "Only God the Creator can crown with glory and honour; creatures are not competent to ascribe dignity to themselves or to other creatures. . . . And because it is rooted in God's free favour alone, creaturely dignity is secure" ("The Dignity of Creatures," 24).

20 Highfield, *The Faithful Creator*, 113–30.

21. *AH* 5 (*ANF* 1:526). I will explore this theme in greater detail in chapter 11.

him. And God loves his Son and all those whom the Son loves. Looking at the creation of humanity from this perspective, we can see that God loves us for the sake of his Son, and he sees in us the image of his Son, which is our destiny to become. Hence, it is neither true to say that God loves us for what we are nor that God loves us for no reason. *He loves us for what we will become through our union with his Son*, and this love is the ground and assurance of our infinite worth to God, our dignity in the world, and the greatness of our endowments.

Even in our own self-examination we discover hints of our great potential that evoke longings for something greater, better, and more enduring. But our longing extends far beyond our powers of attainment. In the Christian story, we are told about the origin of our potential and the purpose of our endowments. We are given a vision of full actualization of that potential and the means by which it will be accomplished. We are images of God whose task is to make the divine nature visible in the created world. Our ultimate end is to become so united to God that we share in his glory, immortality, and incorruptibility. I dare say a greater end cannot be imagined, that is, to be given everything God has and by grace to share in everything he is. Jesus Christ crucified and risen from the dead is the means by which this end will be accomplished.

4

Into a Distant Country[1]

The Biblical View of Human Wretchedness

CHRISTIANITY ACKNOWLEDGES THE KIND of wretchedness we explored in part one of this book: unhappiness, ignorance, disappointment, discontent, suffering, guilt, death, anxiety, and all the rest. The Bible includes the Old Testament book of Ecclesiastes, the third line of which laments, "Meaningless! Meaningless! . . . Utterly meaningless! Everything is meaningless!" (1:2). The author sees nothing in life but vanity, death, and frustration. The New Testament adds nothing new to the moralists of its day when it describes such crimes as murder, theft, and adultery as great evils. Nor does it innovate by condemning the vices of envy, jealousy, pride, lust, and greed. It breaks no new ground when it praises self-control, patience, prudence, and courage. Aristotle, Cicero, Epictetus, and many others do this. The New Testament authors do not invent a new vocabulary to describe human wretchedness but use common Greek terms for crimes, vices, and virtues. The important word *"hamartia"* (mistake, fault), translated most often in the New Testament as "sin," has a long history in Greek moral thought.[2]

What makes Christianity's understanding of human wretchedness distinct is the way all these acts, virtues, and vices are set in relation to the God revealed in the Old Testament law, the prophets, and Jesus Christ. It was not uncommon in the ancient world to view certain moral laws as handed down by a god and to consider violation of the law an offence not only to the state

---

1. Travel into a distant country as a metaphor for the fall into sin comes from Luke 15:11–32.

2. See Grundmann et al., "ἁμαρτάνω, ἁμάρτημα, ἁμαρτία," *TDNT* 1:267–316.

34

but also to the god.[3] In Greek and Roman religious thought, certain acts were believed to be offensive to the gods—acts of rashness and dishonor *(hubris)*, injustice *(adikia)*, and other sins, whether intentional or unintentional, moral or ritual.[4] In the Old Testament, "the God" is the God of Abraham, Isaac, and Jacob who freed the people of Israel from Egyptian slavery and made a gracious covenant with them to be their God. God's laws are the conditions of the relationship laid down in that covenant (Exod 20:1–17).[5] In the New Testament, God makes a new covenant open to all people through the life, death, and resurrection of Jesus Christ. For Christianity, the human relationship with God envisioned in the new covenant embodies the highest good, absolute right, and ultimate fulfillment of humanity. Hence, for Christianity, the central core of human wretchedness to which all other dimensions must be subordinated is violation of that gracious covenant and consequent alienation from God. The New Testament designates those acts of violation "sin," the resulting condition of alienation "death," and the power that holds us in this wretched condition the "devil."

Sin

Sin is among those terms I mentioned in the introduction with which everyone is familiar but few understand to any depth. Since the church presents the message of salvation for the most part as salvation from sin and its consequences, superficial understandings of sin go hand in hand with superficial understandings of salvation, the means of salvation, and the savior. In this section, I aim to deepen our understanding of the Christian doctrine of sin, though in this short space I cannot present a comprehensive study of the doctrine. Such a project would involve extensive analyses of biblical materials and their backgrounds in ancient cultures. We would need to examine the history of the church's doctrine and theology of sin and enter the controversies that have arisen in that history. Instead of a comprehensive study, I want to present Christianity's basic teaching about what sin is, what its effects on the sinner and the world are, and why we need divine help to get free of it.[6]

3. For example, in the prologue to the code of Hammurabi, Hammurabi says, "When Marduk commissioned me to guide the people aright, to direct the land, I established law and justice in the language of the land, thereby promoting the welfare of the people. At that time (I decreed):" Then follows the statutes (*ANET*, 165).

4. *OCD*, 3rd ed., s.v. "sin."

5. See Grundmann et al., "ἁμαρτάνω, ἁμάρτημα, ἁμαρτία," *TDNT* 1:271–86.

6. My thinking on the doctrine of sin has been influenced by studying the thought of two of the twentieth century's most influential theologians, Karl Barth and Karl

Sin Is an Act

A sin is an act, voluntary, bad, and wrong. The first thing to get clear is that sins are human *acts,* not aspects of human nature. According to the first chapter of Genesis, God pronounced the whole creation *very good,* meaning not that it is perfect but that it can serve God's good purpose. In a strange transition I will address below, God's good creatures abandon God's service and work against his purposes and their wellbeing. However, this abandonment does not destroy and recreate human beings as evil creatures. Sins are *bad* because they work against the true human end. They harm the actor and those whom the acts affect. Voluntary acts are *wrong* when they contradict the will of God. To be sinful, movements must be voluntary and active, not involuntary and passive.[7] Developing heart disease or being struck by a falling tree limb are not sins even though they are "bad" in a certain sense.[8] Such biblical themes as law, prophetic threats of divine judgment, calls for repentance, confession of sins, and forgiveness of sins highlight this view of sin. Throughout the Old Testament, the commandments of God are extolled as good and right and obedience is held up as praiseworthy. Abraham is praised for his willingness to give up his son Isaac in obedience to the LORD's command (Gen 22:16–17). Repeatedly, Exodus tells us that Moses "did just as the LORD commanded him" (Exod 7:6–20; 39:32–42). Moses explains the meaning of the commands he received from the LORD:

> What does the LORD your God ask of you but to fear the LORD your God, to walk in all his ways, to love him, to serve the LORD your God with all your heart and with all your soul, and to observe the LORD's commands and decrees that I am giving you today for your own good? (Deut 10:12–13)

Jesus adopts the attitude of an obedient son: "The world must learn that I love the Father and that I do exactly what my Father has commanded me" (John 14:31; cf. 15:10). And "My food is to do the will of him who sent me and to finish his work" (John 4:34). Jesus completes a life of obedience by giving his fate utterly to the will of his Father (Luke 22:42). Paul, even as he explains how the law cannot save us, says, "So then, the law is holy, and the commandment is holy, righteous, and good" (Rom 7:12). Although the New Testament clearly teaches that no one can be saved by keeping the law,

---

Rahner. See my studies, *Barth and Rahner* and "The Freedom to Say 'No'?" 485–505.

7. According to Günther, guilt, fate, and suffering were "inextricably woven together" in the classical Greek period ("Sin," *NIDNT* 3:577).

8. That is to say, they thwart penultimate ends, such as temporal happiness, physical health, and long life.

it is just as clear that it is never good and right to break the commandments. John explains, "Everyone who sins breaks the law; in fact, sin is lawlessness" (1 John 3:4). Over and over, the prophets Amos, Hosea, Isaiah, Jeremiah, and Ezekiel charge the people of Judah and Israel with breaking the covenant's stipulations. These prophets demand repentance and threaten God's punishment. Jesus began his ministry with a prophet-like message of repentance. "The time has come," he said. "The kingdom of God has come near. Repent and believe the good news!" (Mark 1:15). The instructions for the yearly Day of Atonement's activities included a moment of confession of sins. After Aaron makes the sin offering, he performs the rite of the scapegoat: "He is to lay both hands on the head of the live goat and confess over it all the wickedness and rebellion of the Israelites—all their sins—and put them on the goat's head" (Lev 16:21). The Psalms contain many instances of confession of sins. Psalm 32:5 reads:

> Then I acknowledged my sin to you
> and did not cover up my iniquity.
> I said, "I will confess
> my transgressions to the LORD."
> And you forgave
> the guilt of my sin.

When John the Baptist appeared preaching repentance, many people responded by "confessing their sins" and being baptized in the Jordan River (Mark 1:5). Finally, John explains,

> If we claim to be without sin, we deceive ourselves and the truth
> is not in us. If we confess our sins, he is faithful and just and will
> forgive us our sins and purify us from all unrighteousness. If we
> claim we have not sinned, we make him out to be a liar and his
> word is not in us. (1 John 1:9–10)

If the Scriptures teach that sin is transgression of the law, that repentance is required, that confession is mandatory, and that forgiveness is possible and necessary, our first thesis, that *sin is a voluntary, bad, and wrong act*, is confirmed. If it were not voluntary, no blame could be assigned and repentance, confession, and forgiveness would make no sense. Likewise, if it were not bad and wrong there would be nothing to repent of, confess, or seek forgiveness for.

Sin Is an Internal Act

So far I have spoken of sin only as an external act, a voluntary movement manifested in the physical world by means of the body—a look, a word, a deed. However, I made it clear that such externally directed acts must be voluntary if we are to consider them sins. In confessing and repenting of our sins, we look back on our external acts and confess *ourselves* as the origin of our actions, that is, that our bad and wrong external acts really were ours; they externalized our inner desires. For an act to be voluntary it need not arise from cold, calculated malice. It may be accompanied by all sorts of external and internal conditions that facilitate the act—inclinations, habits, ignorance, temptations, and provocations. However, as long as these conditions do not necessitate or render our actions accidental, they do not absolve us of responsibility. In confessing our sins, we may not be able to specify a moment of deliberation or decision distinguishable from the moment of the act. Nonetheless, confession and repentance presuppose that the act was carried out willingly.

The most obvious internal act is thinking, perhaps because it is most under our conscious control. Desires and feelings, though internal, spring spontaneously into our awareness. But this distinction should not be pressed. We think even when we are not aware of it, and we know that our desires and feelings are not devoid of rational aspects. Even though the operation of thinking is an aspect of human nature, it can be used for good or evil. Hence the Scriptures speak of "evil thoughts," which we enact when we use our rational powers to envision means of doing wrong things (Mark 7:21; Matt 15:19). In the Scriptures, many internal acts of thought, desire, and feeling are designated sinful. The Tenth Commandment declares, "You shall not covet" (Exod 20:17). The New Testament condemns greed, envy, lust, jealousy, impatience, pride, hatred, anger, and many more passions, desires, and feelings. Jesus's moral teaching in the Sermon on the Mount (Matt 5–7) and elsewhere connects inward and outward sins and virtues in an unbroken continuum. "Every good tree," Jesus observes, "bears good fruit, but a bad tree bears bad fruit. A good tree cannot bear bad fruit, and a bad tree cannot bear good fruit" (Matt 7:17–18). Paul also connects internal and external sins and virtues seamlessly and designates both as acts:[9]

> The acts of the flesh are obvious: sexual immorality, impurity and debauchery; idolatry and witchcraft; hatred, discord, jealousy, fits of rage, selfish ambition, dissensions, factions, and envy; drunkenness, orgies, and the like. I warn you, as I did

9. Gal 5:19–24 and Col 3:5–14.

before, that those who live like this will not inherit the kingdom of God. But the fruit of the Spirit is love, joy, peace, forbearance, kindness, goodness, faithfulness, gentleness, and self-control. Against such things there is no law. Those who belong to Christ Jesus have crucified the flesh with its passions and desires.

Already, with the notion that such negative emotions as hate and envy merit condemnation and such positive ones as love and patience merit praise, we are getting close to the limits of what introspection can detect and psychology can explain. We understand readily when we are told that Sam flew into a rage because he was jealous of the attention his wife received from Harry. We can also understand when we are told that Sam was jealous because he was unsure of his wife's love. But why was Sam unsure of his wife's love? Perhaps she had been untrue in the past. Or, perhaps Sam can never rest in the certainty of his wife's love because he does not love her truly. And he cannot love her truly because he cannot love anyone truly. Where do explanations stop? Such psychological explanations usually progress until they arrive at the beginning of a motivational chain that is not an act at all but a fate. The self has been damaged by violence or illness or in some other way is under the compulsion of necessity. Hence, psychological analysis always ends up rooting sinful acts in a cause *other than the sinner*. The Christian doctrine of sin comes to a different conclusion by a different method.

The Christian doctrine of sin asserts that, in the fundamental act out of which all other sinful acts flow, God's good creature turns away from the good and rebels against the right. This first and basic act has no cause other than the human self.[10] From a rational point of view this act is absurd, because in it we turn away from our highest good and reject the grace and love of the creator. This basic sin has been called unbelief, pride, or ingratitude. Whatever we call it, it is the act of breaking fellowship with God, denying our dependence on God, and asserting independence from God. This act is not under our conscious control as external acts are. We cannot simply choose not to do it. Nor is it available for introspection or psychological analysis as are other internal acts. Sin's radical nature is revealed only in the radical remedy enacted by God in Jesus Christ.[11] In the ordinary flow of life we first encounter a problem and then pursue a solution. The knowledge of the solution is implicit in the problem, just as the antidote to a poison

10. In commenting on Romans chapters 1 and 7, Grundmann says, "Assertion against the claim of God" is for Paul "the original sin" (Grundmann et al., "ἁμαρτάνω, ἁμάρτημα, ἁμαρτία," *TDNT* 1:310–11).

11. I agree with Karl Barth when he says, "We maintain the simple thesis that only when we know Jesus Christ do we really know that man is the man of sin, and what sin is, and what it means for man" (*CD* 4/1:389).

is implicit in the composition of the poison. In the Christian doctrine of sin, the method is reversed. Only after God's salvation appeared in Jesus Christ could the problem of sin be known in its fullness. Salvation from sin required the death and resurrection of the incarnate Son of God, and it requires our own death and resurrection in union with Jesus. To escape sin and its consequences we must die and be recreated by the power of the Holy Spirit. In sum, sin is a primal act that taints every subsequent act, but it is not the essence of human beings. This act creates a kind of second nature whose further acts are based on an imaginary world ordered not to God as the highest good but centered on the self as a kind of false god. We are at a loss to find psychological, anthropological, existential, or metaphysical language to describe this situation.

Sin as a Nest of Paradoxes

I referred above to the basic act of sin as absurd, that is, as contradictory to the welfare of the sinner. The very idea of a voluntary act is inconceivable unless we think of the actors as envisioning a better state to be gained through their act. No one can desire their own unhappiness. Sin's absurdity, however, does not appear to the sinner as the absurdity it really is. Here is the first paradox: *we sin knowingly and unknowingly.* Christian thinkers from Paul to Kierkegaard lament this wretched paradox. Paul complains, "For although they knew God, they neither glorified him as God nor gave thanks to him, but their thinking became futile and their foolish hearts were darkened" (Rom 1:21). In *Confessions,* Augustine asks why human beings, whose happiness can be found only in truth, reject manifest truth. "The answer must be this," he muses, "their love for truth takes the form that they love something else and want this object of their love to be the truth; and because they do not wish to be deceived, they do not wish to be persuaded that they are mistaken."[12] Kierkegaard deals with the problem of self-deception in *The Sickness unto Death,* in a chapter devoted to "the Socratic definition of sin."[13] The Socratic view roots bad behavior in lack of understanding. Kierkegaard agrees "to a certain degree," but asserts that Christianity roots this ignorance in the will. That is to say, Christianity "shows that sin is rooted in willing and arrives at the concept of defiance."[14] Traditional philosophy and theology speak of the sinner as willing evil *sub*

12. Augustine, *Confessions* 10.34, Chadwick, *Saint Augustine,* 199–200.

13. Kierkegaard, *Sickness unto Death,* 87–96.

14. Kierkegaard, *Sickness unto Death,* 93. For analysis of Kierkegaard's thinking on self-deception, see Mullen, *Kierkegaard's Philosophy,* 59–72.

specie boni, that is, willing what is evil as if it were good.[15] On the one hand, if we were completely deceived into thinking that the objective of our act is good when it is in fact evil, our responsibility for the act would be removed. On the other hand, to will evil *as evil*—that is, with full knowledge of its utter nothingness—would imply that we were by nature irredeemably evil. This implication opposes the goodness of creation and God's offer of repentance, forgiveness, and redemption. It seems, then, that we who know better deceive ourselves. We will evil *sub specie boni,* but we are not completely deceived by its appearance. Both sides of the paradox must be true, but we do not know how to reconcile them.

The second paradox is this: *sin is universal, but not essential.* The Scriptures everywhere assume and sometimes affirm that everyone sins (Rom 3:23, 5:12; 1 John 1:7–10).[16] How do Paul, John, and others know this? Ordinarily, when we uncover a universal characteristic of a species we consider this trait to be an essential part of its nature, not an accidental property or a voluntary feature. However, according to the Bible, sin is not part of the human essence. It is an *accidental* but *universal* accompaniment to human nature rooted in voluntary action. While there is no logical or physical law that makes it impossible for accidental features or voluntary acts to be universal across a species, we would not expect things to turn out that way. An *accidental* universal or a *universal* accident seems a very strange concept. Yet, that is what the Bible affirms about sin. Why are New Testament authors so sure of this? We get a clue from 1 John 1:7–10:

> But if we walk in the light, as he is in the light, we have fellowship with one another, and the blood of Jesus, his Son, purifies us from all sin. If we claim to be without sin, we deceive ourselves and the truth is not in us. If we confess our sins, he is faithful and just and will forgive us our sins and purify us from all unrighteousness. If we claim we have not sinned, we make him out to be a liar and his word is not in us.

According to John, those who claim to be "without sin" are wrong and can only be deceiving themselves. Not only that, this claim makes God out to be a liar, because we have rejected "his word." John does not appeal to his observations of actual sins in an inductive argument to refute claims of

15. Berkouwer, *Sin,* 236. See also the discussion in Kant, *Critique of Practical Reason,* 62. Kant used the term *sub ratione boni.*

16. The exception in the New Testament is Jesus. Paul (Rom 3:10–12) quotes Psalm 14:1–3, which declares "there is no one who does good, not even one." In Second Temple Judaism, sin was considered nearly universal. However, such OT figures as Moses, Abraham, and Elijah, were exempted from sin (Grundmann et al., "ἁμαρτάνω, ἁμάρτημα, ἁμαρτία," *TDNT* 1:291).

sinlessness. He appeals, rather, to something God has said and done as the ground of his confidence that everyone sins. God knows the truth, and God has declared everyone guilty. Hence, we know that everyone has sinned. To what "word" of divine judgment is John appealing? Given what he says in verse 7 about the blood of Jesus purifying "us from all sin," it seems that John is referring to God's act of providing universal atonement for sin in the action of Jesus Christ. In offering grace, forgiveness, and purification to all, God declares everyone to be in need of grace, forgiveness, and purification. Hence, all have sinned. To claim exemption from sin is to claim not to need grace, forgiveness, and purification and, so, to make God into a liar.

Paul often declares the universality of sin. In the conclusion to the arguments of Romans 1–3, he declares, "There is no difference between Jew and Gentile, for all have sinned and fall short of the glory of God, and all are justified freely by his grace through the redemption that came by Christ Jesus" (3:22b–24). Notice the relationship between the universal judgment that "all have sinned" and the assertion "all are freely justified . . . by Christ Jesus." We find this same relationship in Romans 11 at the end of Paul's reflection on the unfaithfulness of Israel: "For God has bound everyone over to disobedience so that he may have mercy on them all" (11:32). That is to say, God ignores the relative seriousness of different sins and places all sinners in the same category so that he might show the same mercy to all.

In a third paradox, *we sin voluntarily, but not deliberately.* In its basic form, sin is misdirected and deceived self-love, an act of willing turned away from the good. We cannot simply decide not to sin because all our decisions derive from our misdirected wills. Willing always precedes deciding. A decision to stop sinning would be another instance of misdirected and deceived self-love. Such thinking leads to an infinite regression. It is impossible to wrest ourselves free from sin because we do not wholly will such freedom. According to the New Testament, we cannot truly will our freedom from sin until the grace of Christ and the love of the Spirit break down the prison doors.

Sin as Offense to God

So far, we have seen that Christianity understands sin as a basic act directed away from good and right toward bad and wrong from which flow other internal and external acts of the same character. Now we need to explore the biblical and traditional teaching that sin is offense to God. Berkouwer speaks for much traditional theology when he says, "Scripture describes sin in a variety of ways. . . . But it is obvious that in all the multiformity of sin there is always a common trait: sin is always *against God*."[17] The will of God is the law of being, and God wills as right only that which is good. So, when human beings act to achieve something contrary to the good and right they oppose God. Opposing God differs in quality from opposing the laws of physics. We may imagine a different world where our will is the law of nature. But we cannot evade physical law. Opposing our wills to unchangeable law can bring only destruction to ourselves. Such opposition is foolish but not insulting. Offense has to do with personal relationships, and God's relationship to us is personal. The creator graciously gives life and all good things to us. We learn from the message of the cross that God cares for the world with love that knows no limits. In the basic act of sin we refuse to acknowledge the most precious gift from the creator and decline to trust the source of all truth. In doing so, we relate to God as if he were deceptive, unloving, unwise, and unjust. This implication is the reason most Christian thinkers consider sin an offense to God and make it liable to divine punishment and in need of divine forgiveness.[18]

Death

Everyone sins and everyone dies, but not everyone sees the connection between the two. For Christian faith, the multidimensional nature of death comes into view only in relation to sin.[19]

Sin and Death in the Bible

In the biblical drama of wretchedness, death and sin play mutually supporting roles. In the story of the fall, Adam is told that he must not eat fruit from the "tree of the knowledge of good and evil, for when you eat from it you will certainly die" (Gen 3:17). God's warning to Adam does not imply that he was created immortal and threatened with loss of immortality. To the contrary, this story assumes that physical death is natural and that immortality is a possibility forfeited by disobedience. Adam's

---

17. Berkouwer, *Sin,* 242. Emphasis original.

18. The *Heidelberg Catechism* asserts "that sin, which is committed against the most high majesty of God, be also punished with . . . everlasting punishment" (Schaff, *CC* 3:309). Turretin states an opinion common among Post-Reformation Reformed theologians: "every sin is opposed to the glory of God and injurious to his infinite majesty. Thus it has in its measure infinite culpability. . . . If, therefore, the culpability is infinite, the punishment also due to it must be infinite" (*IET* 1:598–99).

19. Barth, *CD* 3/2:587–640.

sin did not change his physical body from immortal to mortal. Instead, it alienated him from God and transformed natural death into something unnatural, that is, a punishment for sin.[20] Paul tells us that sin made its appearance in the world through Adam and that death came "through sin, and in this way death came to all people, because all sinned" (Rom 5:12). In the verses that follow, Paul speaks about death in a way that indicates he means something more by this term than mere death of the body.[21] He speaks three times of death "reigning" over sinners (5:14, 17, 21) and contrasts the reign of death with the reign of those who receive God's gift of grace and righteousness through Jesus Christ (5:17). In verse 21, he speaks of God's grace "reigning through righteousness to bring eternal life through Jesus Christ our Lord." Just as the "eternal life" made possible through Jesus is more than mere continued biological existence, the death that came through sin is more than cessation of biological life.

In what does this "more" consist? We may find a partial answer in Romans 7:8b–11, 21–24:

> For apart from the law, sin was dead. Once I was alive apart from the law; but when the commandment came, sin sprang to life and I died. I found that the very commandment that was intended to bring life actually brought death. For sin, seizing the opportunity afforded by the commandment, deceived me, and through the commandment put me to death. . . . So I find this law at work: Although I want to do good, evil is right there with me. For in my inner being I delight in God's law; but I see another law at work in me, waging war against the law of my mind and making me a prisoner of the law of sin at work within me. What a wretched man I am! Who will rescue me from this body that is subject to death?

In this famously complicated chapter, Paul uses the concept of death and dying in at least four senses. First, he speaks of the physical death of a husband, which frees the wife from the law of marriage (7:2–3). Second, he speaks of our dying to the law by being united to the death of Christ (7:4–6). We do not die to the law through physical death but by coming under a new covenant through Christ's death. In this new covenant, we "die" to the law in the sense that we escape its jurisdiction. Third, he speaks of sin being dead apart from the law (7:8). Here "death" must mean dormancy or inactivity. Finally, he speaks three times of sin killing him by taking advantage of the law's power to awaken sin (7:9–11). Clearly, for Paul, there are many types

---

20. Abel, "Death As The Last Enemy," *CV* 58/1:19–54.

21. Bouteneff, *Beginnings*, 42–44.

of death. The fourth kind is of special relevance to this section on death's relationship to sin. Paul cannot be referring to physical death. He must be thinking about the death of something in his relationship to God. Here death seems almost identical to the destructive effects of sin on the sinner. By provoking people to sin, the law "kills" them, that is, it plunges them into a condition of alienation and condemnation. Paul makes the connection between sin and death also in other places (Rom 6:20–23, 8:1–3; Eph 2:1–5; 5:14; Col 2:12–13). In his Parable of the Prodigal Son, Jesus uses the terms death and life in a spiritual sense. When the wayward son returned home, the father orders that preparations be made to celebrate, "For this son of mine was dead and is alive again; he was lost and is found" (Luke 16:24, 32). The word death is used also by James (1:14–15; 5:19–20) and Revelation (3:1) in a metaphorical sense.

The Problem of Physical Death

Physical death is natural in that it fits into the pattern of the physical universe. All physical things change, and the law of entropy applies everywhere. As a whole, the universe tends toward disorder, even though in certain locations entropy temporarily decreases. Each individual thing eventually disintegrates, and all living things die. Yet human beings have always feared and loathed death and have never accepted it as a good thing. Even though "normal" and "natural" from a physical point of view, from a humanistic perspective death seems abnormal and unnatural. The measure of human dignity and potential seems out of proportion to the brevity of life. For no finite length of time can satisfy the human thirst for life or fulfill the virtually infinite human potential. Termination of our existence at any point, no matter how far into the future, threatens the meaning of the present and every other moment of our lives. We know that whatever we accomplish will come to nothing. Whatever good we enjoy, we know there is much more we will never experience.[22]

The Bible views physical death as unnatural. God created human beings in his image, established a relationship with them through reason and revelation, and demands that they love him and each other. How does death fit into this pattern? Why would God create a world that goes nowhere but to death? God does not need anything. Only if creation itself is the beneficiary of God's goodness does divine creation make sense. It makes sense, then, to hypothesize that God intends to produce beings that can enjoy God

22. See Küng, *Eternal Life?* 34–43, for his simple exposition of three philosophical treatments of meaning and death: Martin Heidegger, Jean Paul Sartre, and Karl Jaspers.

forever. We are not limited to hypothesizing, however. The New Testament proclaims the resurrection of the dead as a historical fact in the case of Jesus of Nazareth. Before this event, the resurrection of the dead stood as a theological hypothesis, well grounded in the character of God but unproven. However, the death and resurrection of Jesus demonstrated that the creator loves us and intends to take us through death into eternal life. The resurrection of Jesus exposes the unnaturalness of physical death. In Jesus Christ, death has been incorporated into God's larger plan for our salvation and the redemption of creation, so that Paul can say, quoting Isaiah 25:8, "Death has been swallowed up in victory" (1 Cor 15:54).

Death as Estrangement from God

In our survey of the biblical theme of death's relationship to sin, we concluded that though physical death does not result from sin's effect on the body, sin endows death with a negative quality beyond its threat as an absolute end; it makes death a punishment for sin.[23] What accounts for this additional negative quality? As I argued above, sin is the basic act of turning away from God to lesser goods. Sin declares independence from God, refuses to believe and trust God, and in this way insults God. But God is the giver of life, apart from whose generosity there is no being at all. If the creature really could remove itself from God's hands, if God allowed sin to achieve its projected goal, the sinner would die. However, since God continues graciously to sustain our lives despite our sin, we deceive ourselves into thinking we can live without God. But this self-deception can never blind us completely to the truths that God is life and sin is death. Hence, death always hangs over the heads of sinners as their self-chosen fate.

Spiritual death is the condition of being sustained by God while in active rebellion against God. Why does this condition deserve to be called death? The most basic reason is the one discussed above, that is, that the act of sin embraces nothingness, *sub specie boni,* as its desired destiny. In doing this, it opposes God, who is the principle of unity, the highest good, and the ground of human dignity. Though God sustains the unity of the sinner's life, it is bereft of all positive awareness and love for God. Without love for God it falls prey to many competing and disordered phenomena clamoring

---

23. Wright, *Surprised by Hope,* 95. Barth seems hesitant to speak of death as a "divine punishment." He speaks, rather, of death as a "sign of God's judgment on us" (*CD* 3/2:596). However, the two interpretations may not be all that far apart. Punishment need not mean "retributive" punishment. It can mean disciplinary and reformatory infliction of pain.

for attention and promising happiness. Disunity, fragmentation, confusion, dullness, insecurity, and conflict characterize its intentional life. Since death comes to a living being when it loses its integrity, death is an appropriate name for this spiritual state of disintegration. However, because God does not let it fall into nothingness, the death effected by sin is a living death, a wretched existence from which only God can rescue (Rom 7:24). Out of this condition of conflict, rebellion, insecurity, and confusion come all other inner and outer acts of violence and despair. Pride, envy, greed, hatred, and lust are internal but outward bound acts destined to expand the realm of death, first to the emotional and conscious life of the self and then to the world of other selves. Murder, theft, adultery, gossip, lying, war, and all other acts of violence toward others arise from poverty and conflict within. The entire world, as Paul concludes, is under the reign of death.

Death as a Consequence and Punishment for Sin

If we include in its definition all the consequences that flow from the basic act of sin, then we can conclude that sin is its own punishment. Every change in the self and in the world caused by sin is bad, destructive, and painful. Rahner argues that, "the punishments of sin are the persistent objectivations of the bad moral decision, being themselves hurtful because contrary to the true nature of the free subject."[24] No good can result from abandoning the absolute source of good, because such abandonment embraces the bad. A thing is bad because it harms the integrity of the nature it affects. As long as that nature remains intact, it recoils against the harmful thing, thereby experiencing pain. The prospect of pain is a negative motivator, and the experience of pain warns against repeating the destructive behavior. These negative consequences can be placed into three categories: internal, external, and social. As we saw above, sin creates internal conflict, sadness, despair, contradiction, guilt, anxiety, confusion, and other painful disturbances. When internal "death" makes its way into the physical world, it causes damage to our bodies and to the bodies and souls of others. Robbery, murder, and other violent acts destroy the physical and psychic health of others. When others perceive us as the cause of their internal and external injuries, they often respond with abandonment of friendship, good will, and civility. Under threat, others rise up to defend themselves with preemptory or retaliatory violence against the threatening individual. Every act of injury is also an insult to the dignity of the one under attack, and insult creates

24. Rahner, "Sin II: Punishment of Sin," 1587.

desire for revenge in the one insulted. In these ways, the basic act of sin recoils on the sinner and causes damage, pain, and death.

Ordinarily we think of punishment as infliction of loss and pain on people for their bad acts in addition to the loss and pain that accrues as a result of the acts' natural consequences.[25] The judicial idea of punishment assumes that sometimes the natural effects of sinful acts on the sinner are not proportionate to the damage their sin does to others. They are too mild or their full effect is in doubt or may be delayed until the far distant future. Usually, punishment is inflicted for one of two purposes, retribution or deterrence. Retribution inflicts pain to maintain a balance between pain suffered by the sinner and that inflicted on others by the sinner. Though philosophers distinguish as many as nine types of retributive justice,[26] most conclude that such punishment is just because the wrongdoer "deserves" it.[27] It does not feel right for a criminal to "get away with" a crime or to "get off light." The threat of pain may also deter future sinful acts. In this case, the balance between sin and punishment is not as important as in the previous case, because the goal is not justice but deterrence. The level of pain necessary for deterrence is determined by whether or not it creates enough fear to discourage future behavior. However, justice requires that the threat not go beyond the level needed to deter the behavior in question.

In what sense, then, are the destructive and painful consequences of sin *punishments*? Because punishment is a judicial concept, the natural consequences of sin count as punishments only if the creator intends them as an element of justice within the natural order. The creator orders nature so that it deters and punishes sin.[28] But one might object that nature does not seem to do a very good job balancing the pain the sinner inflicts on others with the pain sin causes to the sinner. Do not some people "get away" with horrible crimes? Are not some greedy and selfish people relatively happy for their entire lives? Such complaints are common and understandable, and one finds them in many of the Psalms and Old

---

25. Rahner warns against taking a concept of punishment from the civil, secular sphere and applying it to God's relationship to sinners ("Guilt, Responsibility, and Punishment," 197–217).

26. Cottingham, "Varieties of Retribution," 238–46.

27. Walen, "Retributive Justice."

28. Rahner argues that the pain caused by the contradiction between the nature of the free agent and the moral order can be considered divine punishment because "God is the guardian of the moral order." Such punishments are "retributive" only in the sense that God maintains the order that rebounds on the sinner painfully ("Sin II: Punishment of Sin," 1587).

Testament Wisdom Literature. In Psalm 73:1–14 the writer complains about the prosperity of the wicked:

Surely God is good to Israel,

to those who are pure in heart.

But as for me, my feet had almost slipped;

I had nearly lost my foothold.

For I envied the arrogant

when I saw the prosperity of the wicked.

They have no struggles;

their bodies are healthy and strong.

They are free from common human burdens;

they are not plagued by human ills.

Therefore pride is their necklace;

they clothe themselves with violence.

From their callous hearts comes iniquity;

their evil imaginations have no limits . . .

This is what the wicked are like—

always free of care, they go on amassing wealth.

Surely in vain I have kept my heart pure

and have washed my hands in innocence.

All day long I have been afflicted,

and every morning brings new punishments.

In the book of Ecclesiastes the writer makes many observations about the apparent lack of justice in the natural flow of things:

"In this meaningless life of mine I have seen both of these: the righteous perishing in their righteousness, and the wicked living long in their wickedness." (7:15)

"When the sentence for a crime is not quickly carried out, people's hearts are filled with schemes to do wrong." (8:11)

"There is something else meaningless that occurs on earth: the righteous who get what the wicked deserve, and the wicked who get what the righteous deserve. This too, I say, is meaningless." (8:14)

In many cases, these complaints seem justified. But this is true only if one takes a short-term view; for in negating God, sin also negates life and meaning. Everything gained through acts of sin will be taken away—possessions, honor, and even remembrance. From a human point of view, however, leaving punishment to God in this way does not satisfy. Fear of divine punishment in the form of the natural consequences of sin does not deter everyone from committing crimes. Nor does it satisfy most people's desire to see punishment follow in closer succession to crime. Hence, many Christian thinkers have argued that death is not enough punishment to balance the accounts. To satisfy the demands of justice, God must add post-mortem pain in hell to the natural consequences of sin. Because I am interested at this stage only in preparing our minds for the doctrine of atonement, let us lay aside the debate about the nature of hell and focus on the question of retributive punishment. The general argument for the necessity of additional punishment goes something like this: The Scriptures teach that God will inflict the punishment of hell on some people. God is unquestionably just, hence such punishment is just. To say that a punishment is just is to affirm that it is deserved, which is the definition of retributive justice. From there, we could speculate about why such punishment is deserved. We could argue that some especially outrageous sins against humanity—mass murder, genocide, and rape—deserve greater punishment than death. But the most common reason given for the necessity of this greater punishment is that sin insults God. Condemning unrepentant sinners to hell is a just action because insulting God is the worst possible sin, since it blasphemes the greatest possible good. To negate the greatest good is to affirm the greatest evil and, hence, deserves the greatest possible punishment. And experiencing the pain of hell forever is greater than extinction at physical death.[29] I will delay further discussion of the notion of retributive justice until I address the penal substitutionary view of the atonement.

The Devil

The Devil in the Bible

In the New Testament's description of the wretchedness of the human condition, Satan and other demonic forces play a prominent role as the "third

---

29. MacDonald surveys the debate about "infinite retributive punishment" (*The Evangelical Universalist*, 11–15). Though MacDonald rejects the argument that all sin deserves infinite punishment because of its "infinite demerit," he accepts the idea of *finite* retributive punishment for sin's "finite demerit" (*The Evangelical Universalist*, 166). Gregory MacDonald is a pseudonym for Robin Parry.

actor" in the drama of salvation.[30] As soon as Jesus was baptized by John, the Spirit drove him into the wilderness where he was tempted by "Satan" (Mark 1:13; Matt 4:1–11; Luke 4:1–13), and his first miracle recorded by Mark was casting out an "impure spirit," which cried out, "What do you want with us, Jesus of Nazareth? Have you come to destroy us? I know who you are—the Holy One of God!" Jesus rebuked the spirit and cast it out, and the onlookers were amazed that he possessed such authority (Mark 1:21–28). In other encounters with demons, the evil spirits exclaimed, "You are the Son of God," whereupon Jesus orders them to be quiet (Mark 3:11–12). When the Jerusalem authorities heard of Jesus's power over the demons they accused him of being in league with Beelzebul, the prince of the demons. In reply to this charge, Jesus asked,

> How can Satan drive out Satan? If a kingdom is divided against itself, that kingdom cannot stand. If a house is divided against itself, that house cannot stand. And if Satan opposes himself and is divided, he cannot stand; his end has come. (Mark 3:23–26)

Mark devotes twenty verses to the story of Jesus's encounter with the man possessed by the legion of demons (Mark 5:1–20). When Peter rebuked Jesus for speaking of his impending suffering and death, Jesus said, "Get behind me Satan!" (Mark 8:33). As Jesus sent his disciples to preach in the surrounding villages and towns, he gave them authority to cast out demons (Mark 3:14–15; Matt 10:8). When the missionaries returned, overjoyed that the demons were subject to them, Jesus said, "I saw Satan fall like lightning from heaven" (Luke 10:18). Jesus's ministry of liberating people from demonic powers became part of the post-resurrection preaching of the apostles, as we hear in Peter's message to the Roman centurion Cornelius:

> You know what has happened throughout the province of Judea, beginning in Galilee after the baptism that John preached— how God anointed Jesus of Nazareth with the Holy Spirit and power, and how he went around doing good and healing all who were under the power of the devil, because God was with him. (Acts 10:37–38)

Wright concludes that "the Gospels then tell the story of the deeper, darker forces which operate at *a suprapersonal level*, forces which the language of the demonic, despite all its problems, is still the least inadequate."[31]

The New Testament letters refer often to the works of Satan and the forces of evil. In Romans, Paul speaks of sin and death as if they were

30. Rutledge, *The Crucifixion*, 355, fn. 17.
31. Wright, *Evil and the Justice of God*, 81.

personal malevolent forces from which Christ came to liberate humanity (Rom 5–8).[32] In Ephesians, Paul reminds believers that when they were dead in sin they used to follow "the ways of this world and of the ruler of the kingdom of the air, the spirit who is now at work in those who are disobedient" (Eph 2:2). He warns them in chapter 6 about the continuing threat from those powers: "Put on the full armor of God, so that you can take your stand against the devil's schemes. For our struggle is not against flesh and blood, but against the rulers, against the authorities, against the powers of this dark world and against the spiritual forces of evil in the heavenly realms" (Eph 6:11–12). In 2 Corinthians 4:4, Paul speaks of the "god of this age" who blinds the minds of unbelievers. The author of Hebrews explains that Jesus came to share our lot "so that by his death he might break the power of him who holds the power of death—that is, the devil—and free those who all their lives were held in slavery by their fear of death" (Heb 2:14–15). Peter urges readers to remain alert and prepared to resist the devil who roams the neighborhood like "a roaring lion looking for someone to devour" (1 Pet 5:8). John tells us that the Son of God came "to destroy the devil's work" (1 John 3:8). Satan is involved in setting "traps" (1 Tim 3:7), seeing that people are put in prison (Rev 2:10), "leading the whole world astray" (Rev 12:9), and deceiving the nations (Rev 20:7, 10).

Before I attempt to fit the activity of Satan into the New Testament's picture of the human condition, I need to make some general observations about the treatment of this theme in the New Testament: (1) The New Testament does not develop a systematic Satanology or demonology.[33] It shows no interest in the nature or history of Satan or demons. They appear and play a role without explanation; the readers needed none. Christ's saving work is the focus. (2) Though the powers of evil threaten human beings, they do not possess power to threaten God. To the contrary, Jesus Christ defeats them completely (Heb 2:14–15; 1 John 3:8). (3) In nearly every place that deals with the work of the devil or the activity of demons, human beings are the

32. Gaventa, *Our Mother Saint Paul*, 125–36.

33. Clearly, the New Testament draws on intertestamental Jewish literature, especially apocalyptic literature, for its view of the superhuman spiritual world. For the pre-Christian Jewish background to the New Testament's material on the devil and demons, see Lee, *The Cosmic Drama*, 5–38. For a study of this theme in Paul, see Brown, *The God of This Age*. Brown argues that Paul modifies concurrent Jewish apocalyptic views in view of the death and resurrection of Christ. The main difference between Paul's view of the devil and the demonic powers and concurrent Jewish views is that Christ has already in principle defeated them. According to Brown, Paul views Satan as his personal adversary opposing him because of his apostolic mission to preach and care for his churches. For the possibility that Paul draws on Middle Platonism, see Forbes, "Pauline Demonology and/or Cosmology?"

agents through whom they work. The devil does not work directly in the physical world. Satan did not crucify Jesus directly but entered into Judas's heart prompting him to betray Jesus (John 13:2, 27). When Jesus tells the church at Smyrna that the devil will put some of them in prison we need not imagine that the devil runs a prison system. He inspires hatred in human officials who have this power (Rev 2:10). It seems that there is no clear line between the activity of the invisible evil powers and their human agents. (4) In all this "work," the evil powers do not physically coerce human beings but work consistently with human nature and psychology. The devil influences sinners by enticing, tempting, threatening, prompting, scheming, and lying. Deception seems to be the main tool of this enemy.

The Devil in Theology

Tradition and popular culture picture the devil as a created but fallen angel.[34] However, thinking of the power of evil in this way generates some theological difficulties. In the New Testament, (1) the devil can tempt anyone, anywhere, anytime. He can be in more than one place at a time and work on an unlimited number of people at the same time. If the devil is an independent person, his omnipresence and ability to communicate to the whole world at one time seem to give him divine attributes and a god-like universal consciousness. No finite being possesses such attributes. (2) The devil and the demons seem to lead a parasitic existence. They need a host in order to become fully active. Their only activity is working against God's purpose for creation, against all that is good and right. There is no mention of them having a life in addition to these negative functions. (3) The devil and demons seem to be purely evil. There is no hint that they could repent and be saved. How can any creature become so purely evil that healing is impossible, that is, there are no possible conditions under which it could be saved?

These three subthemes in the New Testament materials about the devil's work could better be explained by the theory that the devil is a parasitic personality that comes to exist and exists only in and along with that absurd basic act of sin that all human beings voluntarily enact.[35] The devil could be "omnipresent" because he exists and acts in this parasitic way wherever sinners exist and act. His personality, rooted in the universal act of sin, could become monstrous and genocidal in the corporate existence of gangs,

34. Geisler, "Satan, Reality of," 681–83.

35. Barth, CD 3/3:519–31, argues that the devil and demons exist only as manifestations of nothingness, which also takes form as sin and death. They are real only in their negation of God and creation. They exist only as falsehood exists.

empires, and mad dictators. Viewing him as purely evil and irredeemable would make sense within this framework because he exists only in sin and its disturbance. In his parasitic existence, he is as real as the apologists for a "real, personal devil" argue that he is. Unlike the traditional view of Satan, the parasitic understanding can be made plausible to modern people who have no knowledge, feel, or belief in the ancient hierarchical cosmology in which the universe is populated with a gradation of beings between the highest and lowest and have no sympathy for an apocalyptic view of history. In addition, it can be evaluated to some extent by human experience of the subtlety, power, and monstrosity of evil.

Whichever of these theories we find most plausible, perhaps it is best to take a cautious path and focus not on the devil as an independent object of interest but on the human experience that suggests that a "quasi-personal" force operating at a "suprahuman" level is at work.[36] The central point is the anthropological condition of helplessness in relation to sin and death. The basic, absurd act of sin works itself out in such monstrous, unhuman, insane, and hideous ways that it seems impossible that it is the result of free human action. Even though our sin is absurd and self-destructive we find it impossible to escape its power. It divides us against ourselves and darkens our self-knowledge. It corrupts, sickens, deceives, and enslaves; yet it is our own voluntary act. Death, corruption, deceit, sickness, and sin take on a kind of autonomous power, personality, and reality in our inner and outer acts. In its teaching about sin, death, and the devil, the New Testament makes clear that human wretchedness is so deep, strong, and pervasive that we need a savior who can reach into the human soul and liberate it from its self-incurred slavery, overcome death in all its dimensions, and expel the devil from his stronghold.

Looking Ahead

In the first two parts of this book I described the condition from which we need saving and sketched a preliminary image of the definitive realization of human greatness. Even our phenomenological description of human wretchedness and greatness makes clear that salvation from our woes cannot arise from the human sphere. Only a God can save us. The biblical categories of sin, death, and the devil are not esoteric and exclusively "religious." They radicalize our ordinary experience of wretchedness by placing it within a universal frame of reference determined by the God–world relation as it is

36. Here and throughout his writings Wright speaks of "the satan" (i.e., the accuser) and not of Satan the person (*Evil and the Justice of God*, 81).

unfolded in the biblical history. The Christian view of salvation becomes understandable only within this horizon of meaning. It addresses explicitly our need for salvation from sin, death, and the devil. Implicitly, however, it addresses the problems of contingency and anxiety, embodiment and confinement, desire and discontent, ignorance and vulnerability, guilt and shame, death and meaninglessness, and every other form of limitation and unhappiness we experience. The New Testament proclaims that in the birth, life, teaching, death, and resurrection of Jesus Christ, God has rewritten the sad history of sin and death. As the son of Abraham and David, Jesus rewrites Israel's story, makes a new covenant, and renews the people of God. As the son of Adam, Jesus rewrites the human history of disobedience and idolatry, and through his faithful service reverses Adam's fall to become a new beginning of the human family. Through his death and resurrection Jesus leaves behind the sphere where sin, death, and the devil reign. From this place, he is able to rescue us from these powers and endow us with glory, incorruptibility, and immortality.

—— *Part Three* ——

Christian Soteriology

5

The Resurrection of Jesus

As a child, Athanasius (296–373) lived through the infamous Diocletian persecution, which began in 303 and ended in 313 with the Edict of Milan. With images of those dark days etched in his memory, he wrote about the change that had come over the world since the resurrection of Christ:

> And if, while previously death was strong, and for that reason terrible, now after the sojourn of the Saviour and the death and Resurrection of His body it is despised, it must be evident that death has been brought to nought and conquered by the very Christ that ascended the Cross. For as, if after night-time the sun rises, and the whole region of earth is illumined by him, it is at any rate not open to doubt that it is the sun who has revealed his light everywhere, that has also driven away the dark and given light to all things; so, now that death has come into contempt, and been trodden under foot, from the time when the Saviour's saving manifestation in the flesh and His death on the Cross took place, it must be quite plain that it is the very Saviour that also appeared in the body, Who has brought death to nought, and Who displays the signs of victory over him day by day in His own disciples. For when one sees men, weak by nature, leaping forward to death, and not fearing its corruption nor frightened of the descent into Hades, but with eager soul challenging it; and not flinching from torture, but on the contrary, for Christ's sake electing to rush upon death in preference to life upon earth, or even if one be an eye-witness of men and females and young children rushing and leaping upon death for the sake of Christ's religion; who is so silly, or who is so incredulous, or who so maimed in his mind, as not to

see and infer that Christ, to Whom the people witness, Himself
supplies and gives to each the victory over death, depriving
him of all his power in each one of them that hold His faith and
bear the sign of the Cross.[1]

If it really happened, the resurrection of Jesus is the most revolutionary event in human history. Death, says Paul, is the "last enemy" (1 Cor
15:26). If death wins the last battle it wins the war. Everything is lost. But if
Jesus was raised from the dead, the decisive battle is won and the outcome
determined. It will be salvation, not destruction, victory, not defeat. Hope
routs despair. Courage casts out fear, and power overcomes weakness. Life
triumphs over death.

The Priority of the Resurrection

In order of time, Jesus's death preceded his resurrection, but in relation to
faith the resurrection comes first. The event of Jesus's resurrection changed
the perceived meaning of his death. For had Jesus not been raised, his death
could not have been given the significance the early church gave it. The
Roman authorities' view that Jesus was nothing more than a Jewish rebel
would have been confirmed, and the religious leaders' view of Jesus as a
blasphemer would stand unrefuted. This point is so obvious I hardly need
to show that other theologians agree. But Thomas Weinandy expresses this
truth so well I want to quote him:

> If the Father had not raised Jesus from the dead, it would not
> merely mean that we would never have known that on the cross
> our condemnation has been annulled, nor that we had been rec-
> onciled to the Father, nor that our sinful humanity had been put
> to death. More profoundly, the absence of Jesus's resurrection
> would simply, but frankly, attest that none of these had actually
> been accomplished. Jesus would rightly stand discredited and
> condemned as a blasphemous fraud.[2]

According to the Gospels, Jesus became aware at some point that he
must go to Jerusalem and "be rejected by the elders, the chief priests and the
teachers of the law, and that he must be killed and after three days rise again"
(Mark 8:31; 9:31; 10:33–34). Even after Jesus's second passion prediction, the
disciples did not understand his words and were not prepared for what happened (Mark 9:32). Nor do the Gospels allow us to think that the disciples

1. *On the Incarnation* 29.1–4 (*NPNF2* 4:51–52).

2 Weinandy, *Jesus The Christ*, 117.

came to see Jesus's death as a saving event during the three days between Good Friday and Easter. To the contrary, Jesus's crucifixion surprised, disappointed, and confused his followers. It refuted the hope they had placed in him. Luke tells of a conversation the resurrected Jesus had with two disciples on their way to the village of Emmaus. Not knowing that it was Jesus with whom they spoke, they described how Jesus had been handed over to the Romans by the "chief priests and rulers of the people." The two expressed their disappointment in these words: "but we had hoped that he was the one who was going to redeem Israel" (Luke 24:21).

The priority of the resurrection for faith is illustrated dramatically by the conversion of Saul of Tarsus. Saul was convinced that Jesus was justly executed as a blasphemer right up until the moment Jesus appeared to him on the Damascus Road. To him, the thought that God's Messiah could be crucified on a Roman cross was scandalous to the point of outrage. From the thrice-told story of his conversion in Acts 9, 22, and 24 and from his own letters we learn that Paul came to believe that Jesus is the Messiah only after Jesus appeared to him alive (Gal 1:11–17; 1 Cor 9:1; 15:3–8). The events of the resurrection and the appearances of the glorified Jesus made it necessary for Jesus's original disciples and Paul to rethink the meaning of his death. Only if Jesus really has been raised, really is Messiah, Son of God, and Lord could his death have been a saving event. In Paul's letters—written perhaps eighteen to twenty-five years after his conversion—we see the death of Jesus on the cross placed at the center of the message of salvation. The man who before his conversion found the idea of a crucified Messiah blasphemous now sees in the cross the most profound revelation of God's nature, wisdom, and plan for salvation (1 Cor 1:18–25).

The resurrection takes priority in a second sense. Unlike the death of Jesus, the resurrection was unambiguously a divine act of salvation and a witness to the Messiahship of Jesus. Hence coming to faith in the resurrection is the first step toward conversion. The resurrection of Jesus was clearly a divine act, a miracle loaded with transparent theological significance. Those who saw the empty tomb and encountered the resurrected Jesus knew that God had acted to save Jesus from death and refute the charges that led to his crucifixion. As we will see below, much of the Christology unfolded within the New Testament was implicit in the events of the resurrection and glorification of the crucified Jesus. In contrast, the divine activity in the death of Jesus was completely hidden to human eyes at the time of its occurrence. Before the resurrection it would have occurred to no one to see God's saving wisdom in Jesus's crucifixion. It is still true today that the salvific meaning of the cross can be seen only from within the resurrection faith. In support of this distinction, I find it noteworthy that no sermon in Acts or any other place in the New Testament demands belief in the saving significance of Jesus's death as the *first* act of faith. Those sermons always ask first for belief in Jesus's resurrection or in Jesus as Messiah and Lord as implications of the resurrection (Rom 4:24; 10:9). Hence, belief in the apostolic witness to the resurrection of Jesus is the foundational act of Christian faith. Indeed, the gospel proclaims forgiveness of sins along with the demand for faith in Jesus, but it offers forgiveness as a blessing conditioned on the recipient's faith in Jesus. It is clearly understood that Jesus, now revealed as Lord and Messiah, is the source of forgiveness of sins. However, we are not asked as a *first* act of faith to confess a particular teaching about the relationship of Jesus's death to Jesus's ability to bestow forgiveness of sins.

The Significance of the Resurrection of Jesus

What is the significance of Jesus's resurrection? Of course, if Jesus was not raised from the dead, it matters little what meaning the apostles assigned it. But grasping its significance before we ask about its facticity has advantages, for unless we see the true magnitude of the resurrection's implications we will have little reason to investigate whether or not it happened.

Meaning in History

Christian faith sees in the resurrection of Jesus an event of universal significance, an event that redefines the identity of God and reveals the final meaning of history. How can an event that occurs within the flow of history have the universal significance Christianity attributes to the resurrection of Jesus? Are there any analogies? Clearly, an event at the origin of the universe—the event that initiated the Big Bang, for example—would determine every subsequent event within the universe. Likewise, an event that brought the universe to its final end would also have universal significance. But how can an event that occurs somewhere within the flow of events have such significance? It could not have retroactive effect on events that came before it. The law of historical cause and effect works in the opposite direction. The universe is so vast that any localized event's effect on the whole universe is negligible. We hardly notice events as huge as supernovae in our own galaxy, much less in other galaxies. However, an event that occurred in the middle of time might reveal something about the nature of the universe and, thereby, possess indirect significance for the whole universe. Hence, we can lay down a principle at this point: *the scope of an event's meaning is determined by how much it reveals about the fundamental nature of the universe or how widely it determines other events within the universe.*

On a humanistic level, we look to some individuals—Socrates, Buddha, and Confucius—as revelatory paradigms for human possibility. We acknowledge some people as exceptional models of courage, love, insight, creativity, and endurance. Their lives and actions become significant because they reveal the great potential of human nature. Other human beings' great deeds or revolutionary discoveries—such as those of Plato, Aristotle, Alexander the Great, Caesar Augustus, Shakespeare, Isaac Newton, Napoleon Bonaparte, and George Washington—determine the fate of nations and civilizations for millennia. Many people think of Jesus's significance along these lines, and no doubt in some ways Jesus fits the paradigm of a great human being. Billions of people admire Jesus for his exceptional virtues and heroic deeds. However, Christian faith does not weigh his significance on these scales. Though from a humanistic perspective the influence of Jesus's life on subsequent world history is arguably greater than any other individual, it cannot be shown to be of universal significance by inductive means. Christianity asserts that Jesus's significance reaches from the beginning of creation to the end, to all time and space. Jesus's life, death, and resurrection possess retroactive force into the past and extend to the absolute future. Jesus's resurrection reveals the true origin, nature, and end of humanity. For only the creator can give life and bring it to its definitive end. In Jesus, the creator has opened the way to salvation from human wretchedness into realized greatness and glory.

The Resurrection in Context

Why did the New Testament writers attribute universal significance to Jesus, and were they justified in so doing? The event of Jesus's resurrection occurred in a historical context, and it is the immediate context of an event that gives it its initial meaning.[3] For events within nature, the context is the set of proximate and remote physical causes for the event and its proximate and remote physical effects. But for human actions, motives, beliefs, and values must also be taken into account. If you drive up to my house and find me on my hands and knees in my front yard, your first thoughts may be, "What is he doing? Is he ill? Has he fallen? Has he lost something? Is he weeding?" Taking note of an isolated event is not enough

---

3. I say its "initial" meaning because the resurrection of Jesus is so unique and profound that it bursts all previous categories and must finally be understood from itself. Torrance drives this point home in his *Space, Time and Resurrection*.

to explain its meaning. Likewise, if we stripped away the historical context from the resurrection, we could assign it no precise meaning. No doubt, it would appear unusual and marvelous. Perhaps we could conclude that miracles are possible, that supernatural power is at work. But further significance in that event would remain hidden. Such a bare marvel could not ground the Christology we find in the New Testament. Only within the wider context at that moment does the resurrection take on the universal significance given it in the New Testament.[4] We can divide this context into three parts: (1) the life of Jesus as experienced and remembered by his disciples; (2) concurrent speculations, beliefs, and hopes surrounding death and resurrection and beliefs about God's plan for defeating evil and saving his people; and (3) the impact of the empty tomb and the resurrection appearances on those who witnessed them.

The life of Jesus

Clearly, it matters *who* died, *whose* tomb was found empty, *who* appeared alive and to whom. As Pannenberg expresses it, "For Christian faith it is not a matter of indifference who it was that was raised from the dead, namely, the Crucified, . . . the crucified Jesus of Nazareth."[5] Apart from a few references in the New Testament letters, Acts, Revelation, and Hebrews, we know the disciples' experiences and remembrances of Jesus from the four Gospels. Clearly, the Gospels were written after the resurrection and in view of its significance for the identity of Jesus as Messiah and Lord. Apart from the resurrection faith there would be no point in writing them. We cannot remove the post-resurrection perspective from the Gospels without destroying their integrity, engaging in speculation, and creating needless uncertainty. No doubt the material preserved in the Gospels was used by the early church for multiple purposes, such as evangelism, moral teaching, and catechesis. But in reading the Gospel of Mark, it is hard to miss Mark's aim of explaining why Jesus, the Son of God (Mark 1:1) was judged a blasphemer by the Jewish rulers and crucified as a rebel by the Romans. Jesus entered the public eye when he began preaching, "The kingdom of God is near. Repent and believe the good news" (1:15). He calls disciples to become "fishers of men" (1:17). He exorcises demons from the possessed, and they recognize him as "the Holy One of God" (1:24). Jesus heals a leper (1:40–45). When he heals a paralyzed man, Jesus accompanies his healing command with "Son, your

4. Pannenberg, "On Historical and Theological Method," 137–81. See also Pannenberg, *Jesus,* 66–88, and Pannenberg, *Systematic Theology* 2:343–63.

5. Pannenberg, *Systematic Theology* 2:344.

sins are forgiven" (2:5). He declares himself "Lord of the Sabbath" (2:28) and calms the storm on the Sea of Galilee with the words "Quiet, be still" (4:39). A woman received healing by touching his robe (5:29), and a little girl was raised back to life when Jesus said, "Little girl, I say to you, get up" (5:41). He healed the deaf and blind and fed 5,000 and 4,000 in the desert. He takes Peter, James, and John up to a secluded place on a mountain and is transfigured before them (9:2–13). When the frightened disciples offer to build shrines to Moses, Elijah, and Jesus, the divine voice says, "This is my Son, whom I love. Listen to him!" (9:7).

Jesus spoke with personal authority unlike any rabbi or prophet ever spoke. As we saw above, in dealing with demons, death, and disease, he spoke in his own name. We can see this also in the Gospel of Matthew in the Sermon on the Mount. Jesus says that you have heard it said, but "*I* say to you" (Matt 5:39, 44). And at the end of that sermon, the crowds were amazed because "he taught as one who had authority, and not as the teachers of the law" (Matt 7:28–29). Jesus performed symbolic actions that pronounced judgment on the ruling powers. He rode into Jerusalem on a donkey in triumphal procession. He cursed the fig tree for bearing no fruit and entered the temple and drove out the money changers. In Mark 13, Jesus spoke of the coming judgment on the city of Jerusalem and identified himself as the judge who will bring this judgment (13:26–27). On the night he was betrayed, Jesus celebrated the Passover with his disciples. During this memorial of God's great act of deliverance from Egypt, Jesus changed the meaning of the Passover ceremony. As he shared the bread and wine of the Passover, he said, "This is my body" and "This is the blood of the new covenant which is poured out for many" (Mark 14:22–25). In this act, Jesus claimed that his impending death would bring about a new deliverance and a new covenant.

That night Judas betrayed Jesus and Peter denied him three times. At his trial before the Sanhedrin, the High Priest asked Jesus, "Are you the Christ, the Son of the Blessed One?" (Mark 14:61). Jesus answered unambiguously, "I am. And you will see the Son of Man sitting on the right hand of the Mighty One and coming on the clouds of heaven" (14:62). The next morning Jesus was crucified as a rebel by the Roman authorities. Joseph of Arimathea, a "prominent member of the Council" asked Pilate to release the body of Jesus. Joseph placed Jesus's body in a tomb cut out of rock. Mary Magdalene and Mary the mother of Joses "saw where he was laid" (Mark 15:47). There is so much more we could say about Jesus's life and death, but we now have before us the first part of the context that determines the meaning of the resurrection of Jesus. It was *Jesus* who died, that is, the one who had proclaimed the coming kingdom of God and performed signs that pointed to the fulfilment of that hope. And it was *Jesus* who was resurrected, the person the disciples knew intimately.

Concurrent thought about death and resurrection

The second context within which we must interpret the resurrection faith is the *concurrent speculations, beliefs, and hopes surrounding death and resurrection and beliefs about God's plan for defeating evil and saving his people.*[6] When the first disciples concluded from the resurrection appearances and the discovery of the empty tomb that Jesus had been raised from the dead, what did they think about its significance? The most important data relevant to this question come from the New Testament itself. There are also relevant data in documents contemporary with the New Testament, but we must be cautious about generalizations. The Sadducees, whom we meet in the pages of the New Testament, did not believe in a future resurrection or perhaps in any form of life beyond death.[7] Others, influenced by Hellenistic ideas, may have believed in a state of "blessed (disembodied) immortality" after death.[8] Wright points out that for those first-century Jews who believed in the future resurrection of the dead, resurrection does not happen right after death but at the end of the "present age" and at the beginning of the "age to come."[9] In the New Testament era, everyone who believed in resurrection also believed in an "interim" state between death and resurrection. In Wright's words, resurrection is not about "life after death" but about "life after life after death."[10] As we see in the New Testament, Pharisees believed that God would bring about a future in which the righteous dead would be raised bodily to everlasting life. For the Pharisees, the resurrection of the dead signaled the end of the age of death, sin, disease, and oppression and the dawning of a new age of life and righteousness. Though not every first-century Jew believed in the resurrection, belief in the future resurrection was the dominant view. In Wright's judgment, "Resurrection was not

---

6. See p. 64.

7. Though it is clear that the Sadducees did not believe in the resurrection, it is hard to know for certain whether or not they expected some other form of post-mortem life. Our sources for their views come from their critics. See Wright, *RSG*, 131–40.

8. Wright, *RSG*, 140–46.

9. Wright, *RSG*, 205.

10. Wright, *RSG*, 199.

a strange belief added to the outside of first-century Judaism[;] . . . resurrection had been woven into the very fabric of first-century Jewish praying, living, hoping and acting."[11]

Jesus's teaching on the resurrection is clearly nearer to the view of the Pharisees than to that of the Sadducees. He argues for the resurrection, claiming that the Sadducees do not understand Scripture or the power of God (Matt 22:23–32). As is made obvious by his proclamation of the coming kingdom of God, Jesus expects a new age of righteousness to bring an end to the present evil age. If you follow Jesus in this age, enduring the suffering that accompanies discipleship, you will be rewarded "in the resurrection of the righteous" (Luke 14:14). Paul argues with those in Corinth who doubt the resurrection of the dead (1 Cor 15), refuting the caricatures that picture the resurrection as restoration of our present corruptible bodies. Nevertheless, he argues for a *bodily* resurrection at the end of the age. The resurrection overcomes death and transforms the corruptible body into an incorruptible one. Paul affirms the resurrection of the body, not merely the survival of the spirit. But the resurrection of the body also involves its radical transformation. For Paul, resurrection brings restoration of life in continuity with the identity, history, and bodily existence that otherwise would be destroyed forever by physical death. Also, like the Pharisees, Paul sees the resurrection as signaling the end of the age and the definitive transformation of the world. Set in this context, it stands out clearly that Paul and the rest of the New Testament writers view the "resurrection" of Jesus as restoration of his life and transformation of his physical body into a mode of life expected only at the end of the age, namely incorruptibility, immortality, and glory. The notion that Paul could have conceived of Jesus's "resurrection" merely as survival of his spirit or the justness of his cause is highly implausible. According to Wright, use of the term "resurrection" whether in first-century Judaism or in Christianity, is always set in opposition to such views and never means anything but "bodily resurrection."[12]

We now have before us the second context within which the significance of Jesus's resurrection can be specified. The first Christians understood Jesus's resurrection as an "end-time" event. It signaled the end of "the present age" and the dawn of "the age to come." In the resurrection, God restored Jesus's life and transformed the very body in which he had lived, worked, and died on a cross. Jesus is the beginning of the resurrection of the dead, the end of the age of sin and death, and the dawn of the new age of eternal life. His resurrection designated him as the "Son of God"

11. Wright, *RSG*, 204.
12. Wright, *RSG*, 209.

(Rom 1:4).[13] Through resurrection and ascension, God made him "both Lord and Messiah" (Acts 2:36). Through his resurrection, Jesus's universal significance becomes clear, for the resurrection of the dead is about the destiny of the whole world, all time and space, and everyone. Because his resurrection possesses universal significance, so do his death, his teaching, his acts, and his birth. These conclusions did not require subtle logical inferences. They "did not first need to be interpreted" but were immediately evident given the context and the events.[14]

The empty tomb and resurrection appearances

Apart from the third factor, that is, the discovery of the empty tomb and the resurrection appearances, the first two factors lead nowhere. Prenter emphasizes this point in opposition to those who affirm a "resurrection" but doubt the empty tomb. He explains:

> The empty tomb is, however, an indispensable part of faith's conception of the resurrection as eschatological reality. Through the message of the empty tomb faith hears the proclamation that Christ is really risen, that his resurrection does not mean that he merely lives on spiritually in the religiously conditioned memory of his disciples, but that it is the real beginning of the resurrection of all men. The reference to the empty tomb is not primarily apologetics, but eschatological.[15]

Whatever Jesus taught, claimed, and did, and whatever were the concurrent hopes for resurrection at the end of the age, if Jesus's tomb remained occupied and no one ever saw him again, his life could not have the universal significance the church attributed to it. Every book in the New Testament presupposes or explicitly refers to the resurrection of Jesus. The four Gospels narrate Jesus's appearances to the women who visited the tomb, to Peter and John, and to the rest of the original disciples. The Book of Acts documents the early testimony of Peter and Paul concerning the resurrection. A good case can be made that these accounts derive from people who actually experienced the appearances first hand. But Paul gives his testimony in his own words in letters written by him. Some might argue that the narrations in the Gospels or Acts or Hebrews are second or third-hand, and therefore could differ from the original witnesses' testimony. No such argument can

---

13. See Wright, *RSG*, 242–43, for the significance of this text.

14. Pannenberg, *Jesus*, 67.

15. Prenter, *Creation and Redemption*, 427.

be made about Paul's testimony in 1 Thessalonians, 1 and 2 Corinthians, Galatians, Romans, and Philippians.[16] In these cases, we must either believe Paul or not, since there are no gaps that allow legendary elements to creep in over time. Paul teaches about the significance of the resurrection of Jesus in many places (Phil 3:10–11, 20–21; 1 Thess 1:9b–10; 4:13–18; Rom 1:1–4; 4:18–25; 6:1–10; 8:9–11, 22–26; 10:9–10; 14:7–9; 2 Cor 4:7–15), but he refers to his own experience of the risen Jesus three times, twice in 1 Corinthians and once in Galatians: "Am I not free? Am I not an apostle? Have I not seen Jesus our Lord? Are you not the result of my work in the Lord?" (1 Cor 9:1). With these words Paul begins a chapter-long defense of his apostleship against detractors. He asks four rhetorical questions to which his readers know the answers. These questions can also be stated as assertions that remind the Corinthian believers of what they already know: "You know I am free. You know I am an apostle. You know I have seen Jesus our Lord. You know you are the result of my work." In the third assertion, Paul draws on what the Corinthians already know of Paul's conversion and commissioning by the risen Jesus. His experience of the resurrected Jesus is a matter of public record and defines Paul's identity as an apostle. Hence, a rhetorical question is enough to bring the entire story to mind.

From what he says in 1 Cor 15:3–8, we can see that Paul's personal testimony to the resurrection of Jesus was woven into the message he taught the Corinthians from the very beginning:

> For what I received I passed on to you as of first importance: that Christ died for our sins according to the Scriptures, that he was buried, that he was raised on the third day according to the Scriptures, and that he appeared to Cephas, and then to the Twelve. After that, he appeared to more than five hundred of the brothers and sisters at the same time, most of whom are still living, though some have fallen asleep. Then he appeared to James, then to all the apostles, and last of all he appeared to me also, as to one abnormally born.

Paul places Jesus's appearance to him in the same category as those experienced by Peter, James, and many others before him. We need not think he is asserting that everyone experienced the same accompanying phenomena. The common element among the witnesses is that Jesus appeared to them in a way that proved he had risen bodily from the dead. The resurrection of Jesus and his appearances to his disciples and Paul are of "first importance"

16. Licona addresses how the unique position of Paul in relation to the resurrection has been recognized by those examining the historical question of the resurrection (*The Resurrection of Jesus*, 437–40).

to the Christian message. Throughout the argument of 1 Corinthians 15, Paul assumes that every believer knows that God raised Jesus from the dead; he never argues to that fact. Jesus's resurrection and his appearances are assumptions from which the arguments are drawn.

The third first-hand testimony to a resurrection appearance comes from Galatians 1:11–17:

> I want you to know, brothers and sisters, that the gospel I preached is not of human origin. I did not receive it from any man, nor was I taught it; rather, I received it by revelation from Jesus Christ. For you have heard of my previous way of life in Judaism, how intensely I persecuted the church of God and tried to destroy it. I was advancing in Judaism beyond many of my own age among my people and was extremely zealous for the traditions of my fathers. But when God, who set me apart from my mother's womb and called me by his grace, was pleased to reveal his Son in me so that I might preach him among the Gentiles, my immediate response was not to consult any human being. I did not go up to Jerusalem to see those who were apostles before I was, but I went into Arabia. Later I returned to Damascus.

The two references to "revelation" in this text, considered along with the other two texts from 1 Corinthians, clearly refer to the appearance of the resurrected Jesus to Paul. In verse 12, Paul says he received his gospel by revelation. He did not rely on the testimony of others for his belief that Jesus had been raised from the dead and is Messiah and Lord. In verses 13–16, he elaborates on this revelation, its context and results. Before this revelation, Paul thought he should persecute the church and be zealous for the traditions of his fathers. But God intervened and graciously revealed "his Son in me." Paul experienced the resurrected Jesus as divine grace and as God's choice to have mercy on a sinner and an enemy, and it definitively shaped his understanding of the gospel.

When we view the resurrection of Jesus in its total context it becomes clear that the resurrection is not a brute fact, a miracle whose meaning is exhausted by its unusual nature. Given its context in the life of Jesus, the religious thought of the day, and in the lives of those to whom the resurrected Jesus appeared, Jesus's resurrection implied a religious revolution that has in fact changed the world.

The Resurrection of Jesus as Salvation

Salvation from Death.

According to the New Testament, Jesus had been in the condition of true death for thirty-six to forty-eight hours when God raised him from the dead. Unlike his death on the cross, which in itself is opaque, we can see clearly that his rescue from death was an act of salvation. The author of Hebrews makes explicit reference to Jesus's salvation from death: "During the days of Jesus's life on earth, he offered up prayers and petitions with fervent cries and tears to the one who could *save him from death*, and he was heard because of his reverent submission" (Heb 5:7). Before we ask how Jesus's resurrection contributes to our salvation from sin, death, and the devil, we must first consider it as *his own* salvation. Though Jesus did not deserve what happened to him, he died and needed someone to save him from death. Jesus's resurrection was not about saving a life at the edge of death and restoring it to its full vigor. Jesus was saved from the whole realm of death, from the power of death, from the causes of death and everything associated with death, and from the present age where sin, death, and the devil reign. He was exonerated of the false charges that led to his execution.[17] He was raised into glory, honor, and immortality. In his resurrection, Jesus became the first truly saved and glorified human being. Jesus's resurrection proclaims "God's creative fidelity to the covenant with Israel, and through Israel to all human history and all creation, as that creative fidelity came to a climax in the divine saving action in Jesus."[18] For the apostle Paul, all the promises of God come to realization in Christ (2 Cor 1:20).

How does God's act of saving Jesus also save us and bring us to glory? Clearly, we have not yet been saved in the same way that Jesus was saved. However, God's act of saving and glorifying Jesus inaugurates and antici- pates the resurrection and glorification of all the dead. That God saved Jesus from death shows that God possesses power, willingness, and intention to defeat death, sin, and the devil. In the resurrection of Jesus from the dead, "it is finally revealed who God is: he whose power embraces life and death, existence and non-existence, who is creative love and faithfulness, the pow- er of the new life, on which there is complete reliance even in the collapse of all human potentialities."[19] Even as a sign from God, as the "firstfruits of those who have fallen asleep" (1 Cor 15:20), Jesus's resurrection weakens

17. Pannenberg, *Systematic Theology* 2:344.
18. McDermott, SJ, *Word Become Flesh*, 130.
19. Kasper, *Jesus the Christ*, 145.

the power of sin and death in our lives, imparts freedom, and instills hope.[20] But God's act of raising Jesus from the dead is not merely a sign of events wholly in the future. In Jesus's resurrection, the power of the coming age intrudes into the present. As Prenter puts it, the resurrection of Christ is "the unity of historical and eschatological reality."[21] Jesus is not merely one human being among others who happened to "make it to heaven" before the rest of us. He is the *means* through which God will actually accomplish his goal. Through the resurrection, Jesus has been "appointed" "Son of God," Lord, and Messiah (Rom 1:4). He sits at the right hand of God (Acts 2:33; Rom 8:34; Col 3:1) carrying out the work of salvation in the world. Christ now reigns over God's kingdom and will reign until death itself is "destroyed" (1 Cor 15:24–25; Phil 2:9–11). And he has poured out the Holy Spirit on those who believe (Acts 2:33), so that the power by which God raised him from the dead is already at work (Rom 8:11; Eph 1:19–21). Through his resurrection Jesus not only experienced salvation for himself, he was given the right and power to save those who trust in him. Jesus has been united to God and is present wherever God is present. In McDermott's words, "The presence he offered others during his life is now transformed by God's Spirit into a universal presence."[22] The sphere of his resurrection life will expand until it includes all creation and all things are united in him (Eph 1:10). Even in the present, the Spirit unites us to Christ through faith and baptism. Christ comes to live in us, and we begin to be conformed to his image. We participate in the events of his death and resurrection and their effects (Rom 6:1–4). His resurrection is not merely the assurance but the *cause* of our salvation from death. Our future resurrection will be an effect, an extension, of his resurrection.

Salvation from Sin

We have little difficulty understanding that God's act of raising Jesus from the dead guarantees our future resurrection, and it is obvious that being raised from the dead saves us from physical death. Does Jesus's resurrection also play a part in saving us from sin? Was not that problem dealt with at the cross? However, this dichotomy between the cross and the resurrection obscures rather than illuminates the saving work of Jesus. As we concluded earlier, sin and death are not two totally different problems that could be dealt with by separate means. The absurd, basic act of sin already

---

20. Kasper, *Jesus the Christ*, 154–59.

21. Prenter, *Creation and Redemption*, 428.

22. McDermott, SJ, *Word Become Flesh*, 124.

participates in death, and its deadly effects and consequences radiate outward to soul and body and into the world so that "death reigns" over all people (Rom 5:14). Solving one of those problems requires dealing with the other as well. As we draw all the salvation perspectives together toward the end of this book we will see that all of Jesus's saving activity in his teaching, healing, dying, and rising is one multifaceted act resulting in one multidimensional state of salvation.

In one sense, Jesus's resurrection saved even him from sin. Though Jesus was not a sinner and did not need forgiveness, he came into the world "in the likeness of sinful flesh" (Rom 8:3) and was judged and condemned as a sinner. His resurrection left the "sinful flesh" behind, overturned that judgment, and reversed that condemnation. Unlike Jesus, we *are* sinners. For us, resurrection must deal with this fact and with the internal effects of our sins. It is not a matter of overturning a false judgment and healing wounds inflicted by the sins of others. Since death in the biblical understanding also includes the spiritual consequences of sin, renewal of physical life alone would not be effective in dealing with all aspects of death. To live physically while remaining a sinner would condemn us to a living death. But Jesus's resurrection demonstrated that resurrection is a radical transformation into a new form of life exempt not only from physical death but also from the internal and external effects of sin. In the judgment of Torrance, "It is in the resurrection, then, that the ultimate content and purpose of atonement and reconciliation come to fruition and to view. . . . [The resurrection of Christ] is the ontological side of redemption, the healing and restoring of being in relation to the creative source of all being."[23] Not only so, it delivers us from the conditions that make sin possible: vulnerability, lack, ignorance, error, and falsehood. The resurrection will complete the life-giving, sanctifying, and liberating work of the Spirit begun in this life (Rom 8:9–11) and perfect our transformation into the image of Christ. As John puts it, "We shall be like him, for we shall see him as he is" (1 John 3:2).

The Resurrection of Jesus as a Historical Fact

The Resurrection Narrative

According to the earliest church, the resurrection of Jesus signifies the passing of the present evil age and the dawn of the kingdom of God. It guarantees the future resurrection of the dead and the forgiveness of sins. But the church is correct only if it really happened. So, we must ask the question,

23. Torrance, *Space, Time and Resurrection*, 79.

"Did God really raise Jesus from the dead?" Our answer to this question will be determined by whether or not we believe the word of those original witnesses who made this claim. It happened in the past and only people contemporary with the event had access to it. Only if those with access left a record of their experience are we in a position to make a judgment. But it is not quite as simple as deciding to believe or not. First, not every assertion of fact is equally important. Suppose we find an old letter in which someone casually observes that mail delivery came to their house two hours earlier than usual on the second Tuesday of January 1901. We would not think to doubt it because nothing important is at stake. But the claim that God raised Jesus from the dead demands radical change. It should not be treated lightly. Second, we believe people readily when they speak about ordinary matters of fact unless we have reason not to do so. However, if a claim contradicts our beliefs about how things usually go or demands that we take great risks, our critical sensitivities come alive and we find reasons to doubt. Everyone rejects the principle that we should believe a claim simply because it is asserted. People lie, make mistakes, and pass on second- and third-hand reports, rumors, traditions, and other unverified beliefs in a credulous way. It makes sense, then, to examine the credibility and the placement of those who claimed to know that God raised Jesus from the dead.

Perhaps we ought to visit again the actual claims of the early church. The reasons given by the original witnesses for their belief in the bodily resurrection of Jesus were: (1) the tomb in which Jesus was buried on a Friday afternoon was found empty early the following Sunday. (2) He was seen alive by the women who came to visit the tomb that morning, and a while later he showed himself to Peter, John, James, and many others, including Paul. In sum, the church claimed that Jesus died and was buried, on the third day the tomb was empty, and on Easter morning and on numerous occasions until and including Paul's Damascus Road encounter Jesus appeared in ways that proved it really was Jesus and that he really was alive. Torrance is worth quoting again on this point:

> Everything in the Christian Gospel, now regarded in the light of
> Easter, was seen to pivot finally upon *the empty tomb*—that Jesus
> arose in body, arose as very man in the fullness and integrity of
> his human nature, but human nature which through the Spirit
> of holiness had been stripped of corroding forces of corruption
> and clad in the incorruptible garment of deathlessness.[24]

Reiterating the actual claim would hardly be worth doing—it is so obvious—except that some writers contend that the earliest witnesses used

24. Torrance, *Space, Time and Resurrection*, 83.

the word "resurrection" not for the event of the body coming back to life after having experience true death, but for some type of survival beyond death. In my view, Wright's study of the literature of Second Temple Judaism and of every New Testament reference to resurrection has demolished this view. Resurrection in Judaism and in the New Testament *never* means anything but bodily resurrection. The idea of a non-bodily "resurrection" is a contradiction in terms that would strike any first-century Jew, Christian, and even pagan as absurd.[25] If someone wishes to deny the bodily resurrection of Jesus, there is no other honest option but to admit to disagreeing with Paul and the unanimous belief of the early church. If Jesus did not rise *bodily* from death, the resurrection faith is a lie or a mistake.

Arguments for the Facticity of the Resurrection

N. T. Wright on the resurrection

It is not possible within the limits of this section to construct an elaborate argument for the facticity of the bodily resurrection of Jesus, one that methodically compiled and evaluated the historical evidence and answered all serious objections. Thankfully, many others have already done this.[26] Toward the end of his book *The Resurrection of the Son of God,* Wright formulates an argument for the resurrection that he describes as *"inference to the best explanation."*[27] The historical question is, what is the best explanation for the historical data relevant to the resurrection of Jesus that can be established by critical historical examination of the New Testament? Those data include (1) the tomb of Jesus was empty on Sunday morning and (2) many people, including Peter, James the Lord's brother, John, and Paul claimed to have seen Jesus alive after his death and burial. Wright uses the logical distinction between necessary and sufficient conditions to give shape to his argument. Taken individually, both (1) and (2) are necessary but not sufficient for originating belief in the bodily resurrection of Jesus. Unless the tomb was known to be empty no one could have concluded to the bodily resurrection, even on the basis of Jesus's appearances. But without the resurrection appearances, discovery of the empty tomb would not lead first to belief in the resurrection. Other explanations would take

25. Wright, *RSG.* Wright argues this point in so many places that I need not cite any particular one.

26. Perhaps the most comprehensive and methodical is that of Licona, *The Resurrection of Jesus.*

27. Wright, *RSG,* 716.

priority. However, these two necessary conditions taken together rise beyond necessary to sufficient conditions; that is, anyone who believed the
tomb to be empty and saw Jesus in a way that convinced them that Jesus
was alive—given the dominant Jewish belief in the future bodily resurrection of God's people and its eschatological significance—would rightly
conclude that Jesus had risen bodily from the dead. Wright tests this hypothesis by examining some alternative explanations that have been prof-
fered. He concludes that the actual bodily resurrection of Jesus "provides
a sufficient condition of the tomb being empty and the 'meetings' taking
place."[28] Wright continues to make an even stronger claim: "that the bodily
resurrection of Jesus provides a *necessary* condition for these things; in
other words, that no other explanation could or would do. All the efforts to
find alternative explanations fail, and they were bound to do so."[29]

The rhetorical argument for the resurrection

I find Wright's argument impressive, but as my own contribution to the
discussion, I will make a different kind of argument. Wright's approach assumes an implied reader who weighs evidence in an objective fashion and
feels obligated not to go beyond the data, and correspondingly, Wright allows the New Testament to be treated for argument's sake as a source of
evidential data. He makes a case that the bodily resurrection of Jesus is the
"best explanation" for the data of the New Testament. But when you look at
the "data" of the New Testament from a rhetorical point of view, that is, as
persuasive speech, the scientific mood is absent. You find instead witness,
proclamation, and personal appeals. The goal is not to measure up to an
objective standard of "the best explanation" but to *persuade*. In rhetorical
terms, speakers rely on ethos as well as logos to persuade. In my brief argument below, I aim to give as much attention to ethos as to logos. My goal is
to enable the contemporary reader to make a reasonable judgment and a
responsible decision to believe in the resurrection of Jesus.

I will first address the question of historical placement, that is, how
certain are we that the claim derives from someone in a position to witness
the event? Because of his unique placement in history, I will limit my argument to Paul. The letters of Paul undoubtedly contain the strongest historical
evidence for the resurrection of Jesus. Written between twenty and twenty-
nine years after the crucifixion of Jesus and eighteen to twenty-seven years

28. Wright, *RSG*, 717.
29. Wright, *RSG*, 717.

after Paul's conversion,[30] Paul's letters are the earliest preserved documents that mention the resurrection of Jesus. The earliest preserved reference to the resurrection is 1 Thessalonians 1:10.[31] From studying Paul's letters we can conclude that belief in the bodily resurrection of Jesus was universal in the earliest church. He argues *from* it, but never *for* it. Paul's letters are the earliest surviving documents written by someone who claims to have seen the resurrected Jesus. In Paul, we are not dealing with a second- or third-hand tradition accepted on the word of others. In him, we have a direct claim to have seen Jesus (1 Cor 9:1; 15:8; Gal 1:15–17). We cannot dismiss it as a tale unsusceptible of critical evaluation. The options are clear: Paul is lying, mistaken, or telling the truth. Paul's letters are our earliest indirect evidence for Jesus's appearances to Peter, John, James, and others. We read about the resurrection appearances to the original disciples in the four Gospels and Acts, but these documents were written later than Paul's letters by authors who reveal very little about themselves. But Paul's letters place us much closer to the events themselves. Just a few years after he met the risen Jesus—at least three—Paul traveled to Jerusalem "to get acquainted with Peter" and spent fifteen days with him. While there he also met James the Lord's brother (Gal 1:18–19). It is impossible to imagine that Paul did not share with Peter and James the story of his meeting with Jesus and hear from them their story with Jesus, including the empty tomb and resurrection appearances. We know, then, that Paul was in a position to hear about at least some of Jesus's other resurrection appearances from those who witnessed them. With knowledge gained from Paul, we can read the accounts of resurrection appearances in the Gospels and Acts with greater confidence that they are based ultimately on first-hand testimony, even though we do not know how the writers gained access to this testimony. From Paul's letters and other sources we can calculate that his Damascus Road encounter with Jesus probably occurred within two years of the crucifixion.[32] Paul thus became part of the earliest generation of Christians, which places him in a good position to know what the earliest Christians believed and experienced.

---

30. According to Risner, *Paul's Early Period*, 57–58, the most probable date for the crucifixion of Jesus is April 7, 30. This view is held by the majority of scholars of the subject. According to Risner, Paul's conversion most likely happened within two years of Jesus's crucifixion, in the year 32 (73). Risner finds the later date of seven years after the crucifixion less probable. For his reasons for preferring the earlier date, see *Paul's Early Period*, 53–58.

31. First Thessalonians was probably written in the first part of 50, from Corinth. See Risner, *Paul's Early Period*, 364.

32. Risner, *Paul's Early Period*, 73.

In sum, we know Paul, we know what he claimed, and we know he was in a position to gain this knowledge. But can we trust Paul?

Is Paul a credible witness to the resurrection of Jesus? As I pointed out in the methodological paragraphs above, our knowledge of the actions, words, and experiences of those to whom we have no direct access depends on indirect access through the recorded words of others. Ultimately, to be given credibility we must believe that those words derive from a source that has direct access to the events themselves. Assessing the credibility of a source for its factual claims is not an exact science. The credibility of a witness cannot be demonstrated the way a mathematical answer, logical conclusion, or inference to the best explanation can be demonstrated, that is, in an objective fashion. The trust we give to another person depends on the background worldview, personal psychology, social setting, and experiences we bring to our deliberations. In the end, people will make this judgment for themselves, and there is no reason to think that every right-thinking person will come to the same conclusion. Clearly, a source making a factual claim that challenges a person's worldview, personal psychology, social setting, and experiences will face more resistance and undergo more rigorous scrutiny than a source making a claim that fits perfectly into one's preexisting framework; rightly so for any rational person. I am not denying that we can engage in rational discussion of a person's credibility. I wish only to point out that such discussions cannot lead to rational demonstration valid for all, but to persuasion of a particular person. Arguments that persuade one person may not persuade another. In my view, then, speakers who want to persuade others that Paul's witness to the resurrection is believable should frame their argument as an explanation of why they themselves find Paul persuasive, that is, as witness. I am convinced that such an approach can be helpful to those who are undecided. Finally, however, people must read Paul for themselves, allowing Paul to move them toward the resurrection faith or not.

Scholars studying the rhetoric used in the New Testament aim at "exploring how the texts might have functioned persuasively for the audiences to whom they were directed."[33] They often use categories described in the classic handbooks written by Aristotle, Cicero, and Quintilian to analyze the rhetoric of the New Testament.[34] The three classic "modes of persuasion" invented by the rhetorical speaker are ethos, logos, and pathos. In cultivating

---

33. Selby, *Not with Wisdom of Words*, 3. Recent interest in rhetorical criticism of the New Testament was in part stimulated by the publication of Kennedy, *New Testament Interpretation through Rhetorical Criticism*. For a recent guide to rhetorical criticism, see Witherington III, *New Testament Rhetoric*.

34. Hansen, "Rhetorical Criticism."

ethos, the speaker constructs a believable image of a trustworthy person of good sense. Logos argues inductively or deductively from assumptions or evidence to a conclusion. Pathos appeals to the emotions of the audience by dramatizing such passions as pity, anger, envy, and friendship.[35] Many scholars have examined the rhetoric of Paul's letters and found that Paul uses all three categories.[36] However, as stated above, they focus on strategies used in texts to persuade the target audiences. I am interested in ways Paul's letters can help modern audiences see him as a trustworthy witness to the bodily resurrection of Jesus. In some respects, the two audiences—ancient and modern—overlap in what they find persuasive, but not at every point. Olbricht collates four lists of ethos-enhancing moral characteristics compiled from Aristotle, Cicero, Quintilian, and Paul. While we find some overlap between the classic good person and Paul's vision of the ideal Christian, there are significant differences. Missing from the classic lists are Paul's top priorities for the Christian: "Christ-like, suffering servanthood, Spirit-directed, love, joy, peace, forgiveness, frankness, and meekness."[37] Perhaps the Corinthians could be moved to accept Paul's authority by his rhetorical strategy of adopting the persona of an "apocalyptic seer," but modern people do not view apocalyptic seers as reliable guides.[38] Concerning the resurrection, we face another problem with transposing Paul's rhetoric from ancient to modern settings, that is, in his letters he never attempts to persuade his audience that Jesus actually arose from the dead. He assumes they already believe it. So, the standard scholarly analysis of the rhetoric of Paul's letters can help us with our problem only indirectly.

What are the major characteristics of the "Paul" constructed in Paul's letters that may cultivate ethos with a modern audience? Of course, it is impossible to articulate every aspect of why we find some people trustworthy and others not. In the categories of classic rhetoric, ethos cannot be translated fully into logos. Some speakers can inspire admiration, love, and trust, and others cannot. Some can inspire it in one group but not in another. Attempting to discover why is like trying to explain why someone is beautiful, why you love your spouse, or why the beauty of the universe persuades you to believe in God. It might be better to remain silent and let the thing speak for itself. Though I cannot hope to articulate fully the reasons, I have to ask why I and many others find Paul's personal testimony

35. Aristotle, *Rhetoric* 1.2.

36. Selby. "Paul, the Seer," 351–73; Olbricht, "The Foundations of the Ethos in Paul," 138–59; Tobin, *Paul's Rhetoric in its Context*; Mitchell, *Paul and the Rhetoric of Reconciliation;* and Holland, "Delivery, Delivery, Delivery," 119–40.

37. Olbricht, "The Foundation of the Ethos in Paul," 158.

38. Selby. "Paul, the Seer."

to the bodily resurrection compelling. I shall propose three major reasons. First, consider his pre-conversion career. Paul describes his pre-Christian life in three places in his letters:

> For you have heard of my previous way of life in Judaism, how intensely I persecuted the church of God and tried to destroy it. I was advancing in Judaism beyond many of my own age among my people and was extremely zealous for the traditions of my fathers. (Gal 1:13–14)

> For I am the least of the apostles and do not even deserve to be called an apostle, because I persecuted the church of God. (1 Cor 15:9)

> If someone else thinks they have reasons to put confidence in the flesh, I have more: circumcised on the eighth day, of the people of Israel, of the tribe of Benjamin, a Hebrew of Hebrews; in regard to the law, a Pharisee; as for zeal, persecuting the church; as for righteousness based on the law, faultless. (Phil 3:4–6)

Although Paul makes these autobiographical references for other reasons, they paint a picture of a most unlikely convert: proud, ambitious, and fanatical. The church's claim that the crucified Jesus is the Messiah must have seemed to Paul not only blasphemous but absurd. It contradicted his most cherished beliefs about God, the Messiah, the law, and the righteous life. To accept Jesus as Messiah would entail a religious and moral revolution, which he later describes in this way:

> But whatever were gains to me I now consider loss for the sake of Christ. What is more, I consider everything a loss because of the surpassing worth of knowing Christ Jesus my Lord, for whose sake I have lost all things. I consider them garbage, that I may gain Christ and be found in him, not having a righteousness of my own that comes from the law, but that which is through faith in Christ—the righteousness that comes from God on the basis of faith. (Phil 3:7–9)

Hence, when Paul claims that it was seeing the risen Jesus (1 Cor 9:1; 15:9; Gal 1:15) that changed him from persecutor to apostle, we are confident that he is telling the truth. It would take an event of this magnitude to convince Saul of Tarsus that a man crucified for blasphemy and rebellion is the Messiah, the Son of God.

The second reason to accept Paul's testimony to the resurrection is the character of his post-conversion career. Paul never expressed any doubts or regrets about his conversion. His certainty and sincerity were confirmed by what he suffered. Saul the persecutor became Paul the persecuted. In his argument for the general resurrection, which depends on the facticity of the bodily resurrection of Jesus, he asks rhetorically, if there is no resurrection, "why do we endanger ourselves every hour? I face death every day. . . . If I fought wild beasts in Ephesus with no more than human hopes, what have I gained?" (1 Cor 15:30–32). In 2 Corinthians 11, he "boasts" about his sufferings in comparison to his "super-apostle" critics:

> I have worked much harder, been in prison more frequently, been flogged more severely, and been exposed to death again and again. Five times I received from the Jews the forty lashes minus one. Three times I was beaten with rods, once I was pelted with stones, three times I was shipwrecked, I spent a night and a day in the open sea, I have been constantly on the move. I have been in danger from rivers, in danger from bandits, in danger from my fellow Jews, in danger from Gentiles; in danger in the city, in danger in the country, in danger at sea; and in danger from false believers. I have labored and toiled and have often gone without sleep; I have known hunger and thirst and have often gone without food; I have been cold and naked. Besides everything else, I face daily the pressure of my concern for all the churches. (2 Cor 11:23–28)

There have been many religious fanatics willing to suffer for their causes. Paul's willingness to suffer and die for his belief that Jesus is Lord and Messiah argues for the sincerity of his faith. Of course, earnestness alone does not guarantee that his beliefs are true. But combined with knowledge of his pre-conversion life in Judaism, his claim that his conversion was based on first-hand experience of the living Lord, and the next factor, certainty and sincerity carry great weight.

The third ethos-building factor is the brilliance and soberness of Paul's letters. Paul's letters do not read like the ravings of someone unhinged. In his own day, even his critics had to admit that his letters were "weighty and forceful" (2 Cor 10:10). The letter to the Romans is one of the most influential documents ever written. Logic and passion work together to push the reader relentlessly to the conclusion that Jesus Christ is the all-in-all of the God-human relationship. From diatribes against the pagans and the Jews in the first chapters, to his innovative comparison of Adam and Christ (5:12–21), to chapter 7's penetrating analysis of the law's inability to engender true righteousness, to his lyrical praise of God's care for those whom he loves in 8:18–39, to his innovative theology of salvation history in chapters 9–11, to the doxology in 11:33–36, it is difficult to imagine anyone reading Romans without realizing that the book is a masterpiece of theological literature. And who could dismiss the famous hymn in praise of love in 1 Corinthians 13 as the work of a muddle-headed mystic?

The cumulative force of these three ethos-building characteristics is much greater than anyone of them alone. Paul's pre-conversion status in the Pharisaic party, his confidence in the rightness of his original cause, the blasphemous nature of the Christian claims, the cost of converting, the obvious sincerity and certainty of his faith in Jesus, and the intelligence, creativity, and sobriety of his mind combine to rule out the possibility that Paul's testimony is a lie, or that it is based on carelessness or gullibility or opportunism, or that his experiences derive from mental illness or lack of intelligence. The only plausible option left is that when Paul testifies that God raised Jesus from the dead he is telling the truth about something he has good reasons to believe. And in my estimation, his testimony provides us also with good reasons to believe.

6

The Death of Jesus

EARLY IN CHRISTIAN HISTORY the cross became the central symbol of Christianity. Not a manger, a good shepherd, a sage, or an empty tomb.[1] When Western Christians think of salvation they focus almost exclusively on the forgiveness of sins won by Jesus's sacrificial death on the cross. Liberation from the power of sin and death and union with God, though not excluded, are treated as secondary to forgiveness and justification. Protestant churches consider the former aspects of salvation to be the work of sanctification, which continues throughout life and is complete only in the resurrection of the dead. Concerning the means of salvation, the cross overshadows all other aspects of Jesus's work, eclipsing his resurrection, his present reigning as Messiah and Lord, his pouring out the Spirit, and his return in glory. Not surprisingly, Western theologies of salvation place greater emphasis on the doctrine of atonement narrowly conceived than on other aspects of soteriology.[2]

Interpreting the Cross

The New Testament places the cross at the center. The Gospels describe the events of the trial and crucifixion in greater detail than other events in Jesus's life. The Book of Hebrews views Jesus as the new high priest who brings his own blood into heaven as an eternal offering for sins. For John,

1. Wright, *NTPG*, 366–67.

2. The word "atonement" can be used in a narrow or a broad sense. In the narrow sense, it means the action of Jesus's death on the cross in providing the ground for forgiveness of sins. In the broad sense, atonement means the totality of the work of Christ for salvation centered in but not limited to his death on the cross.

God sent his Son "as an atoning sacrifice for our sins" (1 John 4:10). Revelation pictures Jesus as a slain lamb standing in the throne room of God. However, the New Testament does not isolate the cross from other aspects of the work of Christ or focus on forgiveness of sins to the exclusion of other aspects of salvation. To the extent that theologies of atonement treat the cross in isolation, they will produce narrow visions of salvation and distorted theories of atonement, which in turn create the problem I addressed in the introduction to this book, that is, the obscurity of Christian language about sin and salvation.

The event of the crucifixion "does not contain within itself its own interpretation."[3] As I argued in the previous chapter, apart from the resurrection, Jesus's death could not have been understood as an act of salvation. It might have been seen by his friends as martyrdom. His enemies, of course, would think their view of Jesus as deceiver and blasphemer had been confirmed. Whether friend or foe, no one would be thinking of Jesus's death as a divine act of salvation. Jesus's original disciples and Paul were forced to view Jesus's death as part of God's plan for salvation only because they became convinced that God had raised him from the dead. The salvific significance of the resurrection is plain to everyone. And most people will admit that they need forgiveness and liberation to one degree or another. But the relationship between Jesus's death, considered as an isolated event, and forgiveness of sins is anything but plain to most people. As an isolated teaching, the church's message that "Jesus died for our sins" is an empty religious expression that makes no contact with ordinary human experience. To compensate for its lack of transparent meaning, some preachers and songwriters attempt to make the death of Jesus relevant by assimilating it to the age-old motif of heroic self-sacrifice and tell the story in a way crafted to excite emotions of pity, guilt, and gratitude. Confession that Jesus died for our sins becomes an expression of emotion rather than an assertion of truth.

In the previous chapter, I argued that the resurrection of Jesus was the event that motivated the earliest church to seek the salvific meaning of Jesus's death. In this chapter, I will seek to discover the meaning they found.[4] I will avoid reading the patristic and medieval atonement theories and Reformation-era debates back into the New Testament texts. Only in this way can we put ourselves in the place of the first Christians and retrace the path that led them to view Jesus's death as salvific. The significance the first believers saw in Jesus's death can be understood only by considering three contexts

3. Baker and Green, *Recovering the Scandal of the Cross*, 18.

4. My argument in this chapter is influenced by Wright's massive four-volume work on Christian origins: *NTPG*, *JVG*, *RSG*, and *PFG*. I also found his popular work, *Revolution*, helpful.

in which they interpreted the event: (1) the disciples' conviction that God had raised Jesus from the dead, declaring him to be Messiah and Lord; (2) the biblical and concurrent Jewish thought about the plight of God's people, its mission to the world, its hope for salvation, and its understanding of the means of redemption; (3) the life and teaching of Jesus and the circumstances surrounding his trial and crucifixion. By listing these three contexts separately, I do not want to leave the impression that the reasoning that led early Christians to revise their understanding of Jesus's death proceeded in three discrete steps. All three of these contexts probably exerted influence simultaneously. Nor do we know how long it took the church to arrive at the mature view that Jesus's suffering and death were salvific. However, it had to be very early, since by the time Paul writes his letters the view that "Christ died for our sins according to the Scriptures" (1 Cor 15:3) had already become part of a traditional formula. Indeed, the first phase of this development could have occurred almost simultaneously with the process of grasping the significance of the resurrection, so that everything just "fell into place" without the need to put things together in a system. The resurrection was the precipitating event for this reorientation.

The Resurrection Revolution

In the previous chapter, I addressed at length the revolutionary implications of God's act of raising Jesus from the dead. I need only to summarize those implications here. In the resurrection, God declared the crucified Jesus to be Lord and Messiah (Acts 2:36; Rom 1:4). Prior to his resurrection, his disciples could have viewed Jesus's death only as a bewildering defeat. However fondly they might continue to remember Jesus, they could now be sure that he was not the long-expected Messiah. The arrival of the kingdom would again be delayed. Everyone knows that the Messiah will defeat the evil powers of this age, not be crucified by them. But the resurrection of Jesus overturned these sad conclusions. As it turned out, the Messiah *was* crucified and the Crucified One *is* the Messiah, but he defeated the evil powers anyway. Indeed, the powers' act of crucifying "the Lord of glory" was the beginning of their defeat and had they known God's wisdom and power they would not have done it (1 Cor 2:8). Because he submitted himself "to death, even to death on a cross," Jesus Christ, as a human being, was exalted by God "to the highest place and [God] gave him the name that is above every name, that at the name of Jesus every knee should bow, in heaven and on earth and under the earth, and every tongue acknowledge that Jesus Christ is Lord, to the glory of God the Father" (Phil 2:8–11). The spiritual powers who through sin, law, and death had dominated human beings suddenly found themselves ruled by the same human nature they had dominated. The kingdom of God really is at hand just as Jesus had proclaimed, and the power of the coming age is already at work. Jesus defeated sin and death in his own case and will defeat them for us as well. Hence, Jesus's death could not have been a tragic defeat. It must have been part of the divine plan that included the resurrection and the fullness of salvation that is sure to follow. God had to be at work in the death as powerfully as in the resurrection. But how? What part does the Messiah's death play in God's plan of salvation? The resurrection context by itself cannot give us the answer. Only by considering the other two contexts along with the resurrection can we answer this question.

"According to the Scriptures"

The second context that determines the significance of the death of Jesus is *the biblical and concurrent Jewish thought about the plight of God's people, its hope for salvation, and its understanding of the means of redemption.* Careful reading of the New Testament references to Jesus's death shows that the first Christians looked overwhelmingly to the Old Testament for clues as to its meaning. In his summary of the essential gospel message, Paul begins, "Christ died for our sins according to the scriptures" (1 Cor 15:3b). Wright argues that we should take the expression "according to the scriptures" to refer to the grand narrative of the Old Testament, not merely to a few prophetic proof texts. This story includes Adam, Abraham, and David. It is the story of Passover, exodus, and the glory of God, of exile and return, and of God's covenant faithfulness and Israel's unfaithfulness. Of course, certain texts serve as central carriers of this story: Genesis 1–3 tells the story of how human beings were created to be images of God and of their failure to live up to this calling, which led to their exile from the divine presence. Exodus 12–20 tells the story of Passover, exodus from Egypt, and reception of the law. Deuteronomy 29–32 sets out the blessings and curses of the covenant, predicts the exile, and promises to forgive the people if they repent. Second Samuel 7:11–14 speaks of David's desire to "build a house" for God and of God's promise to "build a house" for David. Jeremiah 31 promises that God will make a new covenant with Israel that will include forgiveness of sins and a "new heart" for the people. Isaiah 40–55 shows how the LORD will rescue his exiled people through his suffering servant, forgive their sins, and fulfill his promise to Abraham to make his children a blessing to the nations. Daniel 7–9 predicts the coming of the universal reign of God, the victory of "one like a son of man," and a period of 490 years of exile. The question that faced the early church was this: how does the death of the resurrected Jesus fit into this grand narrative?

Looking back to Israel's history from the first century, the "return" from exile under Ezra and Nehemiah turned out to be disappointing. God did not return to dwell in the new temple, and, except for a brief time (164 BC to 63 BC) after the Maccabean revolution, the nation never regained independence.[5] The exile, it seems, had been extended and was still in force in Jesus's day.[6] The promises to Abraham had not been fulfilled, and Israel had failed in its vocation. Nevertheless, hope remained that God will yet fulfill the promise made to Abraham. In Ezekiel 40–48, Ezekiel recounts a vision he experienced while in Babylonian captivity. The vision describes the new temple, return of the priesthood, return of the glory of the LORD to the temple, and return of the people to the land. The exile happened because of the sins of the people, especially their idolatry and covenant breaking. The possibility of restoration depends on finding a way to deal with their national sins and establish a new covenant. Jeremiah 31 brings this point home:

"The days are coming," declares the LORD,

"when I will make a new covenant

with the people of Israel

and with the people of Judah.

It will not be like the covenant

I made with their ancestors

when I took them by the hand

to lead them out of Egypt,

because they broke my covenant,

though I was a husband to them,"

declares the LORD.

"This is the covenant I will make with the people of Israel

after that time," declares the LORD.

"I will put my law in their minds

and write it on their hearts.

I will be their God,

---

5. For the full story of this turbulent century between the purification and rededication of the temple (164 BC) and the coming of the Romans under Pompey in 63 BC, see Schürer, *The History of the Jewish People* 1:137–242.

6. Wright, *NTPG*, 299–301.

and they will be my people.

No longer will they teach their neighbor,

or say to one another, 'Know the LORD,'

because they will all know me,

from the least of them to the greatest,"

declares the LORD.

"For I will forgive their wickedness

and will remember their sins no more."

(Jer 31:31–34)

And how will all this be accomplished? Of course, God is ultimately the one who will bring these things about, but God's people must also play a part. Wright points to the belief in Second Temple Judaism that the new age "would come about through a time of intense suffering, either for the people as a whole or for a particular group within the people."[7] Daniel speaks of a time just before the end in which "there will be a time of distress such as has not happened from the beginning of nations until then" (Dan 12:1). In the servant songs of Isaiah, the theme of redemptive suffering receives its most extensive and memorable expressions. According to Wright, Isaiah 53 is the only place in the Old Testament where "intense suffering is the *means*, and not simply the *context* of the expected deliverance, of the forgiveness of sins."[8] Isaiah 52–53 speaks of redemption and return of the people from exile, return of the LORD to Jerusalem, forgiveness of sins, and the reign of God. All these blessings result from the representative suffering of God's faithful servant:

He grew up before him like a tender shoot,

and like a root out of dry ground.

He had no beauty or majesty to attract us to him,

nothing in his appearance that we should desire him.

He was despised and rejected by mankind,

a man of suffering, and familiar with pain.

Like one from whom people hide their faces

he was despised, and we held him in low esteem.

Surely he took up our pain

---

7. Wright, *Revolution*, 121. See Wright, *NTPG*, 277–79, for further discussion of this theme in Second Temple Judaism.

8. Wright, *Revolution*, 124–25.

and bore our suffering,

yet we considered him punished by God,

stricken by him, and afflicted.

But he was pierced for our transgressions,

he was crushed for our iniquities;

the punishment that brought us peace was on him,

and by his wounds we are healed.

We all, like sheep, have gone astray,

each of us has turned to our own way;

and the LORD has laid on him

the iniquity of us all.

It is essential for understanding the New Testament doctrine of atonement to look for the meaning of the New Testament phrase "the forgiveness of sins" or its equivalent in the Old Testament and Second Temple Judaism. We should avoid reading into this expression the meaning it has acquired in later Christian theology. The "sins" that need forgiving are not in the first instance violations of the eternal law, that is, the universal human failing to live up to absolute divine perfection. Nor does "forgiveness of sins" focus primarily on the individual. The "sins" that need forgiving are violations of the covenant the LORD made with the people of Israel. For those violations, Israel had forfeited the blessings and fallen under the curses enumerated in the covenant (Deut 28). The divine punishment under consideration was exile from the land and the divine presence, not postmortem punishment in hell. As Wright explains:

> This needs to be emphasized in the strongest possible terms: the most natural meaning of the phrase "the forgiveness of sins" to a first-century Jew is not in the first instance the remission of individual sins [The sacrificial system dealt with these sins], but the putting away of the whole nation's sins. And, since the exile was the punishment for those sins, the only sure sign that the sins had been forgiven would be the clear and certain liberation from exile. This is the major, national, context within which all individual dealing with sin must be understood.[9]

Hence, just as the "sins" that are being punished are defined in relation to the covenant, so the conditions that must be met for Israel to receive "forgiveness" are defined in relation to the covenant, not in relation to eternal

9. Wright, *NTPG*, 273.

law or God's absolute holiness and perfection understood as metaphysical principles or divine attributes. Repentance and righteous suffering viewed as a "sacrifice" are two important means of expiating sin and receiving forgiveness. Deuteronomy 30:2–3 sets out the way of repentance:

> When you and your children return to the LORD your God and obey him with all your heart and with all your soul according to everything I command you today, then the LORD your God will restore your fortunes and have compassion on you and gather you again from all the nations where he scattered you.

The servant songs of Isaiah 40–55, especially 52:3—53:12, quoted above, speak of the sufferings of the exiled, now penitent people or their representative as redemptive in relation to the punishments inflicted on the nation for breaking the covenant. There is no hint here of paying an infinite penalty for violating eternal law or harmonizing divine justice and divine mercy. Indeed, it may be that voluntary suffering and sacrifice are manifestations of the people's deep repentance to which the LORD has promised to respond with compassion (Deut 30:2). The covenant God is always ready to forgive and restore a penitent and obedient people.

From within this context, then, the Messiah Jesus appears as Israel's covenant representative who in his voluntary suffering and death effectively embodies, endures, and expresses Israel's suffering and penitence. In Messiah Jesus, Israel does what it was otherwise unable to do. It returns to God with all its "heart and soul" and, consequently, receives forgiveness for its sins and is offered a new covenant and a new heart.

Jesus and the New Exodus

The third context that determines the significance of the death of Jesus is *the life of Jesus and the circumstances surrounding his trial and crucifixion.* We can imagine that after the resurrection the disciples reflected on their memories of Jesus and his teaching for clues as to the meaning of his death. Jesus entered the scene in the wake of John the Baptist's preaching that people should repent to prepare for the coming kingdom of God. Jesus proclaimed the arrival of the kingdom and the "forgiveness of sins" to all who repented. Jesus thus welcomed "sinners" and "tax collectors."[10] He forgave the sins of a paralyzed man, and to those who criticized him he replied, "It is not the healthy who need a doctor, but the sick. I have not come to call the righteous, but sinners" (Mark 2:7, 15–17). As Wright

10. Wright, *JVG*, 264–68.

repeatedly emphasizes, "forgiveness of sins" is code language for the end of the exile and the arrival of the kingdom. In proclaiming forgiveness, Jesus announced to Israel that "her sins were being punished no more; in other words, were being forgiven."[11]

According to the Gospels, Jesus anticipated his death on behalf of others. On several occasions, Jesus spoke of his coming suffering and death (Mark 8:31; 9:12; 10:32–34; 14:8). In Mark 10:45, Jesus says that the Son of Man came to serve "and to give his life as a ransom for many." In the context of those sayings, Jesus often warns that "whoever wants to save his life will lose it, but whoever loses his life for me and the gospel will save it" (Mark 8:35). According to Wright, it is highly significant that Jesus chose the Passover as the time to enter Jerusalem and challenge the authorities at the "moment when all his fellow Jews were busy celebrating the Exodus from Egypt and praying that God would do again, only on a grander scale, what he had done all those years ago."[12] Jesus's "triumphal entry" into Jerusalem (Mark 11:1–11) and his cleansing the temple (Mark 11:12–19) had messianic significance. His Parable of the Tenants was an obvious attack on the Jerusalem establishment (Mark 12:1–12), and the apocalyptic discourse about the destruction of Jerusalem and the temple clearly speaks of the end of the evil age and the arrival of a new age (Mark 13:1–37). The night before his death, Jesus spoke of the bread and wine of the Passover supper as his body and blood, and designated his blood as "the blood of the covenant" (Mark 14:22–25). In these words, Jesus announces that his death will occasion a new exodus and constitute a new covenant that will end the slavery and exile of the people of God through the forgiveness of their sins (Mark 14:12–26; Matt 26:17–30; Luke 22:7–24; 1 Cor 11:23–26).[13]

In these accounts, themes of representative suffering, Passover and exodus, new covenant, kingdom of God, and forgiveness of sins are woven together. According to Wright, Jesus is announcing that his death "was to be seen as the inauguration of Jeremiah's new covenant, the covenant in which sins would be forgiven and thus, of course, exile would be undone at last."[14] This new age will be ushered in by Jesus's suffering and death as Israel's representative. In Wright's view, Isaiah 53 "was at the very heart of Jesus's understanding of how his vocation would be fulfilled. He would go ahead of his people and take upon himself the suffering that would otherwise fall upon

11. Wright, *JVG*, 268.

12. Wright, *Revolution*, 179.

13 Wright, *Revolution*, 185–88. For a similar interpretation of Jesus's intentions, see Baker and Green, *Recovering the Scandal of the Cross*, 54–63.

14. Wright, *Revolution*, 192.

them."[15] Like Isaiah and Jeremiah, Jesus warned the people of the destruction that awaited them unless they repented (Luke 13:1–5). Jesus "proceeded to act it out, finding himself called, like Ezekiel, symbolically to undergo the fate he had announced, in symbol and word, for Jerusalem as a whole."[16] Jesus's voluntary death was not exclusively directed toward the universal human condition of sin but was also a prophetic act warning of God's judgment and wrath that would soon be unleashed on unfaithful Israel by means of the Roman legions in the same way Babylon had embodied divine wrath in the 587 BC destruction of Jerusalem. So, in this way Jesus suffered divine wrath, that is, *he voluntarily exposed himself to God's abandonment of Israel to the consequences of its abandonment of the covenant.* In letting himself be crucified by the Romans, Jesus foreshadowed the fate of those who embraced the ideology of military rebellion and exposed the corruption of the Jerusalem Temple authorities. But he also demonstrated the powerlessness of Rome over those who do not fear "those who kill the body, and after that have no more that they can do" (Luke 12:4; Matt 10:28). He defeated Satan, the real power, who—through lies and threats—worked through the Jerusalem establishment and Rome. In his death, Jesus faithfully witnessed to the way of peace and love he had taught his disciples to follow and charted a new course for a renewed people of God.

Paul[17]

In 1 Corinthians 15:3, Paul affirms the message he received and passed on "that Christ died for our sins according to the scriptures." Paul is clear that something revolutionary happened on Good Friday. Wright insists that we will misunderstand Paul's view of what happened in the death of Jesus unless we remember that for Paul it was *Israel's Messiah* who died for our sins.[18] The resurrection had declared Jesus to be "the Son of God," the Messiah (Rom 1:4). So, for Paul the question is, why did Israel's *Messiah* die? Paul does not answer in the way many Western Christians expect, that is, that Jesus died to pay for our sins so we can go to heaven when we die. Wright points to a text in Romans for insight into the answer Paul might give us:[19]

---

15. Wright, *Revolution,* 189.

16. Wright, *JVG,* 594.

17. My thinking in this subsection reflects the influence of Wright, *PFG.*

18. Wright, *Revolution,* 233.

19. Wright, *Revolution,* 233. See also Wright, *PFG* 2:1300–1301, where Wright speaks of Paul's beginning greeting (Rom 1:1–7) and his final thoughts (15:7–13) as bookends that emphasize Jesus's Messiahship and his role in fulfilling God's promises

> Accept one another, then, just as Christ accepted you, in order
> to bring praise to God. For I tell you that Christ has become a
> servant of the Jews on behalf of God's truth, so that the promises
> made to the patriarchs might be confirmed and, moreover, that
> the Gentiles might glorify God for his mercy As it is written:
> "Therefore I will praise you among the Gentiles; I will sing the
> praises of your name." (Rom 15:7–9)

For Paul, all the hopes of Israel and all the promises of God about
the kingdom, the forgiveness of sins, the end of the exile, the return of
the glory and presence of God, and the inclusion of the gentiles are being
fulfilled in the Messiah. As he says in 2 Corinthians, "For no matter how
many promises God has made, they are 'Yes' in Christ" (1:19b). Wright
insists that we must read Paul through this lens. When Paul speaks about
the Messiah's work as "redemption" from slavery, as he does for example
in Galatians 4:4–5 and 3:13–14 or Romans 6–8, he is not simply using a
convenient metaphor. He is using Passover-exodus language to describe
the new Passover and exodus that has happened in the Messiah.[20] In this
new exodus, "redemption" is made possible because the Messiah took on
himself the curses written in the law for those who break the covenant
(Gal 3:1–14). Paul refers in this passage to Deuteronomy 21:23, which says
"Cursed is everyone who hangs on a tree." But he also refers to Deuteronomy 27, where Moses rehearses the curses for not adhering to the covenant.
Paul assumes the entire history of disobedience and exile that reigned until
the Messiah came. Wright comments: "The passage, then, declares that the
'exile' is over—because the curse has fallen on the Messiah, the single representative of Israel, and has thereby been exhausted."[21]

Wright gives special attention to Romans 3:21–26.[22] This passage is
seen by many as the clearest support for the traditional Protestant view
of the death of Jesus in which Jesus takes upon himself the wrath of God
against human sin and imputes to us his righteousness, understood as
moral perfection. Wright takes issue with the usual reading of this text and
reinterprets it in light of the Old Testament categories in which he contends
Paul thinks. Notice the difference between the NIV translation and Wright's
translations of key terms, which I have put in Italics. The NIV reads:[23]

---

and Israel's mission to become a light to the nations.

20. Wright, *Revolution*, 237.

21. Wright, *Revolution*, 240. For a similar approach to the subject, see Hays, *Faith of Jesus*, 179–80.

22. In *Revolution*, Wright devotes fifty-two pages (299–351) to this text. The body of literature devoted to this text is vast. I do not claim to have mastered it.

23. Wright's translation of these verses is found in *Revolution*, 306, 318, and 325.

But now apart from the law the *righteousness* of God has been
made known, to which the Law and the Prophets testify. This
righteousness is given through *faith in Jesus Christ* to all who
believe. There is no difference between Jew and Gentile, for all
have sinned and fall short of the glory of God, and all are *justified*
freely by his grace through the redemption that came by Christ
Jesus. God presented Christ as a *sacrifice of atonement* through
the shedding of his blood—to be received by faith. He did this
to demonstrate his *righteousness,* because in his forbearance he
had left the sins committed beforehand unpunished—he did it
to demonstrate his *righteousness* at the present time, so as *to be
just* and the one who *justifies* those who have faith in Jesus.

Wright translates the same text as:

But now, quite apart from the law (though the law and the
prophets bore witness to it) God's *covenant justice* has been
displayed, God's *covenant justice* comes into operation through
the *faithfulness of Jesus the Messiah,* for the benefit of all who
have faith. For there is no distinction: all sinned, and fell short of
God's glory—and by God's grace they are freely *declared to be in
the right,* to be members of the covenant, through the redemption which is found in the Messiah, Jesus. God put Jesus forth as
the place of mercy, through faithfulness, by means of his blood.
He did this to demonstrate his *covenant justice,* because of the
passing over (in divine forbearance) of sins committed beforehand. This was to demonstrate his *covenant justice* in the present
time: that is, that he himself is *in the right,* and that he declares *to
be in the right* everyone who trusts in the faithfulness of Jesus.[24]

The difference between the two interpretations is dramatic. The traditional translation and interpretation gives the impression that the subject
is the general tension between God's holy perfection and universal human
guilt. God's perfect righteousness had been placed in doubt by his failure
in the past to punished sin as it deserves. But now in Jesus's death God
demonstrates his moral perfection and retributive justice (righteousness)
by punishing the innocent Jesus in our place and displaying his mercy
by counting Jesus's moral perfection (righteousness) as the moral perfection (righteousness) of those who put faith in Jesus. In contrast, Wright's
translation and interpretation places the reader within the history of the
covenant and God's promises. God's "righteousness" in this text should be
understood as God's reliability in acting to fulfill his covenant promises,

24. Wright, *Revolution,* 313.

specifically his promise *"to bless the nations through Israel."*[25] In Jesus, God is now demonstrating his reliability by fulfilling his covenant promises in an unexpected way, by accepting Jesus's obedient suffering and death as the acts of a "faithful Israelite" who finally keeps Israel's covenant.[26] To be "justified" does not mean having Jesus's absolute sinlessness imputed to us. It means, rather, to be accepted as a part of the faithful covenant people because of one's trusting relationship to Jesus. The present verdict of "in the right" for all who are in the Messiah, anticipates the eschatological verdict to be announced in the final judgment.[27] In sum, because of the faithfulness of Jesus, the exile has come to an end, a renewed Israel has now received a new covenant and believing Jews and gentiles have been gathered together and designated faithful covenant partners on the same basis, that is, faith. Jesus himself is now "a place of mercy," that is, the place where believers without distinction are invited to experience the transforming presence and glory of God.

We could raise many objections against Wright's reading of Romans 3:21–26, the most serious being the weight he places on his controversial translation of *dia pisteōs Iēsou Christou* in 3:22 as "through the faithfulness of Jesus the Messiah" rather than as " through faith in Jesus Christ."[28] I think Wright and Hays[29] are probably correct in arguing that *dia pisteōs Iēsou Christou* should be viewed as a subjective genitive construction. However, I do not think acknowledging the decisive role of Jesus's faithfulness and obedience in his saving work depends on the translation of this expression. Jesus's faithfulness and obedience are affirmed in many places and assumed everywhere (Rom 5:19; Phil 2:4–8; Heb 3:2–6). Also, Wright's translation of *hilastērion* as a "place of mercy" instead of "propitiation" does not go

25. Wright, *PFG* 2:841. Emphasis original. Wright contends that God's faithfulness to this covenant promise is under discussion in Romans 3 and 4, the immediate context for interpreting 3:21–26 (*PFG* 2:836–51).

26. Wright says, "If the covenant God is going to bless the world through Israel, he needs a faithful Israelite. In 3:21–26 Paul argues that this is exactly what has now been provided" (*PFG* 2:839). Hays comes to a similar conclusion: God has overcome "humanity's unfaithfulness through the faith(fullness) of Jesus Christ" (*The Faith of Jesus*, 161).

27. Wright, *Revolution*, 324.

28. See Jewett, *Romans*, 276–78, for his criticism of the subjective genitive interpretation of the expression as Jesus's own faith and the literature for and against this interpretation. For Wright's defense of his understanding of *dia pisteōs Iēsou Christou* as "through the faithfulness of Jesus the Messiah," see *PFG* 2:836–51. For arguments against taking the genitive as subjective—*"faithfulness of Christ"*—see also Fee, *Pauline Christology*, 223–26.

29. Hays, *Faith of Jesus*.

unchallenged.[30] In my view, however, even if *hilastērion* here means turning away divine wrath, it must still be set within Israel's covenant history rather than in the universal God-human relationship, as traditional Protestantism does. Additionally, it makes good sense to interpret *dikaiosynē* as "covenant justice" because it places the idea within biblical history rather than in a theory of universal moral law rooted in the divine nature. Hence, I do not believe that a covenantal understanding of these texts or of Paul's thought as a whole stands or falls with one's translation of these expressions. I think Wright is correct that this and other Pauline texts ought to be interpreted primarily in light of the history of covenant promises and curses and the problems faced by the earliest church and Jews of the first century rather than within a theological scheme that pits universal human sinfulness against absolute divine justice.

Summary

In this chapter we have explored the significance Jesus's death had for those contemporary with the event, the Gospel writers, and Paul. Because the crucified Jesus had been declared to be the Messiah by his resurrection from the dead, his death had to be part of God's plan to bring about the long expected kingdom of God and the life of the new age, which the resurrection unambiguously inaugurated. Hence, every promise found in the Old Testament that hinted at the kingdom and the new age, focused originally on Israel as a whole, finds its fulfillment in Jesus the Messiah. Viewed as the fulfillment of Deuteronomy 26–32, Jeremiah 31, Isaiah 40–55, and Daniel 7, 9, and 12, the Messiah's faithful service, obedience, suffering, and death are revealed as the righteous action of God in fulfilling his promises to Abraham and, at the same time, the action of Israel in the person of the Messiah Jesus finally fulfilling its side of the covenant. In his faithfulness unto death, Jesus defeats the idolatrous powers that held God's people in slavery, secures forgiveness of sin, instigates a new exodus, initiates a new covenant, and forms a renewed people of God that includes those from every nation who embrace Jesus as Lord. In this way, Jesus's death acquires a positive and salvific meaning. That is to say, by relating the event of Jesus's death to a web of prophetic texts and understanding it as the fulfillment of these hopes, it is given a specific soteriological meaning within the history of God's covenant relationship with Israel. No doubt Paul and the earliest disciples felt as if the riddles of history had been solved. Everything had become clear.

30. On *hilastērion* as "mercy seat" see the influential Cambridge PhD dissertation of Daniel Bailey (1999), summarized in Bailey, "Jesus as the Mercy Seat."

Looking Forward

However if we turn our attention from the first century to today, the salvific meaning of Jesus's death is anything but clear to many people. As I lamented in the introduction to this book, modern Christians may confess and find comfort in the fact that Jesus "died for our sins" (1 Cor 15:3) and that Jesus "loved me and gave himself for me" (Gal 2:20), but most do not have a clear idea of what those expressions mean. Outsiders find this confession strange and incomprehensible. In the history of theology, we find many different attempts to explain how the death of Jesus secures the forgiveness of sins. Different theories were found persuasive in different ages. In the following chapters, I will focus on the two theories that have the most widespread influence in contemporary Western Christianity, the penal substitutionary theory and the moral influence theory. These two, or variations of them, dominate respectively the two theological extremes of Protestant Christianity in the Western world. Oversimplifying matters a bit, evangelical Christianity accepts the penal substitution theory and liberal Christianity opts for the moral influence view. Both theories display great internal coherence, and that in my view is the source of their persuasive power. As you will discover, I am unable to embrace either view wholeheartedly.

7

Jesus as Penal Substitute I

The Classic Protestant Theory

A VIABLE CHRISTIAN DOCTRINE of the atonement must make sense when placed in its threefold context of the New Testament, the history of Christian doctrine, and contemporary theology. We have already considered the first context in the preceding chapter. In this chapter and the next we will examine the other two contexts, giving special consideration to the penal substitutionary doctrine of atonement.

Atonement Theories in History

Seven Textbook Theories

In the course of church history theologians proposed many explanations for how Jesus's suffering and death save us from sin, death, and the devil. Depending on how finely historians distinguish among them, the list of theories can run from three to twenty or more.[1] I will briefly mention seven before I examine in detail the two most influential ones.

(1) *The ransom theory.* In the view of Origen (ca. 185–ca. 254) and Gregory of Nyssa (ca. 330–ca. 395), by sinning human beings sold themselves to the devil and came under his power. Jesus offered his soul to the devil in exchange for all human souls. The devil agreed. But in his greed he was deceived, for after Jesus's death the devil discovered that he did not have enough power to hold the soul of the Son of God. The scriptural basis

1. Aulén, *Christus Victor*, divides atonement theories into three types. McDonald, *The Atonement*, treats sixteen types. Schmiechen, *Saving Power*, lists ten theories.

for this theory is found in 1 John 3:8, Hebrews 2:14–15, and other places. Anselm of Canterbury and Thomas Aquinas rejected the ransom theory as unworthy of God. It is hard to believe anyone could take this idea seriously today. At most, some might take it as a graphic metaphor expressing some generally accepted soteriological truth.

(2) *The Christus Victor theory.* This theory, like the ransom theory, holds that Jesus's death broke the power of evil and freed people from the forces that kept them in slavery. It looks back to the Gospels where Jesus cast out demons and binds Satan (Matt 12:12–29; John 12:31; Gal 1:4; Col 2:15). It focuses not on satisfaction of divine justice or moral reform of human beings but on defeating the forces that hold us in the miserable condition of slavery, weakness, deception, corruption, and death (Rom 8:37–40).[2] This theory, too, can be rehabilitated for modern people only with great modification. Indeed, many people believe in a real, personal devil against whom we need protection. And Jesus achieved a victory over this evil spiritual power. As long as we do not speculate about *how* Jesus defeats this spiritual enemy, this view functions unobtrusively as another dramatic metaphor expressing a dimension of salvation we experience in Christ, that is, Christ liberates us from the mysterious, deceptive, compulsive power of sin. But when we try to imagine a spiritual battle in which Jesus enters the unseen world and defeats the devil, we are plunged into an abyss of myth and superstition.

(3) *Recapitulation.* This theory was given classic form by Irenaeus of Lyon in the late second century. It is founded on Ephesians 1:10, where Christ is said to "gather up all things" in himself. Jesus Christ is a new Adam. By living through all stages of human life and getting it right, Jesus undoes Adam's history and gives humanity a new start (Eph 1:10; Rom 5; 1 Cor 15). This theory holds more promise than the previous ones for making a connection to contemporary people because it derives from faith in the resurrection of Jesus, an event within history and not a supposed event happening within a hidden spiritual realm. Anyone in any age can understand the resurrection of Jesus as an unambiguous divine act that saved him from death and vindicated him from the charges that led to his death. The resurrection designated Jesus as Lord, Messiah, and a new beginning for humanity. By living an authentic human life and passing through death Jesus leaves behind the history of disobedience and death. Through faith and the sacraments, we are united to Christ in this new history.

(4) *Deification or imparting divine life.* Orthodox churches emphasize this view above all others. Through the incarnation, the Son of God enters

---

2. Aulén, *Christus Victor.* Aulén defends this view from critics that dismiss it as crude and mythological.

the human sphere and imparts eternal life to humanity. By living a full human life, dying and rising, the eternal life that is in Jesus becomes available to all who become united to him. The Holy Spirit unites believers to the risen Christ through faith, baptism, and the Eucharist. Important New Testament texts supporting this view can be found in 1 John 3:2, Romans 6, 1 Corinthians 15:48–50, and 2 Peter 1:4. Once we understand that this theory views salvation very much like the recapitulation theory, modern people may find it intelligible.

(5) *Satisfaction*. This theory has roots in the Old and New Testaments and in the first few centuries of the church. But Anselm of Canterbury (1033–1109) gave it classical expression in his book *Why God Became Man*. Anselm attempts to show the reasonableness and necessity of the incarnation for salvation. By sinning against the infinite dignity of God, human beings incur infinite debt, which of course they cannot pay. But God loves human beings and does not want to abandon his eternal plan for creation. The debt is a human debt, so the payment must come from the human side. However, mere humans cannot acquire merit enough to make up for past sins, because they can never do more than their duty. So, God became human and as human merited an infinite reward. Out of love for us, Jesus shared his merit with us (Isa 53; Rom 3:25; 1 John 2:2, 4:10, 3:4–5; Heb 10:4). I will save my evaluation of this theory and the next for the main part of this chapter.

(6) *Penal substitution*. This theory became the favorite of Protestants during and after the Reformation, and it is defended by many evangelicals today. It has much in common with Anselm's satisfaction theory. But instead of restoring God's honor insulted by human sin, Jesus endures in our place the punishment merited by sin's offense against God. In this way, God maintains his justice without punishing us as we deserve. God's mercy is manifested in sending Jesus to take our place, and his justice is demonstrated in having Jesus endure our punishment (Isa 53; 2 Cor 5:18–21). I will analyze and criticize this theory in great detail below.

(7) *Moral influence*. This theory focuses on the transformation worked in us by the vision of divine love demonstrated in the cross. God's love provokes our repentance and evokes our love. This view has roots in the New Testament (Rom 5:6–8; Gal 2:19–20; 1 John 3:16), but Abelard (1079–1142) gave the theory its classic form. The love God demonstrated in the cross becomes real in us through the activity of the Holy Spirit (Rom 5:5). Modern liberal theology interprets the atonement largely under this heading. I will deal with the liberal appropriation of this theory in a separate chapter below.

Historiography of Atonement Theories

Understanding these theories and their interrelationships requires historians to adopt principles of selection and organization. In his classic study of the saving work of Christ, Robert Franks follows the model of the nineteenth-century history of dogma school pioneered by such thinkers as Ferdinand Christian Bauer (1792–1860), Albrecht Ritschl (1822–89), and Adolph von Harnack (1851–1930).[3] Franks organizes history most broadly in four historical epochs: patristic, medieval, older Protestant, and modern Protestant. Historical epochs are subdivided by school of thought, which in some cases correspond to geography or language, the most obvious being the distinction between East and West or Greek and Latin. Thinkers and documents discussed in sub-subdivisions are chosen because of their influence on later developments.

In contemporary Christianity, the broadest distinction in understanding the salvific work of Christ falls between Eastern Orthodoxy and Western Christianity, the latter of which embraces both Roman Catholic and Protestant communions. Orthodoxy emphasizes salvation from *death and corruption* through the union of God with humanity in the incarnation. By being united to Christ through the Spirit and in the sacraments of baptism and Eucharist, the Christian shares in the divine life. Western Christianity in both its Roman Catholic and Protestant forms emphasizes salvation from *guilt* through the merit accrued by Jesus's suffering and death. Orthodoxy does not exclude salvation from guilt through the merit of Christ and Western Christianity does not exclude salvation from death and corruption through union with God in Christ.[4] It is a matter of emphasis. Yet, we would not be far off the mark to say that Eastern Christianity focuses on the *ontological* side of salvation while Western Christianity focuses on the *judicial* side. The debate within Western Christianity between Roman Catholics and Protestants focused not so much on how Christ's death atones for sin but on the way it is applied to the individual, that is, on the nature of justification. Is the righteousness of Christ *infused* into us through the sacrament of baptism so that it becomes a real quality of our souls, as Catholic doctrine

3. Franks, *The Work of Christ*. In the preface to the first edition and in the original introduction, Franks acknowledges these three historians as influences (vii and xviii). See Seeberg, *Text-Book of the History of Doctrines*, 25–27, for a brief history of the origins of the discipline.

4. For the Latin story, see, Ortis, *Deification in the Latin Patristic Tradition*.

teaches,[5] or is it *imputed* to us because of our faith while remaining outside of us, as classic Lutheran and Reformed teaching maintains?[6]

In this chapter, I will lay aside traditional East-West differences and Protestant-Catholic debates to deal with a question at issue among contemporary evangelical Protestants: defense, criticism, and quest for alternatives to the penal substitutionary doctrine of the atonement.

Almost from the beginning, the classic Protestant doctrine of penal substitution found itself under attack from left-wing Protestants, the most prominent being Fausto Socinus (1539–1604). Arminian theologians Phillippus van Limborch (1633–1712) and Hugo Grotius (1583–1645) modified without rejecting the doctrine.[7] Deists like Lord Herbert of Cherbury (1582–1648) saw no need for satisfaction or substitution in any form. Repentance alone sufficed to assure divine forgiveness.[8] Such nineteenth-century liberal theologians as Friedrich Schleiermacher,[9] Albrecht Ritschl,[10] and Adolf von Harnack,[11] along with their present-day heirs, do not view the atoning action of Christ as satisfying God's justice or turning away his wrath. Instead, Christ works a religious and moral change in human beings through some mode of influence: the infectiousness of his religious devotion, loftiness of his moral teaching, or power of his personality.

5. *Catechism of the Catholic Church* 3.1.3.2.1:481–83.

6. Schmid, *Doctrinal Theology,* 424–41. On the basic definition of justification, Reformed theologians agree with the Lutherans, as is shown by this statement by Rijssenius: "Hence Justification is an exterior but not an interior change in man" (Quoted in Heppe, *Reformed Dogmatics,* 543–44).

7. Franks, *The Work of Christ,* 362–407.

8. Franks, *The Work of Christ,* 475–76.

9. Schleiermacher, *The Christian Faith,* 425–37.

10. Ritschl argues that the traditional doctrine presupposes the unbiblical idea of a conflict between God's grace and his righteousness that Christ resolves through his sacrifice (*The Christian Doctrine of Justification,* 473–84).

11. Von Harnack does not explicitly deny the efficacy of Jesus death, and he works to find some "truth and justice" in the traditional doctrines. But he clearly prefers to focus on Jesus's teaching and the love he showed in his sacrifice (*What Is Christianity?* 156–59).

The Protestant-Evangelical Doctrine of Penal Substitution

Classic Statements of Penal Substitution

What are the essential affirmations of the Protestant doctrine of penal substitutionary atonement?[12] How do these affirmations fit together harmoniously and within the larger body of Protestant theology? Why do some contemporary evangelical theologians resist criticism of it? In this section I will answer these questions by summarizing the consensus developed in Protestant scholasticism in the century and a half after the Reformation and examining the work of the most influential contemporary defenders of the doctrine. Protestant theology divided the work of Christ into three functions or offices. Christ acts as prophet, priest, and king. This organizational scheme has roots in the patristic era, but John Calvin made it popular among Protestants.[13] Protestant theology treated the atonement under the heading of the priesthood of Christ. Heppe outlines Reformed theology's teaching on the priesthood of Christ under nineteen different headings, but it will suffice for my purposes to summarize it in three propositions.

First, *because it violates God's holy law, the law of his own being, sin incurs God's wrath and merits his punishment.* Because it challenges and offends the greatest good, sin is a great evil and deserves the greatest punishment possible. Casper Olevanus's (1535–87) statement may be taken as representative of the Reformed scholastics' views on the seriousness of sin:

> So great and mighty an evil is sin, that it merits the eternal destruction of man. Whence it follows that sin is a greater evil than the eternal damnation of man, since that not even by eternal punishments can they expiate or overcome so great an evil. In short, so great an evil it is to have offended the majesty of God by even one sin, that the total destruction of all creatures would be a less evil. For not even the destruction of all creatures and their reduction to nothing would be an equivalent price to pay for expiating a single sin, which cannot be expiated save by the death of the Son of God.[14]

---

12. I will use the abbreviation PSA instead of "penal substitutionary atonement" with greater frequency from now on.

13. See Weber, *Foundations of Dogmatics* 2:172–77, for a brief history of the *munus triplex*, the three-fold office of Christ.

14. Olevanus, *An Exposition of the Symbole of the Apostles*, 7, quoted in Heppe, *Reformed Dogmatics*, 312.

Lutheran Johannes Andreas Quenstedt (1617–88), in line with Anselm of Canterbury and Quenstedt's Reformed contemporaries, speaks of
the *infinite* magnitude of sin's evil:

> The infinite God was offended by sin, and because sin is an of-
> fence, injury, and violation of the Infinite God, and is so to speak,
> a Deicide, it has, in consequence, a certain infinite wickedness
> . . . and deserves infinite penalties; and so far also demanded
> an infinite price as satisfaction which Christ alone could offer.[15]

The punishment merited by sin is death, a three-fold death of physical, spiritual, and eternal death.[16] Nor do the Reformed theologians accept
the Roman Catholic distinction between mortal and venial sin. All sins are
mortal and deserve death. John Calvin made this clear: "Let the children of
God hold that all sins are mortal. For it is rebellion against the will of God,
which of necessity provokes God's wrath and it is a violation of the law, upon
which God's judgment is pronounced without exception."[17] The Heidelberg
Catechism (1563) answers the tenth question of whether God will allow "disobedience and apostasy" to go unpunished in these words: "By no means,
but he is terribly displeased with our inborn as well as actual sins, and will
punish them in just judgment in time and eternity."[18]

The second proposition asserts that *God's eternal justice is so inexorable that God cannot simply overlook sin but must punish it according to its
demerit.* There are two questions at issue here that must be distinguished,
although many discussions run them together. First, could God simply forgive sin out of sheer mercy without satisfaction in any form? Second, could
God save humanity through a means other than the incarnation and death
of the Son of God? The first generation of Reformed theologians followed
Augustine, *On the Trinity,* where he argues against those who question the
necessity of the death of Christ, "not indeed that no other mode was possible to God, to whose power all things are equally subject, but that there
neither was nor need have been any other mode more appropriate for cur-
ing our misery."[19] John Calvin roots the necessity of Christ's sacrifice not in
a "simple" or "absolute necessity" but in God's "decree," that is, in the divine
free will rather than in a law above or within the divine being. In Calvin's

15. Quenstedt, *Theologia didactico-polemica sive systema theologicum,* quoted in
Franks, *The Work of Christ,* 416.

16. Heppe, *Reformed Dogmatics,* 361, 368.

17. Calvin, *Institutes* 2:423.

18. Schaff, CC 3:310.

19. Augustine, *On the Trinity* 13.10.13 (*NPNF1* 9:174). Heppe, *Reformed Dogmatics,*
469, mentions Calvin, the early Beza, Musculus, and Zanchius as holding this position.

words, "Our most merciful Father decreed what was best for us."[20] Later
Reformed theologians in response to the provocations of Socinus returned
to the position of Anselm and asserted the absolute necessity of satisfaction
through Christ.[21] Geneva theologian Francis Turretin (1623–87) combines
discussion of the general necessity of satisfaction with discussion of the
necessity of satisfaction *through Christ.* He rejects the idea that God could
forgive sin without satisfaction and the notion of the "hypothetical necessity" of satisfaction through Christ derived from a divine decision. Turretin
then states his own position, "absolute necessity," which he proposes to defend. "God not only has not willed to remit our sins without a satisfaction
. . . [God] could not do so on account of his justice."[22] Justice is a "natural
and essential" attribute of God, and in relation to the world, God is a judge
bound by the law of his nature, not merely a creditor who could forgive a
debt at will. "God cannot abstain [from punishing the guilty] without detri-
ment to his justice."[23] Unlike mercy, which God can freely give or withhold,
God has no choice about exercising justice, which is defined as giving each
according to what is due.[24] If satisfaction for sin is to be made at all, it must
be made by a creature of the same nature as the offender and "it should be of
an infinite value and worth to take away the infinite demerit of sin."[25] Only
Jesus Christ can satisfy these requirements. Hence, if the necessary satisfaction is to be made, it must be made through Christ. For another example of
the Reformed view of the necessity of satisfaction through Christ, we can
look to the Dutch Reformed theologian Franz Burman (1628–79). Among

20. Calvin, *Institutes* 2:464. As indicated above, Anselm had argued for the absolute
necessity of the incarnation and death of Christ for true satisfaction, that is, on the
assumption of the divine will to save humanity. Peter Lombard, in *Sentences* 3.20.1,
agrees with Augustine's view that another way was possible to the omnipotent God.
See Franks, *The Work of Christ,* 172, for discussion of Lombard. According to Franks,
Thomas Aquinas also agrees with Augustine's less strict type of necessity (Franks, *The
Work of Christ,* 219).

21. In saying that the Reformed theologians "returned" to Anselm on the matter of
the absolute necessity of satisfaction, I do *not* wish to be misunderstood to say that Anselm, like the Reformed theologians, viewed atonement as satisfaction of divine justice
through penal substitution. For Anselm, Christ voided our liability to punishment by
making recompense to God for the infinite debt we incurred by sinning against God's
honor. In his perfect obedience even unto death, Christ did not suffer our punishment;
he paid our debt.

22. Turretin, *IET* 2.14:418. On the Lutheran side, Quenstedt argues to the same
conclusion as Turretin, rejecting the medieval doctrine that God by his absolute power
could forgive sins without satisfaction. See Franks, *The Work of Christ,* 416, and Schmid,
Doctrinal Theology, 348.

23. Turretin, *IET* 2.14:422.

24. Turretin, *IET* 2.14:422.

25. Turretin, *IET* 2.14:421.

the six reasons he proposes for the necessity of satisfaction through Christ's sacrifice, the sixth is especially poignant: "indeed it were a crime unworthy of God to hand over to death an holy man worthy of God's supreme love, if the necessity did not compel."[26]

Third, *the suffering and death of Christ in our place expressed both perfect divine mercy and complete satisfaction of divine justice.* Christ perfectly fulfilled the righteous requirement of the law and endured the full penalty for every violation of the law. The former is called "active" and the latter "passive" obedience/righteousness. According to Swiss theologian Johannes Wolleb (1589–1629), "Christ's obedience extends just as widely as the law extends. Since therefore the law binds us both to punishment and to obedience, he satisfied both its requisitions."[27] Turretin defends the necessity of active as well as passive obedience: "The obedience of Christ has a twofold efficacy, satisfactory and meritorious; the former by which we are freed from the punishments incurred by sin; the latter by which . . . a right to eternal life and salvation is acquired for us."[28] The obedience of Christ provides not a mere gesture that moves God to have mercy on us. It affords the exact equivalent of the positive righteousness we lack through negligence and the debt we have incurred through sin. German theologian Bartholomäus Keckermann (1572–1608) urges that "the incalculable sorrow in Christ's soul, which he suffered toward the end of his life, arose from the magnitude of the sins committed or to be committed successively by the human race . . . [and from] the impression of the divine wrath felt in the highest degree . . . [analogous] and proportionate to this torture, which the damned will feel in hell and in eternal damnation."[29] Christ suffered and died not merely to provide a benefit to those sinners God wished to save but in their place, as a substitute. Swiss Reformed theologian Johannes Heidegger (1633–98) concludes from his study of Bible references to Christ dying "for" (Greek: *hyper*) us that "it is therefore beyond doubt that *huper* [sic] signified the place, representation or substitution of Christ's death in place of our death which was due."[30] Full satisfaction for sin of every level of seriousness and all time was completed in that event; no further satisfaction need be made.

26. Burmann, *Synopsis Theologiae* 5.19: 5–7, quoted in Heppe, *Reformed Dogmatics,* 470.

27. Wolleb, *Christianae Theologiae Compendium,* 82, quoted in Heppe, *Reformed Dogmatics,* 459.

28. *IET* 2.14.12.10:447.

29. Keckermann, *Systema Sacrosanctae Theologiae,* 346, quoted in Heppe, *Reformed Dogmatics,* 464–65.

30. Heidegger, *Corpus Christianae* 19:70, quoted in Heppe, *Reformed Dogmatics,* 469.

Finally, why is it fitting and just that God accept the satisfaction of Christ in our place? In answering this question Protestant scholastic theologians built on their conviction that Scripture plainly teaches the *fact* of this acceptance of Christ as our substitute. Given this fact, then, Turretin attempts to demonstrate the justice of this substitution. God must maintain his justice by punishing sin. No modification is possible on this point. But as to the "manner and circumstances of the punishment" God is not bound; it is, rather, a matter of

> a positive and free right. For a certain forbearance *(epieikeia)* can be admitted here from the goodness of a most wise God, either in relation to time by the delay of punishment; or in relation to the degree by mitigation; or in relation to persons by substitution. For although the person sinning entirely deserves punishment and can justly be punished, yet it is not so necessary and indispensable that for certain weighty reasons it may not be transferred to a surety. And in this sense, it is said by theologians that punishment should necessarily be inflicted impersonally upon every sin, but not therefore personally upon every sinner (since God can indeed through his singular grace exempt some from it by the substitution of a surety in their place).[31]

Turretin's argument deserves careful analysis. In his view, since sinners stand before God in a three-fold relationship of debtors, rebels, and law-breakers, God stands in a threefold relationship to sinners. God is creditor, Lord, and Judge. As creditor to whom a debt is owed and Lord against whom rebellion is being waged, God may forgive according to his pleasure.[32] In contrast, according to his essential justice and in his role as the world's judge, God must punish sinners. How then can sinners be saved? Drawing on the generally accepted principle that an end may be achieved by more than one means, Turretin argues that God enjoys some discretion as to the *manner* of punishment. In his mercy and goodness, God desires to exempt some sinners from punishment and can "for certain weighty reasons" execute just punishment on a substitute. That is to say, punishing a substitute for our sins falls within God's discretion in choosing *how* to exercise his justice. The cogency of this assertion is so decisive for Turretin's argument that we must scrutinize it carefully. I see two aspects that need to be distinguished. First, he argues that God *can* make the substitution while maintaining his justice, and second, he asserts that God possesses *sufficient reasons* to make the substitution. As to the first aspect, it makes no sense

31. Turretin, *IET* 2.14:420.

32. Turretin, *IET* 2.14:419–20.

to discuss the conditions under which God will decide to make substitution until we are clear that doing so would not contradict divine justice. To demonstrate that substitution does not contradict God's justice, Turretin distinguishes between sin in itself and sinners who sin. God's just nature requires that he punish *sin*. No adjustment is possible here. But divine retributive justice does not necessitate that sinners be punished for their sins *in their own persons*. What grounds justify this assertion? Even if we admit that it is possible to distinguish between sinners and their sins, how does this distinction support Turretin's argument? For how can *sin* be punished? Punishment applies to *persons*, and sin is not a person. Apart from sinners, sin is an abstraction. If divine justice necessitates punishment, surely it necessitates punishing *sinners*. The only way out of this difficulty is the doctrine of "imputation" wherein God transfers our legal liability to Jesus Christ. In God's eyes, Jesus becomes the "sinner" whom God punishes for our sins. However, the doctrine of imputation simply repeats in other words the difficulty it is meant to explain, that is, how is it just for God to exempt sinners from necessary punishment and punish an innocent person in their place? It does not seem that Turretin has explained anything:

1. We know that transfer of our guilt to Christ is possible because God made this transfer.

2. We know God made the transfer because Scripture tells us so.

3. The transfer must be just because God is by nature just.[33]

Hence, we return to where we started none the wiser.

Even if the idea of substitution does not assert a logical contradiction and is not obviously inconsistent with divine justice, God must have good reasons to make the substitution and must find a suitable substitute. What are those reasons, and what qualities must a substitute possess? For Turretin, God's desire that some sinners be saved, to the praise of his glory and grace, is a sufficient reason for God to make the substitution. But what sort of substitute would enable God to make a just and effective substitution? Not every candidate could meet the conditions required. Turretin articulates the problem in this way: "But that such a substitution may be made legitimately and without any appearance of injustice, various conditions are required in the surety, all of which are found perfectly in Christ."[34]

Turretin proposes five qualities that justify Christ becoming a substitute. (1) Christ shares a "common nature that sin may be punished in the

33. See Craig, *Atonement,* for his use of legal philosophy to rationalize the concept of imputation.

34. Turretin, *IET* 2.14:421.

same nature which is guilty." (2) Christ consented "spontaneously and willingly" to take the role of surety. (3) Christ possessed "power and domination" over his own life. (4) Being God and human, Christ possessed "the power of bearing all the punishment due to us and of taking it away as much from himself as from us." (5) Being completely innocent and holy, Christ did not "have to offer sacrifice for himself, but only for us."[35]

In assessing Turretin's argument, we must keep in mind that he does not present these five conditions as measures of the *absolute possibility* of substitution. As we saw above, his distinction between sin and sinners grounded this possibility. Nor does Turretin present his five conditions to demonstrate the *fact* of penal substitution. He accepts this fact on the authority of Scripture. Given the absolute possibility and fact of substitution, Turretin argues for the justice—or at least against the manifest injustice—in the specific case of God offering Christ as our substitute. But even apart from any argument, Turretin already believes the substitution is just, because he believes Scripture teaches it. His argument, then, is not a rational proof for the justice of substitution but an exercise in "faith seeking understanding" in which a doctrine of faith is explored in an analytic way.[36] In a later section, I will return to the crucial distinction between sinners and their sins to show that it turns out to be a Trojan Horse for the penal substitution view of atonement.

To sum up, Protestant scholastic theology contended that the absolute necessity of satisfaction for sin is rooted in God's eternal nature. God cannot let sin go unpunished without denying himself. However, since in his mercy God wishes to save some sinners, he provided satisfaction for their sins through the suffering and death of Christ. God's free decision to have mercy on some sinners entailed a decision to provide satisfaction through Christ. For there was no other way both to meet the demand of divine justice and save sinners from divine wrath. The necessity of satisfaction through Christ is indirectly rooted in the divine nature.

Transitional Defenders of Penal Substitution

By the time Turretin wrote his *Institutes of Elenctic Theology* in the mid-seventeenth century, the Protestant doctrine of penal substitution had been given its classic form. Its central claims had been articulated, its presuppositions and implications explored, its relations to other doctrines made explicit, and the most challenging objections answered. Its defenders

35. Turretin, *IET* 2.14:421.

36. Anselm, *Proslogium* 1. Anselm expresses desire to understand what he believes on authority.

in the eighteenth and nineteenth centuries, though abandoning the rigorous scholastic method of logical or causal reasoning, added nothing to its substance. The same is true of twentieth- and twenty-first-century champions. When authors of whatever century, using whatever method, and responding to whatever challenges set out to express and defend PSA, they invariably defend the three classic propositions I articulated above. On our way to the contemporary discussion we will examine briefly two additional thinkers, Jonathan Edwards from the eighteenth and Charles Hodge from the nineteenth century.

Jonathan Edwards (1703–58)

Edwards's thinking on the atonement is scattered throughout his works but is found principally in two extended studies, *A History of the Work of Redemption,* in which he surveys the entire Bible history[37] and his essay "Concerning the Necessity and Reasonableness of the Christian Doctrine of Satisfaction for Sin."[38] I will limit my comments to the latter essay.[39] As the title indicates, Edwards is concerned to show the reasonableness of the traditional doctrine. Although his major opponents are deistic thinkers of the Enlightenment, he does not hesitate to speak the language of enlightened morality and psychology. First, he shows the necessity of punishment for sin. Sin must be punished "because sin deserves punishment," and great crimes deserve great punishment. "It will follow, that it is requisite that God should punish all sin with infinite punishment; because all sin, as it is against God, is infinitely heinous, and has infinite demerit, is justly infinitely hateful to him, and so stirs up infinite abhorrence and indignation in him."[40] All sin "strikes at God" and "may be resolved into hatred of God and our Neighbor."[41] God's holiness and greatness make it necessary that he punish sin. Also, as "Supreme Regulator and Rector of the universe" God must maintain his rights.[42] For reasons rooted in the

37. Edwards, *Works* 1:531–619.

38. Edwards, *Works* 2:565–78. See Williams, "Jonathan Edwards," 467–71, for further, scattered references.

39. Franks, *The Work of Christ.* See also Grensted, *A Short History,* 275–80.

40. Edwards, "Concerning the Necessity," 565.

41. Edwards, "Concerning the Necessity," 566.

42. Edwards, "Concerning the Necessity," 567. According to Williams, Edwards's use of "governmental" language should not lead us to think that Edwards accepted Grotius's governmental theory of the atonement. Many following in his wake fell into this pattern, but Edwards himself remained an "essentialist," arguing that the necessity for atonement lay in God's own nature as just and holy ("Jonathan Edwards," 467–71).

nature of law and the perfection of the lawgiver, sin must be punished with a "condign" punishment. And, as he urged earlier, infinitely serious crime demands infinite punishment.[43]

Second, Edwards addresses the "reasonableness" of satisfaction for sin. "The satisfaction made by Christ in his death is certainly a very rational thing."[44] Edwards begins with an analogy from human experience. Suppose someone I love and who was deeply obligated to me horribly mistreated me year after year. Eventually, however, they stopped their offensive behavior. Edwards admits, "I should not forgive him except on gospel considerations." But suppose, continues Edwards, that a dear friend who was also a "near relation" of the offender should intercede for him. Suppose that my friend, the mediator, went to great trouble to gain my forgiveness and the offender's repentance. "I should be satisfied, and find myself inclined, without any difficulty, to receive him into my entire friendship again."[45] After giving many examples from the Bible of people making satisfaction or substituting themselves for others, Edwards defines the terms merit, demerit, patron, and client, which he will use in the following extended analogy. Edwards then makes nineteen, ever more radical moves to show the reasonableness of one person's (the patron's) merit counting against the demerit of another person (the client). Edwards begins with consideration of behavior that no one would consider "unreasonable or against nature, or without foundation in the reason and nature of things," that is, that respect should be shown to one on account of his relation to, or union and connection to, another."[46] After adding seventeen other qualifications he arrives at the extraordinary case where the patron takes on the same degree of suffering due to the client, showing that the patron loves the client as much as he loves himself. Whereas such love may be unusual, it is by no means unreasonable. Such, Edwards concludes, is the love in which Christ gave himself to cancel our infinite debt.

Charles Hodge (1797–1878)

Charles Hodge was one of the best-educated theologians in the United States in the mid-nineteenth century. He studied at the College of New Jersey and Princeton Seminary and spent some years studying abroad in

---

See also Crisp, "Penal Non-Substitution," 140–68, for the post-Edwards developments in New England theology.

43. Edwards, "Concerning the Necessity," 567–69.
44. Edwards, "Concerning the Necessity," 569.
45. Edwards, "Concerning the Necessity," 569.
46. Edwards, "Concerning the Necessity," 571.

Germany and France. He became Professor of Oriental and Biblical Literature at Princeton Seminary in 1822. He later transferred to the chair of Didactic and Polemical Theology (1851).[47] As an Old School Presbyterian, he defended the traditional doctrine of original sin and limited atonement through the penal substitution of Christ. In his *Systematic Theology,* he treats the work of Christ under the familiar rubric of the three offices: prophetic, priestly, and kingly.[48] He devotes a preliminary chapter to defining the terms in which the discussion will be conducted: atonement, satisfaction, penalty, vicariousness, guilt, redemption, expiation, and propitiation. In the following chapter, he devotes sixty-three pages to exposition and defense of the traditional doctrine of PSA. This doctrine, Hodge points out, is the teaching of all the confessional statements of "Lutheran and Reformed Churches."[49] Against Roman Catholic theology, he argues that Christ's sacrifice is complete, and against the Scotists and Arminians he asserts that it is necessary and equivalent to the penalty for sin, not arbitrary or merely acceptable by grace.[50] The doctrine is rooted in the very nature of God, in his justice and holiness and in the immutability of his law. Hodge summarizes his argument in this way:

> It has been shown, (1.) That the work of Christ for our salvation, was a real satisfaction of infinite inherent dignity and worth. (2.) That it was a satisfaction not to commutative justice (as paying a sum of money would be), nor to the rectoral justice or benevolence of God, but to his distributive and vindicatory justice which renders necessary the punishment of sin; and (3.) That it was satisfaction to the law of God, meeting its demands of a perfect righteousness for the justification on sinners. If these points be admitted, the Church doctrine concerning the satisfaction, or atonement of Christ, is admitted in all that is essential to its integrity.[51]

Hodge continues his positive argument with proofs from Scripture, related doctrines, and religious experience. He then deals with the usual rational and moral objections and those arising from popular misconceptions. In all this, Hodge stays true to the classic doctrine as articulated by

---

47. Wallace, "Charles Hodge," 303–7.
48. Hodge, *Systematic Theology* 2.
49. Hodge, *Systematic Theology* 2:480.
50. Hodge, *Systematic Theology* 2:485–87.
51. Hodge, *Systematic Theology* 2:495–96.

Francis Turretin, whose theology he studied under the tutelage of Archibald Alexander and Samuel Miller while in Princeton.[52]

Other transitional figures

Already on the defensive in the late eighteenth century, the classic doctrine of PSA came under widespread attack in the early nineteenth century.[53] The details of this history are not important for my purpose, which is to get a clear understanding of the classic doctrine of PSA so that we can assess its viability for a theology of the atonement.[54] Despite being on the defensive, the doctrine found able defenders in the late nineteenth and early twentieth centuries. Among those deserving brief mention is the Dutch theologian Herman Bavinck (1854–1921), whose volume on sin and salvation has only recently been translated from Dutch into English.[55] In volume 3 of his *Reformed Dogmatics,* he writes a ninety-four page chapter on Christ's humiliation. Bavinck's chapter includes an extensive review of atonement theology from the patristic era to his own day, devoting special attention to Socinus and the doctrine's recent detractors on both sides of the Atlantic. He treats the scriptural basis and theological coherence of vicarious substitution and seems especially concerned to answer the criticism that the doctrine does not do justice to the love of God. In a statement summarizing the teaching of Scripture on vicarious satisfaction, he says,

> Then we can construe the interconnection between all these scripture pronouncements in no other way than that Christ put himself in our place, has borne the punishment of our sin, satisfied God's justice, and so secured salvation for us.[56]

Also worthy of mention because of their influence on twentieth-century evangelicalism in America are William Shedd (1820–94), Archibald Alexander Hodge (1823–86), son of Charles Hodge, and Louis Berkhof (1873–1957). One of the leading Presbyterian theologians of his day, Shedd wrote a three-volume *Dogmatic theology.* In volume 2, he defended the classic penal substitution view of the atonement. Christ's sufferings "were *penal* in their nature and intent, since they were neither calamitous nor

52. Wallace, "Charles Hodge," 304.

53. Holmes, "Penal Substitution," 308.

54. For this story, see Grensted, *A Short History,* 307–72, Crisp, "Penal Non-Substitution," 140–68, and Franks, *The Work of Christ,* 475–702.

55. Bavinck, *Sin and Salvation.*

56. Bavinck, *Sin and Salvation,* 398.

disciplinary. They were judicial infliction voluntarily endured by Christ, for the purpose of satisfying the claims of the law due from man; and this *purpose* makes them penal."[57] A. A. Hodge became professor of systematic theology at Princeton Seminary in 1878. In his books *Outlines of Theology* and *The Atonement,* Hodge defends the traditional view of atonement. "The sufferings of Christ were penal, therefore, because he suffered that kind and degree of evil that divine justice demanded as a complete satisfaction for all the sins of all his people."[58] In arguing his preference for the clear term "satisfaction" over the ambiguous term "atonement," the younger Hodge says "Christ fully satisfied all that the justice and law of God required, on the part of mankind, as the condition of their being admitted to divine favor and eternal happiness . . . [including] (1) the obedience which the law demands as the condition of life, and (2) that suffering which it demands as the penalty of sin."[59]

Finally, before we turn to the contemporary debate, we mention Louis Berkhof, who in 1906 became Professor of Theology and from 1931 until his death in 1957 served as president of Calvin College. In his *Systematic Theology,* after surveying the history of the question of the necessity of PSA, Berkhof presents five reasons to prefer "absolute necessity" over non-necessity (Duns Scotus) or hypothetical necessity (Calvin, Bavinck) of the atonement. For "the denial of it [of absolute necessity] really involves a denial of the punitive justice of God as one of the inherent perfections of the divine being, though the Reformers, of course, did not mean to deny this at all."[60] According to Berkhof, the atonement was absolutely necessary because Scripture teaches it, the immutability of God's law, rooted in his inherent attribute of justice, demands punishment for transgressions, the veracity of God's decrees concerning the punishment for transgressions guarantees it, guilt requires "personal or vicarious satisfaction," and the greatness of the gift of Christ "implies the necessity of the atonement."[61]

---

57. Shedd, *Dogmatic Theology* 2:457.

58. Hodge, *Outlines of Theology,* 303. In this early work Hodge in large part summarizes his father's theology with extensive quotes.

59. Hodge, *Atonement,* 34.

60. Berkhof, *Systematic Theology,* 310.

61. Berkhof, *Systematic Theology,* 309–11.

8

Jesus as Penal Substitute II

Contemporary Evangelical Theory

THE DOCTRINE OF PENAL substitutionary atonement is alive and well today in the evangelical world. Hundreds of books and articles for and against PSA have been written in the last thirty years, not to mention conferences, online discussions, and blog posts. I can mention only a few and analyze even fewer. As of the date of this writing, the number 1 selling book in the category of Christian theology is Wayne Grudem, *Systematic Theology: An Introduction to Biblical Doctrine.*[1] Grudem is a vociferous defender of PSA. If fact, three of the ten top-selling books in Christian theology are written by advocates of penal substitution.[2] Another defense of the traditional doctrine high on the list is John Murray's 1955 book *Redemption Accomplished and Applied,* which Eerdmans Publishing Company reprinted in 2015. Among the resolutions passed at the 2017 annual meeting of the Southern Baptist Convention is one reaffirming "the truthfulness, efficacy, and beauty of the biblical doctrine of penal substitutionary atonement as the burning core of the Gospel message and the only hope of a fallen race."[3] My sense is that the doctrine, though not understood at a deep level, exercises considerable influence in popular evangelicalism, in song lyrics, sermons, liturgies, and personal devotion.[4]

---

1. Also selling very well is Erickson, *Christian Theology.* Not far behind is Michael Horton, *The Christian Faith.* Both Erickson and Horton defend PSA.

2. Amazon.com statistics for June 03, 2019. The list includes books by Gruden, Albert J. Mohler, and Charles Hodge.

3. Southern Baptist Convention 2017 Resolutions.

4. In the subtitle to his 2018 article in *Christianity Today,* Galli explains "why

Twentieth- and Twenty-First-Century
Advocates of Penal Substitution

Just as hundreds of seventeenth- and eighteenth-century scholastic theologians were provoked by Socinus's attack on substitutionary atonement to defend the doctrine, such mid-twentieth-century evangelicals as Roger Nichol and Leon Morris wrote in response to arguments made by British New Testament scholar C. H. Dodd.[5] In the 1930s, Dodd had argued that the Greek word *hilastērion,* used in the New Testament in reference to the act of atonement only in Romans 3:25 and 1 John 2:2 and 4:10, and often translated "propitiation" in the older English translations, does not mean pacifying divine wrath but removing the guilt and stain of sin. The saving action of Christ works a change in the *sinner,* not in God.[6] In 2003, Steve Chalke and Alan Mann sparked intense controversy with the publication of *The Lost Message of Jesus.* The authors refer to the image of the atonement presented by PSA as a "form of cosmic child abuse."[7] Among the many books written in response to Chalke and Mann and others critical of PSA because of its supposed reliance on divine violence, is *Pierced for Our Transgressions: Rediscovering the Glory of Penal Substitution.*[8] I will speak more about this book below.

Having read extensively in the recent academic and popular literature advocating penal substitution to the point that I find myself reading the same arguments over and over, I have chosen to limit my discussion to three books I consider representative.

J. I. Packer, *In My Place Condemned He Stood*

In my view, J. I. Packer (1926–2020) is PSA's most persuasive contemporary defender. His writing is concise, clear, moderate, and practical. His three most influential essays on the subject are reprinted in a recent book

---

evangelicals give pride of place to penal substitutionary understandings of the Cross" ("It Doesn't Get Any More Personal").

5. Morris, *Apostolic Preaching,* and Nichol, "C. H. Dodd and the Doctrine of Propitiation," 117–57.

6. Dodd, *The Epistle of Paul to the Romans* and *The Johannine Epistles.*

7. Chalke and Mann, *Lost Message of Jesus,* 182. Because Chalke is a well-known evangelical the book caused a stir among his fellow British evangelicals, so much so that the Evangelical Alliance hosted a public debate in October 2004 to discuss the issue. The papers from this symposium were published as Tidball et al. (eds.), *The Atonement Debate.*

8. Jeffrey et al. (eds.), *Pierced.*

coauthored by Mark Dever and covered with a new introduction by Packer.[9] In his introduction, Packer reviews the essentials of the doctrine of penal substitutionary atonement, which is "the best part of the best news that the world has ever heard" [21]. In agreement with Aristotle, Packer asserts that the nature of justice "is essentially giving everyone their due" [23]. God's justice includes "retribution for wrong doing" [23]. We are due "condemnation and rejection" because "human nature is radically twisted into an instinctive yet deliberate and ineradicable habit of God-defying or God-denying self-service" [23]. In the atonement, Christ reconciled us to God by becoming "a *propitiation,* ending God's judicial wrath against us" through his substitution of himself to endure the divine "retribution due to us guilty ones" [23]. Near the end of the introduction, Packer quotes an earlier essay in which he had listed nine "insights basic to personal religion." The first three mirror the three headings under which I summarized the traditional doctrine: (1) God "judges all sin as it deserves; which Scripture affirms, and my conscience confirms, to be right." (2) "My sins merit ultimate penal suffering and rejection from God's presence (conscience also confirms this), and nothing I do can blot them out." And (3) the "penalty due to me for my sins . . . was paid for me by Jesus Christ, the Son of God, in his death on the cross" [25–26]. In the book's first chapter, "The Heart of the Gospel,"[10] Packer argues, against C. H. Dodd, that the New Testament teaches that the cross turned away divine wrath from the sinner. God's anger is a function of his holy rejection of sin. "God is not just" affirms Packer, "unless he inflicts upon sin and wrongdoing the penalty it deserves" [35]. Both salvation and condemnation "manifest the essential, inherent retributive justice that belongs to the divine character" [40]. In the second chapter, "What Did the Cross Achieve: The Logic of Penal Substitution,"[11] Packer begins with some important reflections on method. Though he agrees with the doctrine defended by the seventeenth-century Reformed theologians, he contends that their efforts to refute Socinus led them into speculation:

> In trying to beat the Socinian rationalism at its own game, Reformed theologians were conceding the Socinian assumption that every aspect of God's work of reconciliation will be exhaustively explicable in terms of a natural theology of divine

---

9. Packer and Dever, *In My Place.* Hereafter I will place references to this book in brackets in the text.

10. This chapter is a reprint of chapter 18 from Packer's bestselling book *Knowing God,* first published in 1973.

11. Originally published under the same title in the *Tyndale Bulletin* 25 (1974) 3–45.

government, drawn from the world of contemporary legal and
political thought. [55–56]

Packer sets out to defend the traditional doctrine without falling into
the rationalism of Socinus and the Reformed theologians who responded
to him. We must recognize that our knowledge of God's work of reconciling us is "faith-knowledge" of a mystery that we can comprehend "only
in part" [57–58]. Hence, we should expect that the doctrine of the atonement will always "entail unsolved problems" that can be articulated only in
paradoxical or analogical language [59]. In this way, Packer avoids the ra-
tionalist assumption that defending a theological truth obligates us to solve
all the problems it raises in a complete deductive system of propositions.
Instead, Packer argues that we have to be satisfied with models. Models are,
"we might say, analogies with a purpose, thought-patterns that function in
a particular way, teaching us to focus on one area of reality (relationships
with God) by conceiving of it in terms of another (relationships with each
other)" [63]. Packer differentiates three levels of models theologians must
take into account: the "control" models of Scripture, "dogmatic" models of
church confessions, and "interpretive" models of theology [63]. Knowledge
of the divine mystery of reconciliation comes to us through the "didactic
thought-models given in the Bible [the control level], which in truth are
instruction from God" [64]. Now that Packer has relieved himself of the
obligation to create a perfectly coherent atonement theory and answer all
objections to the satisfaction of objectors, he is free to test the PSA model
against the teaching of Scripture. He performs this test in two stages: (1)
measuring the traditional understanding of *substitution* against New Testament texts and competing explanations, and (2) treating the additional
question of the *penal* nature of the substitution. After establishing to his
satisfaction that the traditional understanding of penal substitution is the
teaching of the Bible, Packer denies that he has succumbed to the temptation of giving a rationalistic explanation of "how" divine justice and love
can be harmonized. Instead, explains Packer,

> the primary function of the concept is to correlate my knowl-
> edge of being guilty before God with my knowledge that, on the
> one hand, no question of my ever being judged for my sins can
> now arise, and, on the other hand, that the risen Christ whom
> I am called to accept as Lord is none other than Jesus, who se-
> cured my immunity from judgment by bearing on the cross the
> penalty that was my due. The effect of this correlation is not in
> any sense to "solve" or dissipate the mystery of the work of God
> (it is not that sort of mystery!); the effect is simply to define that

work with precision, and thus to evoke faith, hope, praise, and responsive love to Jesus Christ. [79–80]

In the rest of this chapter, Packer defends the essential affirmations of the traditional doctrine of penal substitutionary atonement without, he claims, going behind the mysteries of revelation that constitute this model. Those mysteries are "mysterious divine love," "the mysterious necessity" for the cross, the "mysterious solidarity" that enables Christ to bear the penalty for our sins, and the "mysterious mode of union" by which we are united to Christ [88]. Packer claims to have articulated a simple Scripture-based model of PSA unencumbered by elaborate logical analysis of presuppositions, implications, and corollaries. It shows its truth by its resonance with Scripture, and it will persuade those who accept the authority of Scripture.

I do not believe Packer succeeds.[12] His presentation of PSA includes the same three summary points into which I condensed the traditional doctrine: God must punish sin, we deserve hell, and Jesus endured equivalent punishment in our place. Packer claims that these three propositions are the plain assertions of Scripture and involve no speculation such as that in which Socinus and his Protestant opponents indulged. Instead of speculating based on these truths, Packer has, as I quoted him above, merely "correlated" them and "defined that work with precision" [79–80]. However, as I will argue below, establishing the credibility of these propositions requires a great deal of "speculation." Nor are correlation and definition as speculatively innocent as Packer would have us to believe. As I read them, the seventeenth-century theologians also thought they were simply correlating and defining Bible truths in a rigorous way. In my view, Packer's simple PSA model includes in a hidden way the entire traditional doctrine, including the "speculative" parts. I do not think acknowledging the mystery in all God's works relieves theologians of the obligation to use reason to explore the presuppositions, implications, and corollaries of PSA. If reasoning from this model leads to absurdities, contradictions, and obscurities, it makes sense to question the truth of the model. Perhaps reason can drive us back to the Scriptures for a fresh look.

Jeffery, Ovey, and Sach, *Pierced for Our Transgressions*

The next book can be dealt with briefly. *Pierced for Our Transgressions* (2007), co-authored by Jeffery, Ovey, and Sach, was written after the

---

12. Green and Baker, *Recovering the Scandal of the Cross*, 179–82, come to a similar conclusion about Packer's effort to retrieve PSA.

controversy spurred by Chalke and Mann, *The Lost Message of Jesus* (2003), and the 2004-debate sponsored by the Evangelical Alliance of the British Isles. The book contains biblical, theological, and historical arguments for holding the traditional PSA view as "the central aspect of God's redeeming work in Christ."[13] It also addresses traditional and recent criticisms that have been leveled at the doctrine. Despite many positive features, the book is flawed by its continuous overstatement of its case and lack of self-criticism. Though it is not strident in its language, it gives the impression of being written for insiders to reinforce what they already believe. As an example of overstatement, the authors argue that the sacrifice of the Passover lamb and the sacrifices of the Day of Atonement are clear Old Testament examples of penal substitution wherein the sacrificial animal dies in the place of the worshiper [34–52].[14] In the theological section we find the standard elements of PSA: (1) God, as infinite in holiness and justice, is provoked to burning wrath by sin and must punish it according to its deserts [123]. (2) Sin is such an outrage against God that it deserves hell [111–23]. (3) The apparent tension between God's promise to punish sin and his desire to extend mercy to sinners is resolved by Jesus's work of bearing the full consequences of sin in our place [126, 137]. In the historical section, the authors attempt to refute the claim that PSA originated only in the Protestant Reformation by offering many examples of PSA from the patristic period [161–204]. There are no doubt statements within certain church fathers that can be made to fit PSA, just as there are such statements in the New Testament. However, in many cases the patristic authors are quoting or alluding to New Testament texts without drawing them together and constructing a coherent theory of the atonement. If the New Testament does not clearly teach PSA, then neither do the church fathers.[15]

---

13. Jeffrey et al. (eds.), *Pierced*, 147. Hereafter I will place references to this book in brackets in the text.

14. If not wholly mistaken, this view of the Passover and Day of Atonement sacrifices and the scapegoat ritual is oversimplified. See Milgrom, *Leviticus 1–16*, 254–58, 440–41, 704–13, 1079–84, for thorough analysis of the Old Testament sacrifices in their ancient Near Eastern contexts. Gaster concludes, "This view is thoroughly mistaken, for such animals are not in fact substitutes for capital punishment, but merely vehicles for transferring and thereby removing taint and contagion" ("Sacrifices and Offerings, OT," 153).

15. For a series of articles arguing for the presence of PSA in the church fathers, see Ensor, "Justin Martyr and Penal Substitutionary Atonement," 217–32, Ensor, "Clement of Alexandria and Penal Substitutionary Atonement," 19–35, Ensor, "Tertullian and Penal Substitutionary Atonement," 130–42, and Ensor, "Penal Substitutionary Atonement in the Later Ante-Nicene Period," 331–46.

William Lane Craig, *The Atonement*

William Lane Craig's 2018 book, *The Atonement,* deserves study because it uses philosophy of law to reinforce and defend the traditional doctrine of PSA. Unlike Packer, Craig shows no hesitancy in using philosophical methods to defend PSA and nowhere in this book does he appeal to mystery. Craig lays out the traditional PSA view from Scripture and history and, given the disproportionate space devoted to him and the sparsity of criticism, treats Francis Turretin's account as the definitive theological statement on the atonement.[16] The one area where Craig points to a defect in Turretin's doctrine of the atonement is his lack of explanation of how we can be united to Christ in a way that his righteousness can be justly imputed to us and our sin justly imputed to him [47]. And it is this lack that much of Craig's book is designed to rectify. In the second half of the book, Craig answers two philosophical questions, "What is punishment?" and "Is punishment just?" and applies his legal analysis to the atonement. According to some theories, punishment is harsh treatment, intentionally inflicted in response to a wrongful action and expressing condemnation [55–56]. Under this definition, because it involves condemnation, it would seem that punishing Jesus for the sins of others would be an irrational and unjust action. In addressing this concern, Craig points to the notion of "strict liability" as an example of punishment without condemnation. Strict liability is a legal concept that says a person may be liable to punishment for the consequences of an act that itself is not subject to condemnation [58–59]. But even if we were to grant that punishing Jesus involves condemnation, Craig argues, we would not be bound to think Jesus was condemned for *his* sin. The traditional PSA doctrine teaches that our sins were *imputed* to Christ by God. Are we simply to accept such imputation on faith without any analogy within human affairs? Craig points to the concept of a "legal fiction" as such an analogy. A legal fiction is a construct the court knows to be false but finds useful in pursuit of justice. In a famous case, a Mediterranean island was declared to be part of the City of London for the purpose of the trial, and in another case a ship was declared to be a person so that "she" could be held liable for the crimes committed with her [63]. Craig uses this legal construct to illuminate the biblical notion of imputation. It is known to be false that Christ deserved punishment because of wrong he did, but "God adopts for the administration of justice the legal fiction that Christ did such deeds" [62]. Craig finds another helpful analogy in the concept of "vicarious liability." This legal notion enables a judge to find a superior

16. Craig, *The Atonement,* 42–48. Hereafter I will place references to this book in brackets in the text.

liable for the wrongdoing of a subordinate. Craig sees in this concept "a very close analogy to the doctrine of the imputation of our guilt to Christ" [66]. While these analogies do not prove the theological doctrine of imputation they refute "any allegations of incoherence respecting substitution and the definition of punishment" [66].

In examining the issues imbedded in the second question, that is, "Is punishment just?" Craig responds to a six-step argument against penal substitution, which he states in this way:

1. God is perfectly just.

2. If God is perfectly just, He cannot punish an innocent person.

3. Therefore, God cannot punish an innocent person.

4. Christ was an innocent person.

5. Therefore, God cannot punish Christ.

6. If God cannot punish Christ, penal substitution is false. [67]

In responding to this argument, Craig makes several distinctions drawn from philosophy of law that for my purposes we need not discuss. He aims his pivotal challenge to the argument at premise 4, that is, the claim that Christ was an innocent person. Because of God's imputation of our guilt to him, Christ became *legally* guilty and *legally* liable to punishment. Hence, in punishing Christ, God did not punish a legally innocent person. Penal substitution, then, stands undefeated by this argument [75].

Perhaps God is not unjust to punish Christ to whom God has imputed the guilt of our sins, but how does penal substitution satisfy God's positive retributive justice, which requires God to punish the sins of all?[17] Craig sets out the objection in three steps:

1. Unless the person who committed a wrong is punished for that wrong, divine justice is not satisfied.

2. If God practices penal substitution, then the person who committed a wrong is not punished for that wrong.

3. Therefore, if God practices penal substitution, divine justice is not satisfied. [77]

Craig responds to this argument by drawing on his previously discussed concept of vicarious liability, which we met above. According to this

---

17. This question presumes a distinction between *positive* retribution in which the guilty must be punished because they deserve it and *negative* retribution in which the innocent must not be punished because they do not deserve it.

legal concept, retributive justice can be satisfied if the person legally "liable" for a wrong is punished, even if that person is not the doer of the wrong [79]. Craig proposes a revision to premise (1) so that it reads as follows:

1. Unless a person who is liable for a wrong is punished for that wrong, divine justice is not satisfied [79].

The traditional PSA doctrine meets this revised condition. In Craig's words, "But then given the doctrine of imputation of sin, Christ is legally liable for our sins and so may satisfy justice by being duly punished for those sins" [79]. In response to premise 2, Craig invokes the concept of "representation" in which Christ not only takes our place (substitution) but stands as our proxy in which role his actions count as ours. Craig explains the concept of representation: by the will of God the Father, the Son of God "voluntarily consented to serve as our proxy before God by means of his incarnation and baptism, so that by his death he might satisfy the demands of divine justice on our behalf" [81]. The requirement stated in premise 2, then, is satisfied. Those who committed wrong *are* punished in their God-appointed proxy.

Only a few more problems remain for Craig to clear up. Nothing can change the past and the fact that we have sinned. Hence, how can forgiveness remove guilt? Craig again draws on legal theory to distinguish between guilt as *the fact of having done a wrong* and guilt as *"legal liability to punishment"* for that wrong.[18] Craig uses this distinction to address an alleged dilemma. Within legal theory, pardon can be justified only to correct an injustice in the legal process. If God pardons sinners to correct injustice, then God does not act out of grace but out of obligation to justice. But if God pardons sinners graciously and freely without regard to satisfaction of justice, God acts unjustly. According to Craig, resolving this dilemma requires that we adopt something like the position of "Anselm and the Reformers that the satisfaction of divine justice is a necessary condition of salvation" [93]. Craig sets out a modal argument for the necessity of satisfaction of divine justice, if some human beings are to be saved:

1. Necessarily (Retributive justice is essential to God.)

2. Necessarily (If retributive justice is essential to God, then God justly punishes every sin.)

3. Necessarily (If God justly punishes every sin, then divine justice is satisfied.)

4. Therefore, necessarily (Divine justice is satisfied.)

18. Craig, *The Atonement*, 89. Emphasis original.

5. Therefore, necessarily (If some human beings are saved, divine justice is satisfied.) [94]

According to Craig, this argument shows that God's pardoning of sin demands (necessarily) satisfaction of divine justice, and, hence, establishes the conditions that demand construction of the PSA theory. In Craig's view, then, the traditional PSA doctrine brings together divine retributive justice and boundless divine grace in complete unity and harmony. In PSA, God's merciful pardon meets the requirements of justice. "This atoning arrangement is a gift of God to us, not based on human merit. In this sense God's pardon of us, while consistent with divine justice, is a pardon grounded ultimately in mercy" [95].

Critical Assessment of Penal Substitutionary Atonement Theory

As we noticed in the exposition above, PSA came under severe criticism as soon as theologians articulated it in a systematic way. As early as the late sixteenth century, Fausto Socinus launched a systematic attack, and others followed in a continuous stream: deists and theists of the Enlightenment, Unitarians and Protestant liberals of the nineteenth and twentieth centuries, and today, left-of-center evangelicals.[19] I do not have space to document the history of criticisms of PSA, and I will refer to them only as they are relevant to my analysis and criticisms.[20] It would be an exercise in futility to begin assessing PSA by challenging its interpretation of scores of individual texts. As long as the traditional theological system remains intact, we cannot correct the doctrine by disputing its exegesis. Those texts seem to support PSA because they are integrated into a skewed system. The three summary theses uncovered above determine the nature of the traditional penal substitutionary doctrine of atonement and how the texts used to support it are read. The first two propositions describe the problems the atonement solves and the third states the solution to *those* problems. But are those the real problems?

---

19. Deserving of brief mention because its closeness in many ways to my own perspective is Baker and Green, *Recovering the Scandal of the Cross*. Writing from a moderate evangelical perspective, Baker and Green mount a sustained critique of PSA. Their critique of the doctrine is based on analysis of Charles Hodge and brief references to a few contemporary advocates. See Baker and Green, *Recovering the Scandal*, 45, 172.

20. See Rutledge, *The Crucifixion*, 489–506, for her section treating fourteen contemporary objections to PSA.

Justice and the Divine Dilemma

As we saw above, defenders of PSA argue that the death of Christ is the *necessary* means of salvation because it is rooted in the divine nature and not simply in the divine will.[21] As they conceive it, *God's eternal justice is so inexorable that God cannot simply overlook sin, but must punish it according to its demerit.* Of course, no right thinking Christian theologian would deny that God is just. God is the maximum of all excellent properties, and justice is an excellent property.[22] But what does it mean to affirm that God is just? As we saw above, theologian after theologian, from Heidegger and Turretin to Edwards and from Hodge to Packer and Craig, defines God's essential justice as "giving everyone their due." Divine justice issues forth in punishments and rewards according to the deserts of the recipients. Because it is essential to the divine nature, God is not free to forgive sin without satisfaction to his retributive justice. Sin *must* be punished. No defender of PSA I have read questions the definition of divine justice as giving "what is due" or attempts to prove this principle. The view of Robert Letham seems to be typical: "That God will give everyone his due is an axiom of biblical revelation."[23]

Is the definition of divine justice as "giving everyone their due" theologically sound? The answer is *no*, for several reasons. First, this definition is not formal enough to get at the essence of justice and, hence, to cover human and divine justice under one concept. In human societies, rights and duties must be codified in laws legislated by authorized legislators. In any debate about the extent of one's rights and the scope of one's duties, disagreements are settled by appeal to law. If justice is "giving everyone their due," then a just person is one who abides by the laws that determine what each is due and a just judge rules in conformity with those laws. Whether or not an action can be deemed just must be decided by the degree of its correspondence to the relevant laws. Justice in the most formal sense, then, is *a relation of correspondence between an action and the norms for actions of that type.*[24] This definition, I believe, states the essential feature of justice

21. As I noted above, Augustine, Thomas Aquinas, John Calvin, and others root the necessity of Christ's death in a divine *decision*.

22. Indeed, God not only *has* the property of justice, but for God, as Anselm rightly asserted, "it is the same to be just that it is to be justice" (*Monologium* 16, Deane, *Saint Anselm*, 64).

23. Letham, *The Work of Christ*, 127.

24. This definition of justice may strike some as too general in that it applies to non-moral as well as moral actions. For the concepts justice and injustice are ordinarily applied exclusively to *moral* actions, that is, voluntary actions in which the acts of one person affect the wellbeing of another person. If this discussion concerned human

better than the one used most often, that is, "everyone according to their due." Expressed in terms of this refined definition, God's justice should be understood as correspondence between God's actions and the norms that govern divine actions. Everyone in this discussion admits that God's own nature, not a law above him, is the norm for God's actions. God does not act in opposition to his nature and character. Hence, divine justice can best be defined as *the perfect correspondence between God's actions and God's nature.* An act of divine justice puts into action and reflects the entire character of the divine being; indeed, that correspondence constitutes its justice. The preceding somewhat complicated argument can be set out as follows:

1. In general, justice is correspondence between an action and the norms that cover that action.

2. Specifically, divine justice is correspondence between divine action and the norms that cover divine actions.

3. God's nature is the norm that covers God's actions.

4. Hence, divine justice is the correspondence between God's actions and God's nature.

The definition of justice as "giving everyone their due" is vitiated by a second flaw. By including the concept of desert—that is, "what is due"— the traditional definition of justice defines God's justice independent of and in opposition to God's love, grace, and mercy. For love, mercy, and grace exclude desert; they are spontaneous and gratuitous. The traditional definition of justice, then, introduces incompatibility among God's essential attributes. In view of the unwelcome implications of an inner divine conflict, theologians throughout history have advocated the doctrine of divine simplicity. Divine simplicity asserts that God *is* his nature, or that everything God is, God is essentially, or that God is perfectly one with himself.[25] There can be no disharmony within the divine life. As an implication of the doctrine of divine simplicity, God's attributes cannot be rightly understood in isolation from, much less in opposition to, one another. In the case of divine justice, only as we come to know the rich beauty

---

actions only, this objection would be fatal to my definition and the argument based on it. But PSA applies its definition of justice to *divine* as well as human actions, and this move needs to be justified. Perhaps human actions can be divided into moral and non-moral classes, but, in my view, divine action should not be divided in this way. *All* God's "actions" are *one*. Hence an all-encompassing principle of divine action is necessary, and I think mine fits the bill. In this way, justice in the moral realm would be a subclass of a more general type of relation, which I describe in my definition.

25. For my study of divine simplicity, see Highfield, *Great Is the Lord,* 155–56, 255–74.

and goodness of God's nature can we have an inkling of the character of God's justice. Because God's justice is *correspondence between God's actions and God's nature.* That is to say, God's justice is God's self-consistency in action, and God brings his whole being into every act.

Where should a Christian theologian look for a concentrated vision of the nature, glory, and character of the eternal God in action? The answer is obvious: we see "the light of the knowledge of God's glory displayed in the face of Christ" (2 Cor 4:6), because Jesus Christ is "the image of the invisible God" (Col 1:15). God's act in Christ must be deemed just, not because it corresponds to the ideas of distributive and retributive justice, but because it corresponds to the eternal nature and character of God. To anticipate my interpretation of atonement in Christ, what is revealed in Christ is the mystery of the divine life of utter self-giving love. In Christ, God's justice is given concrete character as the perfect correspondence between the visible self-emptying love of Christ and the invisible being and character of God. God is just in that he always loves in all his internal acts within the triune community and in his external acts toward creatures.

There is a third unfortunate result of defining God's justice independent of his other attributes and his revelation in Christ. It introduces division into God's acts in relating to creatures. PSA defenders speak with one voice in asserting that God's justice makes it necessary for him to punish sinners and in denying that God's love makes it necessary for him to love sinners. God, they say, *cannot* act unjustly, but he *can* act unlovingly. However, if we postulate that God always acts both lovingly and justly in every act—that in acting lovingly in every act God *is* acting justly; and in acting unlovingly God would be acting *unjustly*—the PSA system would fall apart. For a divine act of punishing sinners as they deserve cannot simultaneously and in the same sense be an act of loving sinners gratuitously.

In view of this difficulty, PSA advocates draw distinctions between the modes and roles of love and justice in the act of atonement, hoping to harmonize them by making them complementary and cooperative despite their different characters. Christ's endurance of death as punishment for our sins displays divine justice in one sense and divine love in another. God acts justly in that he punishes sinners as they deserve and lovingly in that he graciously substitutes Christ in our place, imputing our sins to him. These distinctions enable PSA advocates to explain how atonement in Christ solves the "divine dilemma."[26] The atonement satisfies divine justice while making

26. Craig, *The Atonement,* 91. Cottrell, *The Faith Once Delivered,* 92–93, speaks of the divine attributes as resting in complete harmony until the fall. When sin entered the world, however, God's attributes of love and holiness were thrown into conflict. With respect to dealing with sinful human beings God faces a dilemma that the atonement

it possible for God to have mercy on those whom he wishes. However it can do so only by making the atonement a compound of heterogeneous elements. Even though love and justice cooperate in the atonement to achieve a practical outcome, they do not have the same foundation in the divine nature or the same mode in divine action: divine justice distributes rewards and punishments according to what is deserved, but divine love bestows gifts without regard to merit. Divine justice acts necessarily, but divine love acts freely. Justice and love remain at odds even in the event of atonement. Hence, PSA only appears to resolve the tension it previously posited in God's eternal nature between the justice that must damn sinners and the love determined to save them. The eternal tension is duplicated in the temporal act of atonement. In fact, retributive justice triumphs over mercy. For God does not really *forgive* sin, for this action would be unjust. He lets sinners go unpunished only because he *punishes* their sins in a proxy.[27]

Rejecting the traditional definition of divine justice as "giving each according to their due," destroys a foundational presupposition of PSA. For the necessity of satisfaction depends on the notion that God *must* punish sin. If, in a way we have not yet clarified, God is not bound to punish sin, neither is God bound to demand satisfaction. And if God is not bound to demand satisfaction, God's act of atonement in Christ could not have been designed to resolve a divine dilemma. We are already beginning to see our way clear to understanding the atonement not as a composite act necessary to resolve a divine dilemma—God wants to do something he cannot do—but as one unified act simultaneously loving and just and designed wholly to address a *human* problem. But to complete the picture we need to address the other foundational premise in the theological system that makes PSA seem necessary.

The Infinite Outrage of Sin and Human Liability
for Infinite Punishment

As we saw in the exposition above, advocates of PSA from the sixteenth century until today measure the evil of sin not by a quantitative gage, such as the amount of damage it causes to creation and the human community, but by its qualitative opposition to the infinite excellence of God. In our praise of God we revel in superlatives, naming all the excellent qualities we know and magnifying them to the infinite degree. In the same way,

---

is designed to solve.

27. The different roles PSA gives to the Father and Son in the atonement merely externalize the supposed internal conflict between retributive justice and merciful love.

defenders of PSA magnify sin, only in the opposite direction. Among the reasons they find this magnification necessary is to answer in advance the objection that God could simply forgive sin without satisfaction or that satisfaction of lesser magnitude than the death of the Son of God would suffice. PSA advocates reply that God would not have required the death of his Son unless it was necessary, and the only possible ground for its necessity is that sin is infinitely outrageous. Only the infinite merit of Christ could make up for the infinite demerit of sin. Additionally, theologians who advocate PSA usually also affirm the doctrine of eternal, conscious torment in the fires of hell as "the wages of sin" (Rom 6:23). If sin deserves the infinitely horrible punishment of hell, it must be infinitely evil. If sin were somehow less than infinitely evil, PSA would be undercut. For in that case, some lesser satisfaction might have sufficed.

In response to the traditional argument for the infinite nature of sin, we must ask, "Is human sin really *infinitely* evil?" Is it really insult and hatred of God, "deicide" of the heart? Of course, no responsible theologian would argue that sin is not a serious matter that only God can handle. But to avoid trivializing sin must we affirm that it is *infinitely* bad? To say that something is infinitely bad is to assert that it could not get worse. How bad is that? It would seem that sinners could keep getting worse until they are as irredeemable as the devil is thought to be. But PSA presupposes that sinners are redeemable. And if sinners are redeemable they cannot be infinitely bad. It seems that we have surfaced a contradiction in the theory.

As the most obvious way out of this dilemma, we could distinguish qualitatively between sin and the sinner.[28] Acts of sin indeed imply the negation of God, but *sinners* do not intend their sinful acts to kill God. They intend things much more mundane: wealth, fame, and pleasure. They act out of fear, anger, and lust in relation to finite goods. That is to say, a finite act of sin implies infinite evil only when its limited scope is expanded to infinity by drawing out its logical implications. But the sinner's intentions should not be identified with the logical implications of the sinner's sin. Hence, making the distinction between sin and the sinner enables us to conceive of sin as the negation of everything good without making sinners irredeemable. Could PSA be saved from contradiction in this way? No, it could not. For this way of putting it makes *sin* not the *sinner* the object of infinite punishment. The problem that the atonement solves has changed. It is no longer the infinite punishment due to the *sinner* but the problem of the sinner's slavery to the power of sin, to the blindness and deception from which they

28. As I documented above, Turretin made this distinction to ground the possibility of transferring our liability to punishment to Christ so that he could justly endure punishment in our place. Here the distinction serves a different purpose.

act. Making the distinction between sin and the sinner transforms the PSA theory into the *Christus Victor* theory.[29] We need redemption and liberation from the alien power that urges us toward the infinite negation that is the projected end of sin. And in his death and resurrection Jesus frees us from this condition. Indeed, we are also guilty and need forgiveness, liable to punishment and in need of pardon. In a way that I have yet to propose, God in Christ discounts the non-existent, projected effects of sin and the unreal and impersonal "intention" of sinful acts, and forgives the actual *finite* guilt incurred and heals the actual limited damage caused by sin.

Penal Substitution as the Solution to the Divine Dilemma and Human Liability to Punishment

Because this third part of PSA theology proposes Christ's death as the solution to the problems specified in parts one and two, I can deal with it in summary fashion. I shall state it as a series of assertions and implications:

1. God is by nature perfectly just; therefore, he must punish sinners according to their deserts.

2. Sin is infinitely wicked; therefore, God must punish sinners with an infinite penalty.

3. However, in his boundless goodness, God wishes to have mercy on some sinners.

4. Therefore, God imputes sinners' guilt (liability to punishment) to Jesus who stands as our substitute and representative, so that God can satisfy his justice by punishing Jesus in our stead, as our proxy, and extend mercy to us in a way that is just.

As I have shown above, premises (1) and (2) are beset with problems; in fact, they are false. Even the truth of premise (3) is weakened by its connection with the previous two. For according to PSA, God must punish sin but need not have mercy on sinners. Clearly, premise (4) does not follow indubitably if premises (1) and (2) are false or doubtful. If we do not define divine justice as "giving everyone their due," if sinners are not guilty of infinitely wicked acts, and if God's love and mercy are as much expressions of God's essential nature as his justice is, there is no divine dilemma and the traditional doctrine of PSA offers itself as a solution to a non-existent problem.

---

29. As I said above in reference to Turretin, the distinction between sin and the sinner can become a Trojan Horse that defeats PSA from within. Now we see how this works.

An Alternative Theological Framework for
Understanding the Atonement

While my critique of the theological framework that makes PSA plausible is fresh on our minds I think it would be wise to state clearly the theological framework from which I write on the atonement. Because I anticipated my views in the critique of PSA, I can be briefer in this positive presentation of my viewpoint.

God's Justice Is Correspondence of
His Action to His Nature.

I argued above that divine justice should not be defined as "giving everyone their due." I argued, instead, that divine justice must be defined as correspondence between God's actions and God's nature. God is faithful to himself in all his actions and relations. Once we accept this formal definition, we need further insight into the being and character of God before we can characterize divine justice in a concrete way. Christian faith points unambiguously to Jesus Christ as the locus of revelation for the character of God. God's love and justice cannot be known truly from abstract concepts but only from their concrete manifestations. The overwhelming message of the New Testament is that God's love is revealed in the death of Jesus. From Christ we learn that God is self-giving in all his actions. Divine justice, then, is the perfect correspondence between God's inner Trinitarian love and all his actions toward his creatures. God is just in that he always loves. Retribution has nothing to do with it.

The Atonement Solves a *Human* Problem

According to traditional PSA theory, the central problem solved by the atonement is the divine dilemma created by the tension between God's desire to extend mercy and the demands of divine justice. But as I argued above, *there is no divine dilemma*. If we reject the definition of divine justice as "giving everyone their due" and replace it with "correspondence between God's acts and God's nature," if we reject the contrived notion that human sin incurs "infinite" guilt that deserves "infinite" punishment, and if we recognize that love and justice are equally essential to God's nature, the "divine dilemma" vanishes. The clear message of the New Testament gospel is that the death and resurrection of Jesus is God's solution to the *human* problem. God does not have a problem. God needs no justification beyond his love to exercise mercy and forgive sins. The atonement is the concrete realization in human existence of God's eternal plan to forgive and heal. Everything is directed toward dealing with human wretchedness and achieving human greatness. In the incarnation, death, and resurrection of Jesus, God makes a new beginning for humanity, establishes a new creation.

The Father's Actions Are One with Those of Christ

PSA posits an unwarranted division between justice and love in the divine action of atonement in Christ. This division was made necessary by a previously posited dilemma between divine justice and divine love within the divine nature. But if we reject the idea of a divine dilemma, the supposed problem solved by the atonement ceases to exist and the problematic idea of an inner Trinitarian exchange of satisfaction becomes unnecessary. In the New Testament, all of God's actions in creation and salvation come *from* the Father *through* the Son *in* the Spirit. God's justice and love rest in eternal harmony and in Christ touch us in the same act, at the same time, directed to the same end, that is, to the salvation of human beings.

I see very little commensurability between the theological framework I set out in these three points and the framework that guides traditional satisfaction theories of whatever form. Nor is it compatible with the liberal Protestant system. Reading the New Testament guided by the theological framework I am advocating paints a dramatically different picture of reconciliation in Christ than either of them paints.

9

Jesus as Example and Inspiration

Liberal Protestant Atonement

As I LAMENTED IN the introduction to this book, Christian language about sin and salvation has grown obscure and stale for many people. For some, even the attempt to understand no longer seems worth the trouble. In the preceding chapters, we explored the heroic efforts of many Protestant evangelicals to defend the traditional doctrine of penal substitution. In this chapter, we will examine the opposite end of the spectrum, modern liberal theology. Liberal theology, in so far as it speaks of Jesus's saving activity at all, speaks of it exclusively as the power of his life and teaching to inspire others to follow his example of piety, love, and justice.

The Liberal Solution

The moral influence theory of atonement has been associated with rationalism, anti-supernaturalism, and heretical Christology. There is some truth to this charge, because deists, unitarians, and other dissenters from orthodoxy tend to adopt some form of the moral influence theory.[1] But there is no inherent conflict between the moral theory and orthodox Christology. In this chapter, however, I will focus on theologians that combined rejection of orthodox Christology with an exclusively moral theory of atonement. The term "liberal theology" is rather nebulous, I admit. It groups together a diverse collection of theological viewpoints that nevertheless hold certain ideas and values in common. They all sense that traditional Christian language about

1. Grensted, *A Short History*, 329–33.

sin and salvation has lost meaning for many contemporary people who are, consequently, tempted to abandon the church and live completely secular lives. Liberals account for this loss of meaning by reference to modern science and progressive morality. Advances in science have made such miracles as the resurrection of Jesus and other manifestations of the supernatural unbelievable. Progress in morality has made the traditional doctrines of atonement and original sin morally repugnant. By "progressive morality," I mean the notion that individuals should be liberated from all oppressive structures. Such freedom will enable them to express their individual authenticity in keeping with their native autonomy. Liberals argue that one can reject these obsolete beliefs but still retain the inner religious meaning of Christianity. Some beliefs can be relegated to the past and forgotten. Others can be reinterpreted to refer to something still accessible to the modern mind. The process of reinterpretation shifts the meaning of a term from an outmoded reference to one more acceptable to the interpreter.

The influence of some liberal theologies is limited to academic settings. Others make no pretense to Christian identity. In my view, only two forms of liberal theology are relevant to my argument. The theological model initiated by Friedrich Schleiermacher (1768–1834) deserves mention because it is the first truly modern, liberal theology with any claim to be authentically Christian and workable in actual church life. Second, we will consider the tradition initiated by Albrecht Ritschl (1822–89), which has had a greater impact on church life than that of Schleiermacher and continues to have an impact on "mainline" Protestant denominations in North America and Europe. Historians of modern theology refer to these two streams of the liberal tradition collectively as "Protestant Liberalism."[2]

Friedrich Schleiermacher

The seventeenth and eighteenth centuries witnessed the dramatic growth of deism and the beginnings of atheism among the educated classes of Europe. The dominant reaction of Christian clergy and theologians was defense of biblical miracles and other such traditional doctrines as original sin and the penal substitutionary doctrine of atonement. The liberal alternative to orthodoxy and deism was pioneered by Friedrich Schleiermacher. As a theological student at the Moravian seminary at Barby, Schleiermacher began to have doubts about the doctrine of the atoning death of Jesus. His faith in orthodoxy was further eroded by his study of the philosophy of Immanuel

2. Grensted, *A Short History*, 333; Livingston, *Modern Christian Thought* 1:270; Rupp, *Culture Protestantism*; Welch, *Protestant Thought in the Nineteenth Century*.

Kant at the University of Halle. In 1796, he became the Reformed preacher at the Charité Hospital in Berlin. During this period Schleiermacher became acquainted with many leading figures in the German Romantic Movement, including the poet Friedrich Schlegel (1772–1829).[3]

Romanticism relies on inward feeling rather than supernatural revelation, rational speculation, or moral sensibility for purest access to the underlying reality of world appearance. Schleiermacher incorporated this emphasis on feeling into his theology. The continuing validity and relevance of the Christian religion is rooted in its most primitive origin in human experience of the infinite within the finite. Human beings have the capacity to become conscious of their inner connection and absolute dependence on the infinite and eternal ground of all finite reality. But what has this Romantic experience of inwardness got to do with Christianity? According to Schleiermacher, Jesus Christ experienced this intimate awareness of God more intensely than any other human being. Jesus is at the same time the most religious human being and the truest manifestation of human possibility. He is unique among human beings in that he not only possessed this consciousness for himself but is able to evoke it in others. The Christian church is the community where the God-consciousness inspired by Jesus is cultivated and passed on to others. Christian doctrines are verbal expressions of different modes of this experience of dependence on the infinite and eternal God, which Jesus originally evoked and continues to evoke in the community he established. In Schleiermacher's mature theology, *The Christian Faith*, he systematically works through traditional Christian doctrines, explaining them as variations on the feeling of absolute dependence.[4] Every manifestation of God is always first a modification of human self-consciousness. Hence, Schleiermacher rejects all reports of supernatural acts that occur in space and time before they impact human consciousness.[5]

It would not be wise to dismiss Schleiermacher without acknowledging that he dealt with a genuine theological problem and used all his creativity and brilliance to solve it. He correctly perceived that traditional orthodoxy was unable at that time to show the educated classes of Europe that its doctrines and practices were grounded in truth and consistent with human flourishing. Hence, he attempted to demonstrate that human beings at the core of their being are connected to the infinite and the eternal. The more conscious we become of this connection, the more in touch we are with our humanity. The process of becoming aware of our dependence on

3. Clements, *Friedrich Schleiermacher*, 7–34.
4. Schleiermacher, *The Christian Faith*.
5. Dabney, "Schleiermacher, Friedrich Daniel Ernst," 450–54.

the infinite, of surrendering to it, and rejoicing in it, is identical to becoming religious. In this way, Schleiermacher answered the major objections of the "cultured despisers" of religion, that is, religion is antiquated, superstitious, dehumanizing, and anti-scientific.[6] Schleiermacher worked to show that experiencing our full humanity and being religious go together. He dealt with skeptical objections to Christian doctrines and practices by showing that these beliefs are grounded in the truth of human self-consciousness of absolute dependence on the infinite. We do not have to accept reports of supernatural interventions into the order of nature or a myth about God becoming human. The truth of Christian teachings can be confirmed by experiencing the very source from which they derive and in which their truth is rooted, our own self-consciousness.

Since I am focusing in this book on the Christian view of sin and salvation, I will concentrate on Schleiermacher's reinterpretation of sin, the redeeming and reconciling work of Christ, and the resurrection of Jesus. According to Schleiermacher, Jesus possessed perfect God-consciousness, which so filled him that it overcame all resistance from the flesh. Sin is defined in opposition to this perfect God-consciousness. Accordingly, sin is "arrestment of the determinative power of the spirit, due to the independence of the sensuous functions," that is, the flesh, which is "the totality of the so-called lower powers of the soul."[7] It is best not to define sin as "violation of the divine law," since this definition does not get to its root, which is resistance to God. A more Christian way of speaking of sin is that "sin consists in our desiring what Christ condemns and *vice versa*."[8]

Christ brings redemption and reconciliation to others by imparting his God-consciousness to his original disciples, who in turn formed the community that became the medium through which later generations participate in it. Participation in Jesus's God-consciousness gives us power to bring the flesh under the control of the spirit.[9] Christ reconciles by drawing us into "the fellowship of his unclouded blessedness." A central aspect of this blessedness is the consciousness of the forgiveness of sins, for in fellowship with Christ "all relation to the law ceases." In union with Christ, the consciousness of "deserving punishment" disappears and we experience his life as ours in such a way "that this possession exists solely as a gift, which, since we receive it simply by His will that we should have it, is His blessing

6. Schleiermacher, *On Religion*.

7. Schleiermacher, *Christian Faith*, 272–73.

8. Schleiermacher, *Christian Faith*, 272–73.

9. Schleiermacher, *Christian Faith*, 425–31.

and His peace."[10] We are redeemed and reconciled by our fellowship with him, and not as traditional theology contends by his suffering and death. His suffering and death play a part only because of the way he endured them. He allowed nothing to stand in the way of his message and mission. His suffering and death place in bold relief the all-encompassing and ir-resistible nature of his God-consciousness.[11]

> For in His suffering unto death, occasioned by His steadfastness, there is manifested to us an absolutely self-denying love; and in this there is represented to us with perfect vividness the way in which God was in Him to reconcile the world to Himself, just as it is in His suffering that we feel most perfectly how imperturb-able was his blessedness.[12]

But it is his God-consciousness itself and not his physical suffering and death that saves us.[13]

Lastly, what part does the resurrection of Jesus play in salvation? Schleiermacher admits that in the New Testament and in the creeds the resurrection of Jesus—along with his ascension and the return in judg-ment—plays a role in salvation. But Schleiermacher denies a necessary connection between the two. Christ's effectiveness as the redeemer depends on his God-consciousness, and faith in him depends on the "impression" he left with us. Belief in the resurrection adds nothing. Indeed, contends Schleiermacher, the original disciples perceived the power of God in him prior to the resurrection. Christ's "incomparable dignity" is securely estab-lished by his consciousness and devotion to God. It does

> not depend upon a visible resurrection or ascension, since of course Christ could have been raised to glory even without these intermediate steps: and so it is impossible to see in what relation both of these can stand to the redeeming efficacy of Christ. . . . Hence we may safely credit everyone who is familiar with dogmatic statements with a recognition of the fact that the

10. Schleiermacher, *Christian Faith*, 433.

11. Schleiermacher, *Christian Faith*, 435–37. Grensted refers to Schleiermacher's theory as "half ethical half mystical" (*A Short History*, 331). See Franks, *The Work of Christ*, 533–60, for a concise summary of Schleiermacher's treatment of the work of Christ.

12. Schleiermacher, *Christian Faith*, 458.

13. Schleiermacher speaks of it as the "real meaning" of belief in the salvific nature of Christ's suffering (*Christian Faith*, 458). For Schleiermacher, the idea of vicarious satisfaction cannot be accepted as traditionally understood. It must be "reinterpreted if it is to be accepted at all" (*Christian Faith*, 461).

right impression of Christ can be, and has been, present in its fullness without a knowledge of these facts.[14]

Schleiermacher, though not explicitly denying the empty tomb and the bodily resurrection of Christ, enables the modern person skeptical of miracles to experience the redeeming and reconciling work of Christ without having to decide whether or not the resurrection really happened. This pattern of sidestepping and reinterpreting miracles and morally offensive ideas is the hallmark of the liberal tradition.

Albrecht Ritschl

A second liberal tradition responded to the educated critics of religion in a different way. The tradition that includes Albrecht Ritschl (1822–89), Adolf von Harnack (1851–1930), and Wilhelm Herrmann (1846–1922), like Schleiermacher, desired to articulate a form of Christianity purified of the supernaturalism, dogmatism, and authoritarianism of traditional orthodoxy. Like Schleiermacher, they wished to ground religious truth in human experiences open to confirmation by individuals. Unlike Schleiermacher, they located the place of human religious experience centrally in the moral sense. Religion is not grounded in the feeling of absolute dependence but in the experience of freedom of spirit in contrast to the deterministic course of nature.[15] But what makes religion Christian? For Ritschl and his followers, Christianity is based on the gospel taught by the historical Jesus and received by the community he founded. The gospel is not about a supernatural Jesus but about Jesus's own religious relation to God and God's goal of bringing the perfect kingdom of righteousness to earth. Jesus's "divinity" can be known only in the salvation we experience through him. To confess that Jesus is "God" means only that we experience him as the revealer of God and the mediator of reconciliation to God:

> But if Christ by what He has done and suffered for my salvation is my Lord, and if, by trusting for my salvation to the power of what He has done for me, I honour Him as my God, then, that is a value-judgment of a direct kind. It is not a judgment which belongs to the sphere of disinterested scientific knowledge, like the formula of Chalcedon. . . . The nature of God and the Divine we can only know in its essence by determining its value for our salvation[;] . . . we know God only by revelation, and

14. Schleiermacher, *Christian Faith*, 418.
15. Ritschl, *The Christian Doctrine of Justification*, 199.

therefore also must understand the Godhead of Christ, if it is to be understood at all, as an attribute revealed to us in His saving influence upon ourselves.[16]

According to Ritschl, sin is disruption of fellowship with God and guilt is a feeling of this lack. Justification is

the acceptance of sinners into that fellowship with God in which their salvation is to be realized and carried out into eternal life[;] . . . it must be conceived as reconciliation . . . [in which] the place of mistrust towards God is taken by the positive assent of the will towards God and his saving purpose.[17]

Ritschl rejects the traditional doctrine of penal substitution. Christ's work does not turn away divine wrath or satisfy divine justice. Such a theory would "drag the being of God down into the process of historical change."[18]

For Christ had no sense of guilt in His sufferings, consequently, He cannot have regarded them as punishment, nor even as punishment accepted in the place of the guilty or in order to deter men from sin.[19]

The saving action of God in Christ is directed wholly to human beings, to restore them to fellowship with God. In the judgment of Grensted, "It is clear from the very outset that the position taken up is entirely ethical in type, and that the resulting theory of Atonement will be wholly manward."[20] However, Ritschl does not propose an individualistic understanding of reconciliation. For only in our lives in the community Jesus established are we able to embrace Christ as the revelation of God's victory over all that opposes us. "The individual believer, therefore, can rightly understand his position relative to God only as meaning that he is reconciled by God through Christ in the community founded by Christ."[21]

As was the case for Schleiermacher and will be true for each of the representatives of liberal Protestantism we will consider, Ritschl reinterprets the New Testament teaching of the bodily resurrection of Jesus in terms of Christ's continued influence in the world through the community he

16. Ritschl, *The Christian Doctrine of Justification*, 398.

17. Ritschl, *The Christian Doctrine of Justification*, 85.

18. Ritschl, *The Christian Doctrine of Justification*, 325.

19. Ritschl, *The Christian Doctrine of Justification*, 479.

20. Grensted, *A Short History*, 333.

21. Ritschl, *Instruction in the Christian Religion*, quoted in Livingston, *Modern Christian Thought* 1:279. I've not been able to find these words in the original source.

founded. Christians do not believe that Christ is Lord and savior because they believe he was raised bodily from the dead; they believe in the resurrection because they experience him as the locus of their salvation:

> For through this suffering he changed the world's opposition to his life purpose into a means of his glorification, i.e., into the certainty of overcoming the world by the very fact of this momentary subjection to its power and of assuring the supramundane continuance of His life. Accordingly, his resurrection through the power of God is the consistent fulfillment, corresponding to the worth of his person, of the revelation effected through him which is final in respect to both the actual will of God and the destiny of man.[22]

Ritschl here reverses the order we find in the New Testament. As I argued in chapter 5 on the resurrection of Christ, views like those of Ritschl and others who spiritualize the resurrection to mean "the supramundane continuance of his life" can in no way account for the origin of Christianity. Nor can they account for the real ontological transformation in the human condition worked by the death and resurrection of Christ such as we find attested in Romans 6 and 8 and 1 Corinthians 15.

Adolf von Harnack

In his classic book *What is Christianity?* first published in 1900, Adolf von Harnack summarizes Jesus's teaching under two headings, that God is our Father and that the individual person is of infinite value. This religion is so pure, simple, and profound *"that it is, therefore, religion itself."*[23] Von Harnack rejects such nature miracles as calming the storm on the Sea of Galilee (Mark 4:35–41), but leaves the door open that Jesus may have cured some people with his "spiritual force."[24] But miracles are not central to Jesus's message, so "do not let yourselves be deterred because this or that miraculous story strikes you as strange or leaves you cold. If there is anything here that you find unintelligible put it quietly aside."[25] In a move that reminds us of Ritschl and Schleiermacher, von Harnack rejects the traditional doctrine of the vicarious suffering and death of Jesus but attempts to retrieve a meaning that makes some psychological and religious sense to modern people. Jesus suffered for us in the sense that suffering was the price he paid for preaching his gospel. Communicating the message of the

22. Ritschl, *Instruction in the Christian Religion*, 230.
23. Von Harnack, *What Is Christianity?* 63. Emphasis original.
24. Von Harnack, *What Is Christianity?* 28.
25. Von Harnack, *What Is Christianity?* 29.

fatherhood of God, not suffering for the sin of the world, was his mission. Nevertheless, the way he suffered and died set a noble example: "But it was by the cross of Jesus Christ that mankind gained such an experience of the power of purity and love true to death that they can never forget it, and that it signifies a new epoch in their history."[26]

In dealing with the resurrection of Jesus, von Harnack distinguishes between the "Easter message" and the "Easter faith." The Easter message focuses on the empty tomb and the resurrection appearances while the Easter faith "is the conviction that the crucified one gained a victory over death."[27] Von Harnack seems anxious to show that the Easter faith does not depend on the Easter message. He is not willing to allow faith in Jesus's message "to rest on a foundation unstable and always exposed to fresh doubts."[28] We can believe that Jesus achieved victory over death without believing that a "deceased body of flesh and blood came to life again."[29] According to von Harnack,

> Whatever may have happened at the grave and in the matter of the appearances, one thing is certain: This grave was the birthplace of the indestructible belief that death is vanquished, that there is a life eternal.[30]

Marcus Borg

The late popularizer of liberal Protestantism in America, Marcus Borg (1942–2015), continues the tradition begun by Schleiermacher and practiced by Ritschl and von Harnack. Jesus did not die as our representative or substitute. This notion is "bad theology and bad history."[31] It is bad theology because it elevates one perspective on the atonement above others and reflects poorly on God by making him desire the death of "this immeasurably great and good man."[32] It is bad history because it views Jesus's death as "part of the plan of God" when a historical explanation is so obvious.[33] He died for sins only in the sense that he was executed because he threatened the powers in charge of his world. "To say that Jesus's death was a sacrifice

26. Von Harnack, *What Is Christianity?* 159.

27. Von Harnack, *What Is Christianity?* 161.

28. Von Harnack, *What Is Christianity?* 162.

29. Von Harnack, *What Is Christianity?* 160.

30. Von Harnack, *What Is Christianity?* 162.

31. Borg, "Executed by Rome," 158.

32. Borg, "Executed by Rome," 158.

33. Borg, "Executed by Rome," 150.

means that his death has become sacred to us."[34] Jesus died in service to the cause of justice for the oppressed. To say "Jesus lives" or "Jesus is Lord" is a way of saying that Jesus's example still compels us to work for the cause of justice. Jesus's resurrection was not the kind of event that could have been observed had we been in the tomb on that Sunday morning, and his appearances were not public facts. Resurrection is a metaphor that expresses the disciples' conviction that Jesus was on the side of right and the dominating powers were on the wrong side.[35] Borg defends his strategy of reinterpreting the event of Jesus's resurrection in these words:

> Rather than focusing on "what happened," this approach focuses on the *meaning* of the resurrection of Jesus in the New Testament. What did it *mean* for his followers in the First Century to say that God raised Jesus from the dead? Believe whatever you want about whether the tomb was really empty, whether you are convinced it was or uncertain or skeptical—what did Easter mean to his early followers? The answer to the question of meaning is clear. In the Gospels and the rest of the New Testament, the resurrection of Jesus has two primary meanings: "Jesus lives" and "Jesus is Lord." . . . Focusing on the empty tomb reduces the meaning of Easter to a spectacular event in the past. It makes the resurrection of Jesus vulnerable to skepticism. . . . This alternative way of understanding Easter sees the Easter stories as parables—parables about Jesus. That is, it understands these stories metaphorically.[36]

Writing two hundred years after Schleiermacher and one hundred years after von Harnack, Borg adds nothing of substance to the soteriology of liberal Protestantism. The language is updated, but the strategy of reinterpretation remains the same. Jesus saves by inspiring us to adopt the great cause for which he gave his life. We know Jesus's cause was right not because God raised him bodily from the dead but because it fits with contemporary moral/ethical views.

Protestant Liberalism versus Orthodox Christian Theology

What is the essential difference between liberal Protestantism and orthodox Christian theology? In the previous paragraphs I mentioned several important differences. Liberal theology has a tendency to deny miracles, reject the

---

34. Borg, "Executed by Rome," 158.
35. Borg, "Executed by Rome," 163.
36. Borg, *Speaking Christian*, 111–12.

incarnation, reinterpret the atoning death of Jesus in psychological terms, and accommodate to the ever-changing moral views of de-Christianized progressivism. These are real and significant differences, but is there one fundamental difference that unites these differences? Yes there is. The apostolic faith and its faithful articulation in orthodoxy assert that in the existence and activity of Jesus Christ an *ontologically real* interaction between God and the world took place. By "ontologically real" I mean that God acts causally to change the *being* of the world, to change the way it exists. In miracles, God actually works on the existence of the lame, the blind, and the dead to change their real, physical being. In the resurrection of Jesus, God actually renewed the life of Jesus's dead body and translated him into a new mode of existence. In the incarnation, God actually united the humanity of Jesus to himself in a way different from all other human beings. The eternal Son of God, the Word, who was with God and was God, became flesh and lived among us (John 1:1–14). In the death and resurrection of Jesus, something actually happened between God and humanity that changed humanity's status from being condemned to death to being set free for life. God really counts and actually makes Jesus's sinless faithfulness ours.

In liberal Christianity, real divine action, causality, and change are missing. For liberal theology, God works no change in the physical space-time world. Every action, every cause, and every change in the world is exclusively natural. The significance of legendary miracle stories is their metaphorical meanings. As parables, they teach moral lessons or illustrate God's benevolence or justice. All change occurs in the human subjective reaction to the story. They are not literally and historically true. Jesus's body was not transformed physically from death to life, from mortality to glory. The resurrection is a metaphor for the rightness of his cause. And the rightness of his cause is the really important thing, the essence of Christianity. How we know that his cause was right apart from the real bodily resurrection liberalism leaves obscure, but the liberal answer is obvious: we know it because of our own moral insight. Jesus Christ is not really the personal union of God and humanity, as the orthodox doctrine of the incarnation teaches. The incarnation is a metaphor for Jesus's complete devotion to God. He is united to God in love, and we too can be united to God in love. Jesus's death and resurrection was not really God acting causally to change the being of sinful humanity. No real change occurred. Jesus died "for us" only in the sense that he died serving a good cause that we also judge to be a good cause. His faithfulness unto death serves as an example of devotion to God and highlights the importance of his moral and religious cause. But his death is no more a divine act of atonement than the deaths of other martyrs. Its power for salvation is limited to the inspiration it provides for others to serve good causes.

Why is liberalism so hesitant to make assertions about real, effective divine action in the world? As is obvious from the preceding sections, liberal theology wants to insulate itself from rational critique of divine causal actions, such as those divine actions cherished by orthodoxy. It wants Christianity to be founded on a source of knowledge that is universally available and rationally unassailable. It does not relish having to defend the ontological aspects of apostolic and orthodox Christianity. Hence, it downplays their importance. In reading liberal Christian theologians we hear a recurring theme, that is, the desire to rid Christianity of vulnerability to rational critique. But why is it so anxious about this vulnerability? Here is my hypothesis. Schleiermacher, Ritschl, von Harnack, Borg, and other liberals realized that Enlightenment rationalism and the progressive moral vision were going to marginalize Christianity and the institutional church in Western culture. Christianity had been the dominant cultural force in the West for over a millennium. What a frightening prospect to envision living in a post-Christian culture. The liberal project centers on making sure that Christianity and the institutional church are not marginalized in progressive culture. For liberal theology, the moral influence of Christianity is its most important contribution to Western civilization. It seemed essential to its survival. Hence, to liberals, sacrificing the ontological doctrines seemed a reasonable price to pay to maintain Christianity's moral influence in a culture on the move.

Borg is correct that asserting a real bodily resurrection makes Christianity vulnerable to falsification. The apostle Paul knew this. "If Christ has not been raised, your faith is futile . . . we are of all people most to be pitied" (1 Cor 15:17–19). But the bodily resurrection also grounds the claims of Christianity in objective reality, in an unambiguous act of God. In contrast, Borg's metaphorical understanding of the resurrection is grounded only in a subjective decision to connect Jesus to human aspirations. Hence, liberal theology is vulnerable to the charge of wishful thinking and making an arbitrary decision to attach subjective meaning to Jesus without a rational warrant. It is vulnerable to the critique that it possesses no real knowledge of God, that its claims about the kingdom of God, God's benevolence, justice, and love are really human aspirations and characteristics projected onto an imaginary God. Liberal theology may look tempting to doubting evangelicals and fleeing fundamentalists. But it looks pathetic, nostalgic, and sentimental to atheists, secularists, nihilists—and to orthodox Christians.

10

Jesus as the New Beginning

Reconciliation as Theōsis *through Recapitulation*

PREVIOUS CHAPTERS SHOW THAT efforts to construct a unified theory of the atonement often result in one-sidedness. The penal substitution theory so emphasizes divine justice that God's love becomes secondary.[1] The liberal moral influence theory reduces the atonement to a human work to be explained wholly in moral, social, and psychological terms. In response to these failures, some theologians think it best to place different biblical perspectives on the atonement beside one another without speculating about the unity that underlies them.[2] Given the history of the topic, I understand the appeal of this cautious attitude. However, I believe it is necessary to say something about the comprehensive unity of the event of atonement. Because it begins and ends in the one God, the event of reconciliation must be one throughout. The unity of any event is revealed in the final end it achieves. In the case of Jesus's death and resurrection, the end is eternal life in union with God. In my view, then, every aspect of God's reconciling work in Christ should be understood as a moment in the process of healing human beings' wretchedness and bringing them to full realization of their created greatness. Colin Gunton's words capture my thoughts exactly:

1. According to PSA, apart from God's free decision to have mercy on some sinners by having Christ suffer their punishment, no sinner could be saved from divine wrath. Hence divine love/mercy is necessary for our salvation. However, its necessity is of a *different kind* from the necessity of divine justice. It is not necessary *for God*. Mercy is conditioned on the divine *will* whereas punishment of sinners is conditioned on the divine *essence*. Hence the divine love/mercy extended in the act of atonement is "secondary" to divine justice because of its hypothetical mode of necessity.

2. For example, see Green, "The Kaleidoscopic View," 157–85.

> Redemption is not merely a removal of disorder but a redirection and a liberation: it is a resurrection. . . . Combining the metaphors, we can say that the sacrifice which the victorious and risen Son makes to the Father *is* the perfected creation. . . . Victory, justification and sacrifice alike are oriented to the end, and they conceive the atonement in terms of the perfection of the creation, in the Son's bringing to the Father a renewed and completed world. . . . [The metaphors for atonement] must be understood from the end as well as from the beginning[;] . . . [they] give up their full meaning only eschatologically.[3]

To express this conviction in traditional language, the overarching unity of the Christian message of salvation is *theōsis* through recapitulation. Union with God is the end to be achieved, and recapitulation of all things in Christ is the means. Within the comprehensive narrative of recapitulation, different aspects of human wretchedness are dealt with: covenant unfaithfulness, sin, death, and the devil. In my view, these problems and their solutions should not be treated in isolated "theories" of atonement but as aspects of the one great act of reconciliation accomplished in Christ.

The Grand Narrative of Reconciliation

I consider God's reconciling the world to himself in Christ to be *one divine act* that can be described in one grand narrative, that is, *recapitulation*. This divine act follows the contours of human wretchedness, dealing with each form of wretchedness as it demands. In what follows, I will describe this divine act as it is refracted by its impact on the human condition and in its narrative unity.

Jesus as Covenant Representative

The first aspect of the atonement focuses on Jesus's activity within the Judaism of his day. As we saw in chapter 6 on the death of Jesus, Jews in the first century longed for redemption from domination by pagan Rome. They yearned for God's glory to return to the temple and the kingdom of God to arrive. They hoped for full realization of God's promises to Abraham and David and anticipated eagerly the fulfillment of the prophecies spoken by Isaiah, Jeremiah, Ezekiel, and Daniel. But everyone understood that the exile, pagan domination, and delay of the restoration were divine

---

3. Gunton, *The Actuality of Atonement*, 150–54.

punishments for Israel's unfaithfulness to the covenant and that the re-demption would not come until the people returned to God with all their hearts and obeyed all his laws (Deut 30:2–3; Jer 29:13). However, most of the people did not keep the law strictly and the Jerusalem Temple was controlled by a corrupt oligarchy. Some groups thought that renewed zeal for the law and persecution of lawbreakers would avert divine punishment the way the "zealous" Phinehas, the grandson of Aaron, averted the divine plague by killing two flagrant offenders (Num 25:1–13). Apparently, Paul's zeal for persecuting the church derived from such theology (Gal 1:14; Phil 3:4–6).[4] Just under the surface seethed such hatred of Rome that it would soon erupt in a disastrous war.

Into this setting, Jesus entered, adopting the somewhat ill-fitting roles of teacher, prophet, martyr, and future Messiah. In his prophetic ministry, he urged people to prepare for the coming kingdom and impending divine judgment by repenting of their sins. As Jeremiah warned in relation to the Babylonian empire, Jesus warned the firebrands among his contempo-raries not to take up arms against Rome, but to follow the way of peace (Jer 27; Mark 13; Luke 13:34–35, 23:28–31). Jesus entered Jerusalem during Passover week and began to act in a way seemingly designed to provoke his own death. He symbolically attacked and cleaned the temple in prepara-tion for God's return and spoke parables against the temple authorities. In the Last Supper, he redefined the Passover in relation to a new exodus and a new covenant he would seal with his blood. Reminiscent of Eze-kiel's symbolic actions anticipating the destruction of Jerusalem by the Babylonians (Ezek 12), Jesus gave himself to suffer the fate of his people in advance. Jesus's voluntary obedience unto death is layered with multiple levels of meaning. On one level, it is an extreme, symbolic act dramatizing the future of rebels against Rome. On another level, he gives himself as a substitute and representative of his people in the spirit of the suffering servant of Isaiah 40–55. Like the Maccabean martyrs, he stands up to the evil empire to show on the one hand that the faithful need not fear death and on the other hand to "bring to an end the wrath of the Almighty that has justly fallen on our whole nation" (2 Macc 7:36–38, cf. 6:12–17; 4 Macc 6:27–29).[5] In his faithful obedience, in his sorrow for his people's sins, and as the one who is and will be the King of the Jews, he represents the whole nation before God. In a way dramatically different from Phinehas, he turns away the wrath of God by absorbing the last blow of divine punishment due to Israel for her unfaithfulness. He opens the way for a new exodus,

4. Wright, *NTPG*, 170–81, and Wright, *PFG* 1:80–84.

5. Wright, *JVG*, 579–84.

new covenant, new kingdom, new temple, and a renewed people of God. Of course, all of these would have been desperate and empty gestures had not God raised Jesus from the dead.

After my sharp criticisms of the penal substitution theory of atonement, it may come as a surprise that I am now speaking of Jesus as substitute and representative and of his voluntary death in terms of punishment, divine curses, and wrath. However, in using these terms I am not revoking my criticisms of PSA. PSA theory interprets these terms within a theological framework I rejected and replaced with another. It sets substitution, representation, punishment, and divine wrath in the context of the supposed metaphysical necessity of divine retribution on the infinite offence of sin. My use of these terms is set in the context of God's covenant with *Israel*, with its divinely chosen stipulations, blessings, and curses. Within this framework, the law's conditions, promises, and curses arise from divine freedom and love and serve a limited purpose. They are educative and disciplinary, not retributive in their functions. The Sinai covenant and the law look beyond themselves to Christ (Gal 3:24). The curses and punishments that follow upon Israel's unfaithfulness aim at an end beyond themselves, that is, repentance, purification, and reformation of the people of God in view of its mission to the world. Jesus took on the fate of his people and endured the stripes that were designed to produce a penitent nation, so that the people as a whole would not be destroyed by the consequences of their own sins. Jesus did indeed turn away divine wrath by allowing that wrath to achieve its covenant purpose, that is, to produce a penitent and obedient people. In keeping with the stipulations of the covenant, Jesus earned forgiveness for those he represented because in his own person he *is* the penitent people now returning to God and obeying him with their whole heart (Deut 30:2). However, the forgiveness Jesus enabled as the people's covenant representative is in the first instance redemption from exile, return of the divine glory, and fulfillment of the divine promises made to Abraham.[6] Jesus did not have to make it possible for God to forgive sin by satisfying eternal, necessary divine justice. He made it possible, rather, *by actualizing repentance* in his new people and so satisfied the covenant stipulations. As long as we keep the covenant context in mind, we can even speak of the atonement as an act of divine justice in that it was a divine promise kept. This punishment was necessary only because it was promised, and it was promised ultimately in view of God's redemption of his covenant people from the worst consequences of their own sin. The promise was kept and the punishment enacted. Covenant justice, rooted in covenant law, was satisfied. God did what he said he would do.

---

6. Wright, *NTPG*, 273.

In contrast to the obscure logic of the PSA theory, the covenant representative idea as I have presented it can be made understandable and morally plausible to contemporary people. Even though we do not experience the history of the old covenant in the way a first-century Jew would have experienced it, we can understand its inner, narrative coherence as it moves from Abraham to Christ. Given its goal of creating a special people to be a "light to the nations" (Isa 51:4; 60:3) we can understand the blessing/curse (Deut 28:1–68), punishment/repentance, and exile/return (Deut 30:1–10) structure of the covenant in moral terms that make sense. Suffering follows sin as its natural consequence, and repentance and reform often follow suffering. The idea of one person representing the whole people makes sense within the covenant narrative. In the Old Testament history, the success of the people of God in fulfilling God's purpose never depended on the faithfulness of every individual within that people. Except for Joshua and a few others, the entire generation that was redeemed from Egypt died in the desert before entering the promised land (Num 14). At times, it seemed as if none was faithful. The LORD punished his people with war and exile. But the people survived, for God always preserved a "remnant." Isaiah is confident that "a remnant will return, a remnant of Jacob will return to the Mighty God" (Isa 10:21; cf. Ezra 9). The faithful remnant may be reduced to just one "servant" (Isa 40–55; cf. Rom 9–11). The Messiah Jesus turned out to be the one truly faithful Israelite, the focal point of the remnant wherein the people of God gets a new start. Within the image of Jesus as covenant representative, the universal scope of the atonement is hidden but implicit in its immediate result, the redemption of God's covenant people. The renewed people can now become what it was meant to be, a blessing to all peoples and a light to the nations. This good news can be proclaimed to the whole world by people living today with just as much joy as it was by Jesus's first disciples. As Paul says near the end of Romans, "For I tell you that Christ has become a servant of the Jews on behalf of God's truth, so that the promises made to the patriarchs might be confirmed and, moreover, that the Gentiles might glorify God for his mercy" (Rom 15:8–9).

Jesus as the New Adam

The second aspect of God's reconciling work looks back from the resurrection of Jesus, which made the life of the new age and justification available to all. From within the Jewish horizon, the problem Jesus solves in his death and resurrection comes into view as the unfaithfulness of God's chosen people and their seemingly permanent exile. Looking back from the resurrection, however, the problem Jesus dealt with is sin's universal and inescapable hold on human beings and the harsh reality of death. In the New Testament, these two horizons are fused together. Such fusion makes sense in that context, because, as I pointed out above, the universal implications of the atonement were hidden but implicit within Jesus's work as covenant representative. Penal substitution and other satisfaction theories treat these two horizons as if they were identical, and this confusion is one source of their errors.

In Romans 5:12–21, Paul compares and contrasts Adam and Christ. They are similar in that they stand at the beginning of new families. Adam's disobedience brought condemnation and death to all his children whereas Christ's obedience brought righteousness to his family. Jesus Christ ends the history set in motion by Adam and makes a new beginning. Adam's family is produced by physical reproduction, but Christ's family is produced by the Spirit. Paul deals with the Adam/Christ contrast again in 1 Corinthians 15: "For as in Adam all die, so in Christ all will be made alive" (15:22). The "first man Adam became a living being; the last Adam a life-giving spirit" (15:45). Clearly, through his death and resurrection, Jesus left behind mortality and the conditions that make sin unavoidable and entered a glorified state as the first completely saved and glorified human being. He is now able to save and give life to all who respond to his call. In Romans 6, Paul reminds his readers that in baptism they died with Christ and were raised with him. This symbolic death and resurrection spiritually unites the believer to the living Christ and anticipates the believer's future death and resurrection. We are to count ourselves dead to sin, free from its mastery. But how does Jesus's death free us from sin? In Romans 6:6–10, we find a hint in answer to this question:

> For we know that our old self was crucified with him so that the body ruled by sin might be done away with, that we should no longer be slaves to sin—because anyone who has died has been set free from sin. Now if we died with Christ, we believe that we will also live with him. For we know that since Christ was raised from the dead, he cannot die again; death no longer has mastery over him. The death he died, he died to sin once for all; but the life he lives, he lives to God. (Rom 6:6–10)

In these verses, Paul works from a general principle: sin has power over someone only as long as they live.[7] In dying, one escapes sin by

---

7. After canvasing several interpretations, including the one that seems obvious to me, Jewett gives up and declares that "no fully satisfactory solution is currently available" (*Romans*, 404–5).

escaping the flesh. Jesus "died to sin," by moving beyond the place where sin reigns. Those who die with Christ by being baptized into his death are beyond the controlling reach of sin. In 7:1–7, Paul argues that death frees a person from the law, and in 8:3, he speaks of God sending his Son in "the likeness of sinful flesh" to deal with sin by "condemning sin in the flesh." Scott puts it this way:

> And in the act of dying He divested Himself of that flesh, the medium through which He had become involved in the human experience of the hostility of evil Potentates and Powers, the spirit-forces which had usurped authority over men. . . . He escaped their dominion, nay more, He broke it; God raised him from the dead.[8]

Indeed, dying will free us from the conditions that make sin possible, but apart from resurrection and justification, it will be a hollow victory. But Jesus invites us to share in his double victory over sin. He passed through death, leaving behind the "likeness of sinful flesh" (Rom 8:3) and in the resurrection received eternal life and vindication from the charges on which he was crucified. He gave himself over to death so that we would not need to die the death of a condemned sinner. We die the death of a sinner only in baptism in which we join with Christ in his death "to sin once for all" (Rom 6:10). He died to condemn sin, to defeat it, to leave it and the conditions under which it thrives behind (Rom 8:1–4). He went through death to purify human nature for a new beginning, freed from the hold of death and the grip of sin to live a new life in the power of the Spirit.

Jesus as Victorious Warrior

As the New Testament authors see it, we need more than new insight and forgiveness for sins. We need liberation from the invisible powers that dominate this "present evil age" (Gal 1:4) before we can get a fresh start. The New Testament designates these evil powers by many names: Satan, the devil, lordships, demons, rulers, thrones, gods, authorities, fallen angels, and many more.[9] We cannot defeat these powers without divine help. As the New Testament authors look back from the cross and resurrection, they proclaim in one voice that in his cross Jesus Christ triumphed over all anti-God, anti-creation, and anti-human powers. Who and what are these powers, and how do they work? How did Jesus's obedience unto death, "even death on a

8. Scott, *Christianity according to St Paul*, 35.

9. Despite its idiosyncratic agenda, Wink's *Naming the Powers* is still a good place to survey the "powers" theme in the New Testament.

cross" (Phil 2:8), defeat them? I do not believe it is enough merely to repeat the narrative of the *Christus Victor* theme in the New Testament and the early church fathers without attempting to make it plausible to a modern audience.[10] The point of this book is to make the saving work of Jesus understandable at least to the point it can be received as good news by people living now. People touched by post-Enlightenment Western thought no longer think in hierarchical or dualist cosmological terms. Our cosmology has reserved no natural place or function for non-divine spiritual beings. Many people believe in these beings and their malevolent work because the Bible mentions them. Some people believe in these beings because they adhere to a spiritualist philosophy. It is hard to tell whether contemporary references to Satan, the devil, and demons in common speech or even in church settings are being used figuratively or literally. Perhaps people simply use these terms without reflection on their status one way or another. It is a matter of debate just how literally the New Testament authors understood these characters. Since they were not asked the questions we moderns would like to ask them, they do not give us answers in a form we desire. As they did with other such ancient cosmological ideas as geocentricity, earth's immobility, or the existence of an underworld, they took them for granted but did not teach them for doctrine.[11] As we can see in the New Testament, the spiritual enemies of God always work through human agents. Hence, in my view, it is best to focus on the anthropological aspects of this message.

There is in the depths of humanity a dark capacity for violence and depravity beyond human control or understanding.[12] It is no myth but a truth demonstrated every day that beneath the refinement and compassion of every Dr. Jekyll, lies the crudeness and cruelty of Mr. Hyde. In *The Brothers Karamazov*, the character Ivan gets at this dark truth when he says,

> People talk sometimes of "bestial" cruelty, but that's a great injustice and insult to the beast, a beast can never be so cruel as a man, so artistically, so artfully cruel. The tiger only tears

10. This is the chosen method of post-liberal narrative theology: tell the story and let it have its impact. Ignore such questions as "Did it really happen?" or "What does it mean"?

11. There is a significant difference between (1) intentionally using a word figuratively to achieve a desired impact, (2) using it unreflectively literally in conformity to its common usage, and (3) using it intentionally literally in opposition to those who deny its truth taken literally. The biblical authors seem to do (1) and (2) often. I am not aware of an instance of (3).

12. Colin Gunton, *The Actuality of Atonement*, 52–82, presents a similar view of Jesus's victory over the powers. Language about the demonic is metaphorical. But the power to which the metaphor refers is so mysterious that it cannot be reduced to the conceptual language of psychology or sociology.

and gnaws, that's all he can do. He would never think of nailing people by the ears, even if he were able to do it. . . . I think if the devil doesn't exist, but man has created him, he has created him in his own image and likeness. . . . [I]n every man, of course, a beast lies hidden, a beast of rage, a beast of sensual inflammation from the screams of the tortured victim, a beast without restraint, let off the chain.[13]

The main tool of "the powers" is the lie.[14] A lie is nothing in itself, but it can misdirect human passion and action toward horrible ends. Human beings naturally seek power, pleasure, life, honor, and glory, and they fear shame, pain, and death. These natural desires and fears are not evil in themselves. In a rightly ordered world, we would seek glory, honor, and immortality in God alone. We would not fear shame, pain, and death more than we love God. But when human beings are deceived into turning away from God, darkness, chaos, and corruption take over. Though evil is nothing in itself, it gains a body, an army, an instrument in the ones who believe the lie. How do you kill a lie? How do you defeat a falsehood? Embrace the truth and never let go! How do you conquer a fear? Face it undeterred, no matter what the cost![15]

How did Jesus defeat the devil and the powers? Not with physical force. Jesus did not go into the underworld like Beowulf to do battle with Grendel. We cannot defeat a lie by force of arms. For the idea that the sword can defeat our most dangerous enemy *is the biggest lie of all.* The lie is that shame, pain, and death are the worst that can befall us. If we believe this lie, we are already slaves to the powers that threaten to inflict these things.[16] How did Jesus defeat the "rulers of this age" (1 Cor 2:8)? He rejected the lie and trusted God absolutely. He went into Jerusalem armed only with truth, faith, and righteousness and let shame, pain, and death engulf him.

---

13. Dostoevsky, *The Brothers Karamazov,* 206–9.

14. I consider it appropriate—despite my ignorance of the natures of the powers—to personify this mysterious power. I know of no other way to express their destructive and enslaving force, which in human beings takes over and works through their persons. In agreement with Wright, the language of the demonic is "the least inadequate" to denominate the "deeper, darker forces which operate *at a suprapersonal level*" (*Evil and the Justice of God,* 81; emphasis original). Anything less would trivialize the monstrosity of evil.

15. Note the list of weapons to be used in defense against the powers in Ephesians 6:10–17: truth, righteousness, peace, faith, salvation, and the Spirit.

16. According to Gunton, "The lie in this context refers to the behavior of anything finite or created—and that includes political and ecclesiastical institutions—which is treated or elevates itself to be of divine status" (*The Actuality of Atonement,* 78).

As Wright says in many places, Jesus let evil "do its worst."[17] It failed. For Jesus remained faithful, and God raised him from the dead. Jesus exposed the Jewish rulers, the Roman emperor, and all who stood with them as liars and slaves of the lie, and thereby deprived them of their power. We can allow Athanasius's words, which we quoted above, to express the change that Jesus's refutation of the lie worked in the world.

> Death used to be strong and terrible, but now, since the sojourn
> of the Savior and the death and resurrection of His body, it is
> despised; and obviously it is by the very Christ Who mounted
> on the cross that it has been destroyed and vanquished finally.
> When the sun rises after the night and the whole world is lit up
> by it, nobody doubts that it is the sun which has thus shed its
> light everywhere and driven away the dark.[18]

Jesus as God in Action

So far, we have considered Jesus's saving work in view of his roles as the faithful Israelite, the new human beginning, and the victorious warrior. Through his death Jesus fulfills the covenant, purifies human nature, and defeats the lying powers. In each area of activity, we have seen God at work in Jesus, confirming his faithfulness and glorifying his humanity by raising him from the dead. Under the first three headings, we concentrated on the human aspect of his activity. In this fourth image, we will examine Jesus's atoning work as a *divine* act.

According to the New Testament, *God* is the main actor in the salvation that comes through Christ. Paul makes this clear in these words from 2 Corinthians 5:17–19:

> Therefore, if anyone is in Christ, the new creation has come; The
> old has gone, the new is here! All this is from God, who recon-
> ciled us to himself through Christ and gave us the ministry of
> reconciliation: that God was reconciling the world to himself in
> Christ, not counting people's sins against them.

I do not need to argue this point at length. It is so obvious: the love, grace, and kindness of Christ are at the same time the love, grace, and kindness of God (Rom 8:35, 39; 2 Cor 8:9; Gal 2:21; Eph 2:7). The mind of Christ is the mind of the Lord (1 Cor 2:15–16). Christ is the image of the invisible God and the fullness of deity (Col 1:15; 2:9). He is the wisdom and power of God (1 Cor 1:24). Christ is the one through whom God created "all things"

---

17. Wright, *Evil and the Justice of God*, 81.

18. Athanasius, *St. Athanasius On the Incarnation*, 59.

(1 Cor 8:6; Heb 1:1–3; Col 1:16–17). God's glory shines forth in the face of Christ (2 Cor 4:6). The kingdom of God is also the kingdom of Christ (Eph 5:5). Christ is the Word of God (John 1:1), "the true God and eternal life" (1 John 5:20). Christ is the "mystery of God" (Col 2:2).

It is the consistent message of the New Testament that God acts in creation, providence, and salvation *through* Jesus Christ. Reconciliation, peace, righteousness, and redemption come *through* Christ (Rom 5:1, 11, 17). Victory over sin and death are achieved *through* our Lord Jesus Christ (1 Cor 15:57). Salvation comes *through* Jesus (1 Thess 5:9). All God's promises are fulfilled *in* Christ (2 Cor 1:20). God's gifts and blessings are found *in* Christ (Rom 6:23; 8:10; 1 Cor 1:2, 4; 15:22; 2 Cor 5:17; Gal 3:26–28; Eph 1:3). We could continue this list about the action of God through Christ and even extend it to document the New Testament teaching about God's work in and through the Spirit. But I have done enough to remind us that the New Testament speaks about God the Father, the Son, and the Spirit in ways that justify our speaking of the economic Trinity. All God's activity in the world—creation, providence, reconciliation, and consummation—originates *from* the Father, is made actual *through* the Son, and is perfected *in* the Spirit. And the creature's praise, worship, and service are returned *in* the Spirit, *through* the Son, *to* the Father. The divine activity is one. The divine being is one. Only the inner Trinitarian relations differ. The Son and the Spirit are no less God in their being and activity than the Father. In my view, then, the church of the early centuries was fully justified in reasoning from the Triune economic activity to the immanent or ontological Trinity of the Nicene Creed.[19]

If we take seriously the unity of divine action in Christ, the implications for the atonement are far-reaching. Christ embodies and manifests the love, justice, mercy, grace, and forgiveness of God in a way that makes them effective in the human sphere. The death of Christ does not evoke, merit, or purchase God's forgiveness. God needs no cause, motive, or justification to love. Nor does Christ's death *satisfy* God's retributive justice. To the contrary, it *manifests* unambiguously God's eternal, essential, and reliable love. Christ reveals for us in time what God is in himself in eternity: creative, self-bestowing love. Jesus's love, forgiveness, humiliation, and suffering in his humanity in time correspond to God's eternal love. Not only is the heart of God revealed in the event of Jesus's *death;* it is revealed in the *manner* of his death (Phil 2:8).[20] By submitting to the utter shame of a criminal's death, Jesus shat-

19. I argue this point in my book on the doctrine of God, *Great is the Lord,* 104–38.

20. A great strength of Rutledge's *The Crucifixion* is her emphasis on this neglected theme: "*The Creator of the universe is shown forth in this gruesome death*" (12, emphasis original; cf. 44). Jesus's death was "*the death of a nobody*" (76, emphasis original). Jesus experienced not merely suffering "but *suffering that degrades*" (78, emphasis original). This manner of death reveals the self-giving nature of God (500), God's utter solidarity

ters the universally cherished notion that dominating power and retributive justice are the defining characteristics of deity. In the cross, divine dignity, justice, glory, wisdom, and power are radically redefined. In the Spirit and through Christ, human beings freely return love, praise, glory, and honor to the Father. The work of redemption achieves its purpose.

How does God's action in Christ relate to our forgiveness? In a private context, to forgive is to forego revenge for insult and injury. In a judicial context, to forgive is to exempt the guilty from punishment. In both cases, the harm done by the guilty party is dealt with in a way other than retribution. When we forgive someone, we "absorb" the insult and injury into ourselves. We deal with them by summoning inner strength and healing power. Forgiveness in the first place means revenge not taken, punishment not inflicted. But the impact of injury and insult and the corresponding energy for revenge must go somewhere. The one who forgives suffers twice, from the original wrong done to them and from the pain of restraining the impulse to take revenge. To love is to forgive, and to forgive is to suffer.

This analogy may help us in some measure understand God's act of forgiveness in Christ. God loves his children and wants their love in return even when they treat him as an enemy. He is not compelled by some inner judicial necessity to take revenge on sinners for their insult and injury. Instead, God forgives and takes insult and injury into his boundless life. *Christ is in time God's eternal act of forgiveness and reconciliation.* Jesus's suffering in his flesh corresponds in time to God's eternal absorption of sin's insult and injury for our salvation and glorification. Christ's death did not *enable* God to forgive; it is the *actualization and concrete* form of that forgiveness.[21] Forgiveness is the negative side of the new life that Christ made actual by passing through death and entering into glory. And we are invited to share through faith and baptism in Christ's death to "the likeness of sinful flesh" (Rom 8:3) and his glorious new life.

Recapitulation: The Grand Narrative

Of all proposals of which I am aware, the idea of salvation through recapitulation as developed by Irenaeus of Lyon[22] is the most helpful at describing

---

with "those who are despised and outcasts in the world" (143), and the true horror of sin (564).

21. The unity of the Father and Son in the Trinity's acts of revelation and salvation is a persistent theme in Rutledge, *The Crucifixion*. In one of many examples I could quote, she says, "The event of the cross is the enactment *in history* of an *eternal* decision within the being of God. God is not changed by the historical event but has always been going out from God's self in sacrificial love" (*The Crucifixion*, 500).

22. Lawson points out that apart from the doctrine of recapitulation, the idea of *theōsis* tends to be sundered from the events of the life, death, and resurrection of Jesus

the comprehensive unity of the work of Christ for salvation. The concept of recapitulation, though not the word itself, is found in Paul's Adam/Christ comparison (Rom 5; 1 Cor 15). It is used explicitly in Ephesians 1:10, where God is said to be planning "to bring unity to all things in heaven and on earth under Christ." According to Eric Osborn, "The idea of recapitulation dominates the theology of the second century. Adumbrated by Justin, it is expounded endlessly by Irenaeus and given decisive place in Tertullian."[23] Recapitulation is a shorthand way of designating the entire history of Jesus Christ from conception through resurrection as the compressed story of creation and salvation. It is not a rational theory but a narrative description of that event from the perspective of its result.

Osborn lists four tasks recapitulation performs in Irenaeus's understanding: "it corrects and perfects mankind; it inaugurates and consummates a new humanity."[24] Recapitulation is an all-inclusive category for God's action in relation to creation, for "everything God does is part of his economy and every part of his economy is defined in relation to recapitulation."[25] Recapitulation involves "a renewing and saving permeation of the whole history of the world and of mankind by 'Christ the Head', from its beginning to its end."[26] John Behr concludes,

> For Irenaeus, then, the work of atonement is not simply a once-for-all act in the past. Rather, it is the one economy of the one God effected by the one Son in the one human race which encompasses both creation and salvation, embracing our apostasy and death, yet turning them inside out, in the mystery of Christ, the Wisdom of God, in which atonement is seen as the bringing into one (at-one-ment) of God and the human being (*Haer.* 5.36.3).[27]

In living human life through all its stages, facing our temptations, enduring our sufferings, and dying our death, all faithfully and without sin, Jesus rewrote the human story, recreated human existence, and brought it to its glorious goal. In opposition to those who deny that Christ really entered into the human condition, Irenaeus never tires of explaining how Jesus experienced every stage of human life:

---

and focused on the bare incarnation, as if salvation were the mere outworking of the effects of the incarnation (*The Biblical Theology of Saint Irenaeus*, 153–54).

23. Osborn, *Irenaeus of Lyon*, 97

24. Osborn, *Irenaeus of Lyon*, 97.

25. Osborn, *Irenaeus of Lyon*, 98. Osborn also speaks of recapitulation as an "inclusive totality" (*Irenaeus of Lyon*, 154).

26. Grillmeier, SJ, *Christ in the Christian Tradition* 1:102.

27. Behr, "Irenaeus of Lyon," 574.

He has therefore, in His work of recapitulation, summed up all things, both waging war against our enemy, and crushing him who had at the beginning led us away captives in Adam. . . . And therefore does the Lord profess Himself to be the Son of man, comprising in Himself that original man out of whom the woman was fashioned . . . in order that, as our species went down to death through a vanquished man, so we may ascend to life again through a victorious one; and as through a man death received the palm [of victory] against us, so again by a man we may receive the palm against death.[28]

For, in what way could we be partaken of the adoption of sons, unless we had received from Him through the Son that fellowship which refers to Himself, unless His Word, having been made flesh, had entered into communion with us? Wherefore also He passed through every stage of life, restoring to all communion with God.[29]

[He came among us] not despising or evading any condition of humanity, nor setting aside in Himself that law which He had appointed for the human race, but sanctifying every age, by that period corresponding to it which belonged to Himself. For He came to save all through means of Himself—all, I say, who through Him are born again to God—infants, and children, and boys, and youths, and old men. He therefore passed through every age, becoming an infant for infants, thus sanctifying infants; a child for children, thus sanctifying those who are of this age, being at the same time made to them an example of piety, righteousness, and submission; a youth for youths, becoming an example to youths, and thus sanctifying them for the Lord. . . . Then, at last, He came on to death itself, that He might be "the first-born from the dead, that in all things He might have the pre-eminence," the Prince of life, existing before all, and going before all.[30]

There is therefore, as I have pointed out, one God the Father, and one Christ Jesus, who came by means of the whole dispensational arrangements [connected with Him], and gathered together all things in Himself. But in every respect, too, He is man, the formation of God; and thus He took up man into Himself, the invisible becoming visible, the incomprehensible being made comprehensible, the impassible becoming capable of suffering, and the Word being made man, thus summing

28. Irenaeus, *AH* 5.21.1 (*ANF* 1:548–49).
29. Irenaeus, *AH* 3.18.7 (*ANF* 1:448).
30. Irenaeus, *AH* 2.22.4 (*ANF* 1:391).

up all things in Himself: so that as in super-celestial, spiritual, and invisible things, the Word of God is supreme, so also in things visible and corporeal He might possess the supremacy, and, taking to Himself the pre-eminence, as well as constituting Himself Head of the Church, He might draw all things to Himself at the proper time.[31]

In passing through death, Jesus left behind even the possibility of sin, and in his resurrection, he saved and glorified our humanity in his person. He became humanity's new beginning, a new Adam, "the firstborn among many brothers and sisters" (Rom 8:29). In the words of Colin Gunton,

> The recapitulation of the human story by Jesus is then the means of perfection in the senses both of restoration and of completion. God re-inaugurates the project of creation by means of the life, death, resurrection and ascension of Jesus.[32]

Jesus's story can become our story and his life our life. The recapitulation narrative incorporates the four aspects of God's act of reconciling the world to himself we discussed above within one story.

- Jesus is the faithful Israelite who finally keeps the covenant.
- He is the new human beginning, who corrects Adam's fall and lives up to the glory of God.
- He is the victorious warrior who defeats our foes.
- From conception to resurrection, he is God in action for us.

In each of these actions and roles, Jesus overcomes a form of human wretchedness by living through it and getting it right. We participate in his victory by allowing ourselves to be caught up in his history and making his identity our own. In Paul's words, "I have been crucified with Christ and I no longer live, but Christ lives in me. The life I now live in the body, I live by faith in the Son of God, who loved me and gave himself for me" (Gal 2:20). We recapitulate his recapitulation, and through him we get it right.

And now it is time to examine directly the end result of Christ's work of salvation from which Irenaeus, Athanasius, and others looked back to interpret the saving significance of the life, death, and resurrection of Jesus.

---

31. Irenaeus, *AH* 3.16.6 (*ANF* 1:442–43).
32. Gunton, *The Triune Creator*, 202.

11

Partakers of the Divine Nature[1]

IN THIS CHAPTER, I want to flesh out the intuitions of Irenaeus, Athanasius, and others on the nature of salvation and argue that we ought to understand the unity of the work of Christ from the perspective of its ultimate aim. The work of salvation aims at *theōsis*, which Christ achieved through recapitulation. Only from this perspective, can we answer the question that haunts any less comprehensive doctrine of salvation: does the Christian vision of salvation remove human wretchedness completely and fulfill human greatness in a way that is unsurpassable?

Christōsis and *Theōsis* in the New Testament

Eschatological Transformation

The Christian message of salvation through Jesus Christ envisions more than forgiveness of sins and peace and hope in this life. In numerous places, the New Testament looks forward to the resurrection of believers to eternal life and grounds this hope in the resurrection of Jesus. Now, says John, we are God's children, even though "what we will be has not yet been made known. But we know that when Christ appears, we shall be like him, for we shall see him as he is" (1 John 3:2). In Romans 6, Paul assures his readers that "if we have been united with him in a death like his, we will certainly also be united with him in a resurrection like his" (6:5). In Romans 8:11, he explains, that "he who raised Christ from the dead will

---

1. This is the way the KJV and the RSV translates the three words *theias koinovoi physeōs* in 1 Peter 1:4. The NIV translates them as "participate in the divine nature."

also give life to your mortal bodies because of his Spirit who lives in you." In Romans 8:23, Paul sees the answer to our suffering and groaning in this present life as a future "redemption of our bodies." In Philippians, Paul speaks of Christ as the one who "by the power that enables him to bring everything under his control, will transform our lowly bodies so that they will be like his glorious body" (3:21).[2]

Paul writes his most sustained treatment of the resurrection of the dead in 1 Corinthians 15. I have space here to explain only briefly Paul's vision of the final stage of salvation in Christ. Some in the Corinthian church deny a future resurrection for believers, and in response to this idea Paul points to the contradiction in affirming the resurrection of Jesus while denying the resurrection of believers (15:16). In response to the Corinthians' "foolish" questions about the nature of the resurrection body, Paul addresses the nature of the transition:

> So will it be with the resurrection of the dead. The body that is
> sown is perishable, it is raised imperishable; it is sown in dishonor,
> it is raised in glory; it is sown in weakness, it is raised in power;
> it is sown a natural body, it is raised a spiritual body. If there is a
> natural body, there is also a spiritual body. (1 Cor 15:42–44)

After all, reasons Paul, we know something about the resurrection body because the Messiah has been raised, and he is the power, model, and sphere of our resurrection from the dead. The resurrection will transform our bodies from one quality of life to another. In the text quoted above, Paul lists four qualitative contrasts between our present bodies and our resurrection bodies: from perishability to imperishability, from dishonor to glory, from weakness to power, and from a "natural" (*psychikon*) body to a "spiritual" (*pneumatikon*) body. I have put the Greek words translated "natural" and "spiritual" by the NIV (2011) in parentheses because they are often misunderstood. According to Paul, we now live in a *sōma psychikon*, but in the resurrection we will receive a *sōma pneumatikon*. In the Greek translation of Genesis 2:7, we read that God breathed into Adam and he became a *psychē zōsan*, a living being. To be a *psychē zōsan* is a blessing, and compared with nonliving things it is glorious and powerful. But a *psychē zōsan* is by nature perishable and destined for dishonor. The term *sōma psychikon* is another way of saying *psychē zōsan*, a body animated in the ordinary way by created life. But in this context it is contrasted with *sōma pneumatikon*, which gives it by comparison a negative connotation unlike the positive one

2. See Wright's survey of Paul's ideas about the resurrection of Christ and that of believers in *RSG*, 209–76. Wright emphasizes the connection between Christ's resurrection and that of believers.

it receives in the creation story. What is a *sōma pneumatikon?* In the popular mind, the word "spiritual" refers to something ghostly, definitely opposed to body. In fact, *sōma pneumatikon* does not mean ghostly existence. It means that the future resurrection will bestow on those who are in the Messiah a body animated not in the ordinary way (*psychikon*) but by God's own Spirit (*pneuma*). A *sōma pneumatikon* is a body filled, sanctified, and animated by the Holy Spirit.[3] Such a body participates in the powers and qualities of God's Spirit, that is, imperishability, glory, and power.

As Paul nears the end of this chapter, the tone changes from argument to praise and triumph:

> I declare to you, brothers and sisters, that flesh and blood cannot inherit the kingdom of God, nor does the perishable inherit the imperishable. Listen, I tell you a mystery: We will not all sleep, but we will all be changed—in a flash, in the twinkling of an eye, at the last trumpet. For the trumpet will sound, the dead will be raised imperishable, and we will be changed. For the perishable must clothe itself with the imperishable, and the mortal with immortality. When the perishable has been clothed with the imperishable, and the mortal with immortality, then the saying that is written will come true: "Death has been swallowed up in victory."
>
> "Where, O death, is your victory?
>
> Where, O death, is your sting?"
>
> The sting of death is sin, and the power of sin is the law. But thanks be to God! He gives us the victory through our Lord Jesus Christ.

When Paul declares that "flesh and blood" cannot inherit the kingdom of God he is not going back on the bodily nature of the resurrection. "Flesh and blood" is simply another way of naming our *sōma psychikon*, our ordinary body, which is incapable of enjoying the glorious life to which we are destined.[4] Flesh and blood is subject to death, and death always wins the relentless fight against the perishable body. Hence, the resurrection-transformation of the body to immortality is a great victory precisely because death is defeated on

---

3. Wright explains further, "Precisely because the soul is *not*, for him, the immortal fiery substance it is to Plato, he [Paul] sees that the true solution to the human plight is to *replace* the 'soul' as the animating principle of the body with the 'spirit'—or rather, the Spirit" (*RSG*, 346). Stephen Finlan takes issue with Wright's interpretation of the "spiritual body" mentioned in 1 Corinthians 15, arguing that Paul has a much more radical change in mind ("Can We Speak of *Theosis* in Paul?" 68–80).

4. Wright, *RSG*, 359.

the battlefield where it appeared to have triumphed, that is, in the whole living being God created in his image. In the resurrection of the dead, the divine Spirit so fills and animates the life of the redeemed that they participate in God's own immortality, glory, and incorruptibility. It is important to emphasize that the *"sōma pneumatikon"* will itself possess these divine properties *as its own.* The creator not only sustains the human reality in a hidden and indirect way as a *sōma psychikon* but now becomes, as it were, a constituent of that reality. In this new mode of existence, God's Spirit is as intimate and constitutive of the human person as the created *psychē* (life principle) had been in the former mode of existence. Clearly, the transformation Paul describes here could without distortion be called *"theōsis."*

Changed into His Image

Through the Spirit, believers become united to Christ even in this life, so that they begin to share his character, qualities, and accomplishments.[5] The idea that Christians should be transformed to be like Christ permeates the New Testament. We find it in Paul, 1 John, 1 Peter, and 2 Peter. In 1 John 2:6 we read, "Whoever claims to live in him must live as Jesus did." As an isolated statement John's instruction sounds like a moralistic rule, that is, Jesus sets us an example to imitate. But there is more to it than that, as John makes clear in 4:3: "This is how we know that we live in him and he in us: He has given us of his Spirit." The Spirit makes Jesus present in us and us in him, so that living like him is the natural outflow of his presence. This non-moralistic reading of 2:6 is confirmed by 3:1–2, where John speaks about our present status as "children of God" in contrast to our eschatological transformation: "But we know that when Christ appears, we shall be like him, for we shall see him as he is." Being a "child of God" is not merely a matter of behavior but of character and being, and the eschatological event of seeing Christ "as he is" will bring about an even more radical ontological transformation. First Peter encourages Christians to pattern their lives after

5. Gorman limits his study of *theōsis* to the Christian life and excludes the eschatological aspect of the doctrine of *theōsis*. Hence, he focuses on the moral/spiritual aspects of "becoming like God." He defines *theōsis* in this way: *"Theosis is the transformative participation in the kenotic, cruciform character and life of God through Spirit-enabled conformity to the incarnate, crucified, and resurrected/glorified Christ, who is the image of God"* (*Inhabiting the Cruciform God,* 125; emphasis original). My chapter focuses much more on the eschatological and ontological transformation of the resurrected and glorified people of God. Blackwell places greater emphasis on the eschatological transformation without neglecting present transformation (*Christosis*).

Jesus, especially in the face of unjust persecution. He advocates living what has come to be called a "cruciform" life:

> To this you were called, because Christ suffered for you, leaving you an example, that you should follow in his steps. "He committed no sin, and no deceit was found in his mouth." When they hurled their insults at him, he did not retaliate; when he suffered, he made no threats. Instead, he entrusted himself to him who judges justly. (1 Pet 2:21–23)

> Therefore, since Christ suffered in his body, arm yourselves also with the same attitude, because whoever suffers in the body is done with sin. (1 Pet 4:1)

> But rejoice inasmuch as you participate in the sufferings of Christ, so that you may be overjoyed when his glory is revealed. (1 Pet 4:13)

I do not think we should interpret these statements in a moralistic way, but leaving that question aside, they at least conform to the general pattern in the New Testament, that Christian salvation involves becoming like Christ in character.

In 2 Peter 1:3–4, we find a classic proof text for the patristic teaching on *theōsis or theopoiēsis*

> His divine power has given us everything we need for a godly life through our knowledge of him who called us by his own glory and goodness. Through these he has given us his very great and precious promises, so that through them you may participate in the divine nature *[theias koinonoi physeōs]*, having escaped the corruption in the world caused by evil desires.[6]

Even though the writer speaks of "sharing in the divine nature," the immediate context focuses on the divine power for liberation from passions and for godly living. As we will see below, some later writers took this text to teach a sort of assimilation to God, human nature being augmented and infused with divine qualities.[7]

In Paul, we find the clearest affirmation that the goal of salvation is becoming like Christ in every way. He expresses this conviction autobiographically in many places:

---

6. Others are Psalms 82:6 and John 10:34–35.

7. Starr, "Does 2 Peter 1:4 Speak of Deification?" 89–92.

> I have been crucified with Christ and I no longer live, but Christ lives in me. The life I now live in the body, I live by faith in the Son of God, who loved me and gave himself for me. (Gal 2:20)

> What is more, I consider everything a loss because of the surpassing worth of knowing Christ Jesus my Lord. . . . I want to know Christ—yes, to know the power of his resurrection and participation in his sufferings, becoming like him in his death, and so, somehow, attaining to the resurrection from the dead. (Phil 3:8–10)

In Romans 6, Paul contends that our initial acts of faith and baptism mark our death, our co-crucifixion with Christ, and our resurrection to new life. We have been "united with him in a death like his," and this union will also manifest itself in "a resurrection like his" (Rom 6:4–5; cf. Col 2:9–12). In Galatians 2:20, quoted above, we discover what Paul means by this new life. Being united to Christ's death leads to being united to his life, that is, co-crucifixion introduces us to co-living. Jesus Christ becomes the real life-principle of the new life. Paul focuses every ounce of his energy on becoming like Christ in cruciform living, dying, and rising.

Second Corinthians 3:17–18 is perhaps the classic text for the idea of transformation into the image of Christ:[8]

> Now the Lord is the Spirit, and where the Spirit of the Lord is, there is freedom. And we all, who with unveiled faces contemplate the Lord's glory, are being transformed into his image with ever-increasing glory, which comes from the Lord, who is the Spirit.

Volumes could be written on this rich text. What is the relationship between the Lord and the Spirit? What does it mean to "contemplate" the Lord's glory?[9] What are the implications of believers being changed into "the same image" as Christ?[10] Are the "glory" and the "image" of the Lord the same

---

8. Stephen Finlan speaks of this passage as "the most frankly theotic passage in Paul" ("Can We Speak of *Theosis* in Paul?" 75). See Blackwell for his study of 2 Corinthians 3:1—5:21, in which he places 3:18 in its larger context (*Christosis*, 174–238).

9. Litwa, "Transformation through a Mirror: Moses in 2 Cor 3.18," 286–97. In this interesting article, Litwa draws on traditional Jewish interpretation, which was troubled by the apparent assertion of Numbers 12:8–9 that Moses saw God in a direct vision. This tradition finds in the text the idea of a mirror through which Moses saw the Lord. In commenting on Exodus 33:13, Philo speaks of Moses seeing God clearly through the "mirror" of the Logos. Litwa hypothesizes that Paul may have something similar in mind. Christ is the perfect, clear mirror, the perfect means, through which God's glory (that is, God's excellence of being) is revealed.

10. The phrase that the NIV translates "are being transformed into his image" can better be translated "are being transformed into the same image" (*tēn autēn eikona*).

reality? Even if the answers to these questions remain obscure, the idea of transformation into the image of Christ is clear. Nor does this transformation come about by mere imitation, for the change is *the work of the Spirit*. It is also clear that the metamorphosis begins and continues in this life. As we contemplate or behold the glory we become the image. Romans 8:29–30 also connects being made into the image of Christ with glorification:

> For those God foreknew he also predestined to be conformed to the image of his Son, that he might be the firstborn among many brothers and sisters. And those he predestined, he also called; those he called, he also justified; those he justified, he also glorified.

As "firstborn," Jesus has ontological and temporal priority, but his brothers and sisters will also become like him. They will bear the same image and share in the same glory.

All Things Summed Up in Christ

In a third biblical theme, Christ is the one through whom God created all things and he is the space within which everything in the cosmos will be brought together and unified in perfect harmony. Jesus Christ is "Lord of all" (Acts 10:36), the one "through whom all things came and through whom we live" (1 Cor 8:6), "through him all things were made" (John 1:3). He "sustains all things" (Heb 1:3), "in him all things hold together" (Col 1:17), and every knee will bow and every tongue confess "that Jesus is Lord" (Phil 2:10–11). The classic texts for this theme are found in Ephesians:

> He made known to us the mystery of his will according to his good pleasure, which he purposed in Christ, to be put into effect when the times reach their fulfillment—to bring unity to all things in heaven and on earth under Christ. . . . And God placed all things under his feet and appointed him to be head over everything for the church, which is his body, the fullness of him who fills everything in every way. (Eph 1:9–10, 22–23)

> He who descended is the very one who ascended higher than all the heavens, in order to fill the whole universe. (Eph 4:10)

Interpreters have hesitated to draw the conclusion that Paul is saying that believers will be transformed into the *same* image and glory of Christ, that is, truly to become divine. For this discussion, see Litwa, "2 Corinthians 3:18 and Its Implications for *Theosis*," 117–33.

These texts from Colossians, Ephesians, and elsewhere connect salvation and creation in an intimate way. The two works flow from the same source. Jesus Christ the savior is the Word through whom God creates and sustains all things. Salvation is the completion of creation, not its destruction.[11] In his new work, Christ heals the wounds and brings the scattered and conflicted universe to unity and harmony in himself. As the creator and sustainer of the universe, he has always been present and at work everywhere, giving being, life, and form to all things. But as the savior, according to Ephesians 1:23, he fills "everything in every way" (*panta en pasin*), or in the words of 4:10, he fills "the whole universe" (*ta panta*). Christ imparts to the universe his unity and life in a way that overcomes all disharmony and decay. He becomes the direct life principle of the redeemed universe in the way the Spirit becomes the direct life principle of resurrected human beings. He works this healing action not merely as the *Logos asarkos*—a cosmic principle—but as Jesus of Nazareth in his *human* living, dying, and being raised.

God Will Be All in All

The unified and all-encompassing kingdom will be handed over to God so that God will be "all in all" (1 Cor 15:28). In the verses leading up to 1 Corinthians 15:28, Paul speaks of the resurrected and reigning Lord as destroying every enemy that sets itself against God. The last enemy, death, will be destroyed at the final resurrection. "When he has done this, then the Son himself will be made subject to him who put everything under him, so that God may be all in all." The ultimate goal of Christ's work is that "God may be *all in all*."[12] The expression "all in all" (*panta en pasin*) should not be interpreted in a pantheistic way to mean that the distinction between God and creation or the Son and the Father will be abrogated. This interpretation abandons the personal and relational categories that otherwise characterize Paul's thought, even in this very chapter. Paul's argument for the resurrection of the dead and their being raised in spiritual *bodies* would make no sense on pantheistic premises. There are no strict parallels outside the New Testament

---

11. The continuity between creation and salvation is a golden thread that runs through Gunton, *The Actuality of Atonement*.

12. Gregory of Nyssa (ca. 330–ca. 395) sees in the phrase "all in all" the promise that God will annihilate all evil from creation. In Gregory's words, "Quite clearly in the last verse of the passage Paul asserts in his argument the nonexistence of evil by saying that God in becoming all things to each comes to be in all. For it is obvious that it will be true that God is in all at that time when nothing evil is discerned in existing things" (Gregory of Nyssa, "On 'Then Also the Son,'" 125).

in which the expression "all in all" is applied to God.[13] But in Greek and Roman literature contemporary with the New Testament the expression is found in contexts of love and friendship. A dear friend or an object of romantic love can be someone's "all in all" as if they needed nothing else for life and happiness. Or, grateful subjects can look to a ruler or a god as their "all in all," that is, as the supplier of all their needs.[14] As creator, God is the source of everything whether creatures recognize it or not. As savior, the Son brings it about that God is lovingly recognized and glorified as this source. God will then be the "all in all" for all creatures, the direct source of all their joy. Everything will be perfectly ordered to the one source of all things. Only then will the work of creation and salvation be complete.

When we put these four New Testament themes together a clear picture of ultimate salvation comes into view. At the resurrection of the dead, the Spirit of God will become the direct life-giving force of our transformed bodies, and thus our metamorphosis into the image and glory of Christ, which began in this life, will be perfected. Christ will fill the universe and God will become every creature's all in all. We are not speaking here of three separate actors, the Spirit, the Son, and God. The Father, Son, and Spirit are *one*, and where the one is there are the others. Where the one acts, the others act. To become like Christ is to become like God, and to be animated by the Spirit of God is to be animated by God. Hence, a significant part of the Christian tradition designates this process of salvation as deification *(theōsis or theopoiēsis),* that is, becoming like God or being made God.[15] If the Spirit of God becomes the immortal life of our persons, the Son of God our image and glory, and God our all in all, what other term could do it justice? The process of taking on Christ's character and participating in the divine attributes of glory, immortality, and incorruptibility occurs in Christ, who sums up all things in himself by the power of the Spirit.

Theōsis in Tradition and Theology

In the early centuries of Christianity, especially in the Greek-speaking church,[16] the theme of salvation as *theōsis* came to sharper focus and was

13. As we saw above in discussing Ephesians 1:23, the expression "all in all" *(panta en pasin)* is applied to Christ.

14. See Fredrickson, "God, Christ, and All Things in 1 Corinthians 15:28," 254–63.

15. See Blackwell, *Christosis.* I am very sympathetic with Blackwell's conclusions. There is no doubt that Paul envisions eschatological salvation as becoming like Christ in the ethical and ontological senses. And if Christ is God and the means of reconciliation with God, *Christōsis* is at the same time *theōsis.*

16. The theme of deification or divinization was also prominent in the Latin

developed into what can be called a "doctrine" of deification.[17] In the survey that follows I will not attempt to trace the complicated development of the doctrine of *theōsis* in detail. Many historians have worked on this project.[18] I wish to highlight a tendency in the patristic church to describe the ultimate salvation worked by Jesus Christ in terms as great as can be imagined. Hence, I will sample representative thinkers from among those who made significant contributions to this theme with this more modest goal in mind.

The church fathers thought about the nature of salvation within two major contexts, the biblical/ecclesiastical and the Greco-Roman religious/ philosophical settings.[19] They followed Paul's teaching about baptism and the Eucharist, the sanctifying and life-giving work of the Holy Spirit, and the gifts of immortality and glory promised in the resurrection, and they followed John on the incarnation of the Word. But they also lived in the Greco-Roman world where the notion of a human hero, king, or emperor being deified after death was commonplace and where divinity was considered a quality that could be shared by many divine beings at different intensities.[20] Many Christian thinkers we will consider were also influenced by philosophical theories of deification, especially those in the Platonic tradition.[21] As one example, we can quote Eudorus (middle to late first century BC), the consolidator of Middle Platonism:

> Socrates and Plato agree with Pythagoras that the *telos* [of human life] is assimilation to God *(homoiōsis theoi)*. Plato defined this more clearly by adding: "according as is possible *(kata to dynaton)*," and it is only possible by wisdom *(phronēsis)*, that is to say, as a result of Virtue.[22]

---

fathers: in the liturgies, in the early martyrologies, Tertullian, Cyprian, Novatian, Hilary of Poitiers, Ambrose of Milan, Jerome, Augustine, Leo the Great, and many others. For this story see, Ortis, *Deification in the Latin Patristic Tradition*. The last chapter, written by Russell, examines the common heritage of East and West on the subject of deification ("A Common Christian Tradition: Deification in the Greek and Latin Fathers," 272–94).

17. For the distinction between the theme and the doctrine of deification, see Billings, "John Calvin: United to God through Christ," 205–6.

18. Gross, *The Divinization of the Christian*; Russell, *The Doctrine of Deification*; and Christensen and Wittung, *Partakers of the Divine Nature*.

19. See Litwa, *We Are Being Transformed*. Litwa counsels caution in drawing too big a distinction between the two.

20. See Wright, *PFG* 1:313–43.

21. See Sedley, "The Ideal of Godlikeness," 317, and Sedley, *Creationism and Its Critics in Antiquity*, 98.

22. Quoted in Dillon, *The Middle Platonists*, 122.

Irenaeus of Lyon (ca. 130–ca. 200)

Irenaeus anticipated many ideas later thinkers developed at length and expressed in more nuanced language. In the previous chapter, we examined Irenaeus's idea of recapitulation, which he developed in greater detail than any theologian before him. Irenaeus also envisioned the transformation that later theologians would call *theōsis*. In the preface to Book Five of *Against Heresies,* after encouraging his readers to avoid the heresies he has just refuted, Irenaeus encourages them to remain faithful by "following the only true and stedfast Teacher, the Word of God, our Lord Jesus Christ, who did, through His transcendent love, become what we are, that He might bring us to be even what He is Himself."[23] This way of expressing the relationship between Christ and the believer has come to be known as the "exchange formula."[24] In earlier parts of *Against Heresies* Irenaeus had observed, "When a man sees God, the vision confers incorruptibility, because it glorifies the creature with divine glory" (*AH* 4.38. 3) and "The Word of God was made man and he who was the Son of God was made Son of Man united to the Word of God, in order that man should receive adoption and thereby become the Son of God. How else could he have received incorruption?" (*AH* 3.19.1).[25] Irenaeus uses Psalm 82:6 on three occasions: to prove that there is only one God (*AH* 3.6.1), to prove the divinity of the Son (*AH* 3.19.1), and to explain why human beings were not created "gods" from the beginning (*AH* 4.38.4).

Clement of Alexandria (150–215)

Well versed in Middle Platonism and in the Platonizing biblical exegesis of Philo of Alexandria, Clement of Alexandria was the first Christian writer to use the technical vocabulary of deification when speaking of Christian salvation.[26] His favorite word for deification is *theopoieo* (making God). He speaks of deification as a process facilitated by Jesus's teaching and the sacraments of the church: "Being baptized, we are illuminated; illuminated, we become sons; being made sons, we are made perfect; being made perfect, we

---

23 Irenaeus, *AH* 5 (*ANF* 1:526).

24. See Osborn's discussion of the relationship between participation and exchange in *Irenaeus of Lyon,* 260–62. Athanasius elaborates on this formula in his early work *The Incarnation of the Word* 54: "For He was made man that we might be made God; and He manifested Himself by a body that we might receive the idea of the unseen Father; and He endured the insolence of men that we might inherit immortality" (*NPNF2* 4:65).

25. Quoted in McGuckin, "The Strategic Adaptation of Deification," 95–114, 96–97.

26. Russell, *The Doctrine of Deification,* 122–25.

are made immortal. 'I,' says He, 'have said that ye are gods, and all sons of the Highest.'"[27] Through the Scriptures the divine light shines into the hearts of those who believe, "bestowing on us the truly great, divine, and inalienable inheritance of the Father, deifying man by the heavenly teaching."[28] Just as teachers of crafts make craftsman and dancing instructors make dancers, "so he who obeys the Lord and follows the prophecy given through him is fully perfected after the likeness of his teacher, and thus becomes a god while still moving about in the flesh."[29] Clement can also speak philosophically about deification. In commenting on Psalm 82:6 ("I [God] said, 'You are gods; you are sons of the Most High'"), he says:

> Who are these gods? They are those who are superior to pleasure, who rise above the passions, who have a precise knowledge of everything that they do, who are gnostics, who transcend the world, . . . who have detached themselves as far as possible from everything human.[30]

Later in the same work, Clement articulates his view of deification in language that, according to Russell, reminds us of "the standard philosophical ascent to God through the contemplation of the intelligible world which we find in Philo and other Middle Platonists."[31] Clement acknowledges the insights of Plato on this subject:

> Plato therefore rightly says too that he who devotes himself to the contemplation of the ideas will live as a god among men. The intellect is the place of ideas, and the intellect is God. He therefore called him who contemplates the invisible God a living god among men. . . . For when the soul has transcended the created world and is alone by itself and associates with the Ideas . . . it has already become like an angel and will be with Christ, since it has become contemplative and always contemplates the will of God."[32]

Clement does not admit a contradiction between these two models of deification, the philosophical and the biblical. Indeed, the perfected Christian, the one who has become a god "while still moving about in the flesh,"[33]

---

27. Clement, *The Instructor* 1.6 (*ANF* 2:215).

28. *Exhortation to the Heathen* 11 (*ANF* 2:203).

29. *Miscellanies* 7.101.4, quoted in Russell, *Doctrine of Deification*, 125.

30. *Miscellanies* 2.125.4–5, quoted in Russell, *Doctrine of Deification*, 129.

31. Russell, *Doctrine of Deification*, 131.

32. *Miscellanies* 4.155, quoted in Russell, *Doctrine of Deification*, 131.

33. *Miscellanies* 7.101.4, quoted in Russell, *Doctrine of Deification*, 125.

must follow the way of contemplation and asceticism. But that way is made possible only by divine grace.[34]

Athanasius (ca. 296–373)

An exhaustive study of deification in the church fathers would examine the thought of Origen (185–253) and other third-century thinkers. But I have space only to consider him briefly as a background to Athanasius. Origen was the first writer to incorporate 2 Peter 1:4 ("partakers of the divine nature") into his thinking about deification.[35] He made the Platonist concept of "participation" central to his understanding of deification. The concept of participation explains how a derived reality can possess properties that exist separately and eternally. For example, all living things live by participating in life itself. Things are wise to the extent that they share in wisdom itself. For Origen, only the Father is God (*ho theos* and *autotheos*) in the absolute sense. The Son and the Spirit are divine (*theos*) by participation.[36] And human beings can be deified by participating in the Son and sanctified by participating in the Spirit.

Athanasius inherited a well-established tradition of deification, but unlike previous writers, his thought on this subject was decisively determined by the Arian controversy over the deity of the Son and Spirit.[37] Whereas Origen thought that divinity can be participated in to various degrees, Athanasius made a clear distinction between the uncreated (*agenētos*) and the created (*genētos*) orders. The humanity that the Logos assumed was deified by the union, but the Logos himself is God by nature and does not need to be deified. In contrast, Arius placed both natures on the created side of the divide. Athanasius used the accepted teaching of deification through the Son as an argument for the deity of the Son, contending against Arius that only that which is God by nature can deify. In his early work *On the Incarnation of the Word*, Athanasius uses an "exchange formula" that reminds us of Irenaeus: "For He was made man that we might be made God."[38] In his *Discourses Against the Arians*, he argues that the Logos assumed human nature that he might deify it and thus make possible our deification:

---

34. Russell, *Doctrine of Deification*, 134.

35. Russell, *Doctrine of Deification*, 151.

36. Russell, *Doctrine of Deification*, 145.

37. According to Russell, *Doctrine of Deification*, 170–71, the notion of deification through the Son was accepted by the Arians as well as by Athanasius.

38. Athanasius, *Incarnation of the Word* 54 (NPNF2 4:65).

For man had not been deified if joined to a creature, or unless the Son were very God; nor had man been brought into the Father's presence, unless He had been His natural and true Word who had put on the body. And as we had not been delivered from sin and the curse, unless it had been by nature human flesh, which the Word put on . . . so also the man had not been deified, unless the Word who became flesh had been by nature from the Father and true and proper to Him. For therefore the union was of this kind, that He might unite what is man by nature to Him who is in the nature of the Godhead, and his salvation and deification might be sure.[39]

Athanasius also uses the deification of believers as proof of the deity of the Holy Spirit:

If the Holy Spirit were a creature, we should have no participation of God in him. If indeed we were joined to a creature, we should be strangers to the divine nature inasmuch as we did not partake therein. But, as it is, the fact of our being called partakers of Christ and partakers of God shows that the unction and seal that is in us belongs, not to the nature of things originate, but to the nature of the Son who, through the Spirit who is in him, joins us to the Father. . . . But if, by participation in the Spirit, we are made "sharers in the divine nature," we should be mad to say that the Spirit has a created nature and not the nature of God. For it is on this account that those in whom he is are made divine. If he makes men divine, it is not to be doubted that his nature is of God.[40]

Given the need to refute the Arians, Athanasius was more careful when speaking of deification than some of his predecessors. The Son and the Spirit deify but are not deified. The deified creature remains clearly on the creature side of the divide between created and uncreated. Athanasius's caution can be seen in the way he frequently pairs deification with other terms that explain its meaning and prevent misunderstanding: sonship, renewal, sanctification, grace, transcendence, enlightenment, being made alive, and salvation. Most of these terms are found in the New Testament, and all of them, according to Russell, are "presented as equivalents to deification."[41] In keeping with this caution, Athanasius denies that the concept of participation in the Son indicates a natural "likeness or kinship

---

39. Athanasius, *Discourses Against the Arians* 2.70 (*NPNF*2 4:386).

40. Athanasius, *First Letter to Sarapion* 24:125–26.

41. Russell, *Doctrine of Deification*, 177.

between human beings and God."[42] By participating in the deified humanity of the Son through the sacraments, empowered by the Spirit, we share
in the properties of his deified humanity, but we do not become God in
the literal sense of the term.

What, then, does Athanasius mean by deification? Kharlamov concludes that whereas Athanasius is very clear about *who* can deify creatures,
he does not attempt to explain what it means to be deified.[43] In the words
of Gross, "with Athanasius we would search in vain for a systematic and
well-balanced exposition of the matter."[44] From a rhetorical point of view,
however, Athanasius's lack of precision on the nature of deification may be
an advantage. The entire biblical vision of salvation can be evoked in one
provocative but inclusive expression.[45]

The Cappadocians

The two brothers Basil of Caesarea (ca. 330–79) and Gregory of Nyssa (ca.
330–ca. 395) and their friend Gregory of Nazianzus (329/30–389/90) are
known as "the Cappadocians" because they were born and served as bish-
ops in Cappadocia. They were friends and admirers of Athanasius, and like
him spend most of their careers defending Nicene orthodoxy and refuting
various forms of Arianism. Like Athanasius, Basil uses the Spirit's power to
deify to prove the Spirit's deity. He argues, "Also, if we call gods those who
are perfect in virtue and perfection is through the Spirit, how can that which
lacks deity deify others?"[46] Unlike Athanasius, however, Basil and the other
Cappadocians speak of deification in terms reminiscent of Platonist-influ-
enced Clement and Origen.[47] Basil says,

> Through His aid hearts are lifted up, the weak are held by
> the hand, and they who are advancing are brought to perfec-
> tion. Shining upon those that are cleansed from every spot,
> He makes them spiritual by fellowship with Himself. Just as
> when a sunbeam falls on bright and transparent bodies, they
> themselves become brilliant too, and shed forth a fresh bright-
> ness from themselves, so souls wherein the Spirit dwells, il-
> luminated by the Spirit, themselves become spiritual, and send

42. Russell, *Doctrine of Deification*, 187.

43. Kharlamov, "Rhetorical Application of *Theosis* in Greek Patristic Theology," 120.

44. Gross, *The Divinization of the Christian*, 163.

45. Kharlamov, "Rhetorical Application of *Theosis*," 120.

46. *Against Eunomius* 3.5, quoted in Russell, *Doctrine of Deification*, 208.

47. Russell, *Doctrine of Deification*, 212.

forth their grace to others. Hence comes . . . joy without end, abiding in God, the being made like to God, and, highest of all, the being made God.[48]

Gregory of Nazianzus coined the term *theōsis*,[49] which was not used again until it was taken up by Dionysius at the end of the fifth century. Its use by Maximus the Confessor in the seventh century assured that it would become the standard term for deification in Byzantine theology.[50] Gregory of Nazianzus, like Athanasius, taught that the possibility of deification lay in the incarnation, and that its beginning is communicated in baptism. However, Gregory focuses on advancing in deification by imitation of God in hope of its full realization in the resurrection. Not surprisingly, then, Gregory was attracted to the monastic life and praised those who follow the ascetic way to deification. They are those

> who are immortal through mortifying themselves; who are united with God through release [from the body]; who are separated from desire and are joined to that love which is divine and dispassionate; to whom belongs the fountain of light and who enjoy even now its radiance; to whom belong the angelic psalmodies, the night-long services and the departure of the intellect to God, rapt up before its time; to whom belong purification and being purified; who know no limit in ascending or in being deified.[51]

Gregory of Nyssa seems to have been somewhat more hesitant than Gregory of Nazianzus to use the language of deification. Strictly speaking, only the humanity of Christ has been deified. We participate in his deified humanity through baptism and the Eucharist and in this way share in the properties of his immortal and incorruptible human body. In a section on the Eucharist in his *Address on Religious Instruction*, Gregory explains how the bread and wine that Christ ate during his life on earth was changed into his deified body. Hence, it should not be beyond our imagination to conceive how the bread and wine of the Eucharist could be changed by that same Word into his deified body, which through its consumption allows us to participate in his immortality:

> The reason, moreover, that God, when he revealed himself, united himself with our mortal nature was to deify humanity by this

---

48. Basil, *On the Holy Spirit* 9.23 (*NPNF2* 8:16)
49. Gregory Nazianzus, *Oration 4*.
50. Russell, *Doctrine of Deification*, 215.
51. *Oration 4*, quoted in Russell, *Doctrine of Deification*, 216.

close relation with Deity. In consequence, by means of his flesh, which is constituted by bread and wine, he implants himself in all believers, following out the plan of grace. He unites himself with their bodies so that mankind too, by its union with what is immortal, may share in incorruptibility.[52]

Cyril of Alexandria (d. 444)

Cyril of Alexandria was installed in 412 as the fourth occupant of the episcopal chair of the Alexandrian church after the death of Athanasius in 373. He is said to have been "the most brilliant representative of the Alexandrian theological tradition."[53] With his gift of systematic and comprehensive thinking he brought the doctrine of deification to "full maturity" by integrating Trinitarian perspectives on the divine nature, Eucharistic participation in Christ, and the moral life into a harmonious whole.[54] By Cyril's time, however, the idea of deification had come under suspicion of association with Apollinarianism and Origenism. In the late fourth century, Apollinarius had proposed the theory that the Word became incarnate by replacing the human mind of Christ, limiting deification to the flesh of Christ. His theory was condemned by councils in Rome (377), Antioch (379), and Constantinople (381). Origenism came under intense attack around 400 by Theophilus of Alexandria, Cyril's uncle and predecessor. Evagarius of Pontius (346–99) and his followers developed Origen's ideas to conclude that in the final state of salvation all souls would be deified to become "pure intellects" and "would be equal to Christ himself."[55] It is not surprising, then, that Cyril uses the traditional vocabulary of deification rarely, usually when he is in dialogue with Athanasius. He prefers the language of participation, and accordingly alludes to 2 Peter 1:4 more often than any writer before him.[56] Like Athanasius and the Cappadocians, Cyril defended the deity of the Son and the Spirit by arguing that only God can deify and since the Son and Spirit deify believers, they are God:

> For we have been adopted through entering into a relationship with God and have been deified by him. For if we are called sons of God through having participated in God by grace, what

---

52. Gregory of Nyssa, *Address on Religious Instruction*, 321.

53. *ODCC*, s.v. "Cyril, St," 447.

54. Russell, *Doctrine of Deification*, 192.

55. Russell, *Doctrine of Deification*, 235.

56. Russell, *Doctrine of Deification*, 192.

kind of participation do we attribute to the Word, that he should become Son and God? We are [sons and gods] by participation in the Holy Spirit; to think this of the Son would be absurd.[57]

Again

It is inconceivable that created being should have the power to deify. This is something that can be attributed only to God, who through the Spirit infuses into the souls of the saints a participation in his own property.[58]

In faith and baptism we come to participate in Christ through the power of the Spirit, and we are transformed into his image:

Since they receive the Son through faith, they receive the privilege of being counted among the children of God. For the Son gives what belongs properly to him alone and exists by nature within him as a right. . . . There was no other way for us who have borne the image of the man of dust to escape corruption, unless the beauty of the image of the man of heaven is imprinted upon us through our having been called to sonship. For having become partakers of him through the Spirit, we were sealed into likeness to him and mount up to the archetypal form of the image.[59]

Toward the middle of his term as patriarch, Cyril found himself embroiled in a controversy not faced by Athanasius. Nestorius, patriarch of Constantinople, seemed to Cyril to advocate that Christ's unity was constituted by a conjunction (*synapheia*) of two persons, a human and a divine person. In Cyril's estimation, this idea was seriously defective, both in its Christology and its soteriology, for it made the unity of Christ and the true incarnation of the Word doubtful and it undermined the salvation of humanity. How can believers be truly deified and sanctified if they are united to a human person merely conjoined to but not united in the one person of the Son of God? Such a Christology abandons the "exchange formula" accepted since Irenaeus. Cyril reasserts the traditional exchange formula in this new situation. The Word assumed a complete human nature as his own. He did not merely associate himself with or indwell a human being:

57. *Thesaurus de Trinitate* 4, quoted in Russell, *Doctrine of Deification*, 194.
58. *Dialogues on the Trinity* 7, quoted in Russell, *Doctrine of Deification*, 195.
59. *In Iohannem* 1.9, quoted in Russell, *Doctrine of Deification*, 195.

> Since he became like us (that is, a human being) in order that
> we might become like him (I mean gods and sons), he receives
> our properties into himself and he gives us his own in return.[60]

What does Cyril mean by deification? What does it mean to participate in the divine nature, to share in God's attributes?

> And as we bear the image of the earthy we shall bear the image
> too of the heavenly; calling the image of the earthy, that of our
> forefather Adam, of the heavenly, that of Christ. What then first
> is the image of our forefather? proneness to sin, becoming under
> death and decay. What again that of the heavenly? being in no
> wise o'ercome of passions, not knowing transgression, not being
> subject to death and decay, holiness, righteousness, and what-
> ever are akin to and like these. But these (I suppose) will befit
> the Divine and Untaint Nature to possess: for superior to both
> sin and decay is Holiness and Righteousness. Herein does the
> Word out of God the Father restore us too, rendering us partak-
> ers of His own Divine Nature through the Spirit.[61]

Maximus the Confessor (ca. 580–662)

As I observed above, the dawn of the fifth century saw the partial eclipse of
the language of deification; it had become associated with Origenism and
Apollinarianism. According to Russell, Cyril's death in 444 marked its total
eclipse.[62] It reappeared, however, in the early sixth century in the writings
of the anonymous writer known as Dionysius the Areopagite.[63] Dionysius
was the first writer to construct a formal definition of deification. "Theosis,"
explains Dionysius, "is the attaining of likeness to God and union with him
so far as is possible."[64] The power for deification derives ultimately from God,
but God draws human beings through a hierarchy in which those above help
those below on their upward journey toward union with God and deification.[65] In his *Ecclesiastical Hierarchy*, Dionysius describes how the earthly hi-

60. Cyril of Alexandria, *Commentary on John*, 363.

61. Cyril of Alexandria, *Five Tomes Against Nestorius* 3.2:94.

62. Russell, *The Doctrine of Deification*, 237.

63. Among his works are *The Divine Names, Mystical Theology, Ecclesiastical Hierarchy*, and *Celestial Hierarchy*.

64. Dionysius, *Ecclesiastical Hierarchy* 1.3, quoted in Russell, *Doctrine of Deification*, 248. The resemblance to the definitions of the human *telos* in Plato and Eudorus
is apparent.

65. The word *hierarchy* was coined by Dionysius and is derived from the word for

erarchy—with its officials, liturgy, and sacraments—leads the people toward deification. For Dionysius, the churchly hierarchy works by enlightening the soul through its symbolic power. According to Russell, "this language refers to the intellectual reception of the symbols rather than to corporeal participation in the body and blood of Christ. These symbols raise the mind to unity and simplicity, enabling it to participate in the divine attributes of goodness, wisdom, and deity."[66] Dionysius, in his revival of the language of deification, anticipated the significant work of Maximus.

After a short but highly successful career in government service, the thirty-four-year-old Maximus resigned his post and entered monastic life. His extensive writing on the subject of deification sets out a program of spiritual progress for monks. In his doctrine of deification, he drew on those who came before him, especially Gregory of Nazianzus, Cyril of Alexandria, Dionysius, and Evagarius of Ponticus (346–99). In Maximus, the theme of deification "finds its greatest elaborator and most profound articulation."[67] The idea of deification is the unifying and directing force of Maximus' authorship. Deification is the *telos* toward which all of God's acts in creation and salvation aim, and it is the *telos* toward which all human striving should aim. Divine love drives the process of *theōsis* by reaching down to touch human beings to create in them a likeness of divine love. The love of God is the greatest good we could seek, "since through it God and man are drawn together in a single embrace, and the creator of humankind appears as a human, through the undeviating likeness of the deified to God in the good so far as is possible to humankind."[68] God's all-embracing love infuses and directs all things toward the end he promised:

> Because he is truthful he will give us everything that he has promised. This is "what no eye hath seen, nor ear heard, nor the heart of man conceived, what God has prepared for those who love him" (1 Cor 2:9). For that is also why he made us, that we might "become partakers of the divine nature" (2 Peter 1:4) and sharers in his eternity, and prove to be like him through the deification bestowed by grace.[69]

In his *Commentary on the Lord's Prayer*, Maximus reflects on seven mysteries contained in the prayer. Pursuing each mystery opens us to a different phase of deification. The list begins with "theology" and "adoption"

---

chief priest, hierarch. See Russell, *Doctrine of Deification*, 251.

66. Russell, *Doctrine of Deification*, 261–62.

67. Russell, *Doctrine of Deification*, 262.

68. Maximus, *Epistulae 2*, quoted in Russell, *Doctrine of Deification*, 265.

69. Maximus, *Epistulae 24*, quoted in Russell, *Doctrine of Deification*, 266.

and ends with destruction of the devil.[70] His *Mystagogia* is a spiritual commentary on the Liturgy, similar in many ways to Dionysius' *Ecclesiastical Hierarchy.* In this work, Maximus develops an ingenious psychology of the human soul. The soul divides into the intellectual and the vital aspects, each of which is subdivided into five virtues or capacities: mind and reason, wisdom and prudence, contemplation and action, knowledge and virtue, enduring knowledge and faith. The first member of these pairs or syzygies[71] is intellectual and aims at truth and the second is vital and its *telos* is goodness. In the process of *theōsis,* all these powers and virtues, with the help of divine grace, are unified and directed toward the perfect unity of truth and goodness, which is God:

> It is through them that the soul vigorously keeps its own good inviolable and bravely repels what is alien to it as evil, because it has a rational mind, a prudent wisdom, an active contemplation, a virtuous knowledge, and along with them an enduring knowledge which is both very faithful and unchangeable. And it conveys to God the effects discretely joined to their causes and the acts to their potencies, and in exchange for these it receives the deification that creates simplicity.[72]

For Maximus, like those before him, the exchange formula is central to his doctrine of deification:

> By these [elements of grace] he has inserted himself totally into God alone, and has imprinted the stamp and form of God alone totally upon himself so that he himself may be a god by grace and be called such, just as God is a man by condescension and is called such on his account, and also so that the power of this reciprocal arrangement may be revealed that deifies man for God through this love for man, and by this beautiful correspondence makes God man, for the sake of man's divinization, and man God for the sake of God's humanization.[73]

The mutual interpenetration or *perichōrēsis* of the divine and human natures in the person of Christ as defined in the formula of Chalcedon (451) is Maximus's model for deification. God and humanity wholly indwell each

---

70. Russell, *Doctrine of Deification,* 267–70.

71. Meaning "yoked together." This word is use in astronomy to speak of the alignment of three celestial objects, for example the sun, earth, and moon during solar or lunar eclipses.

72. Maximus, *Mystagogia* 5, quoted in Russell, *Doctrine of Deification,* 271.

73. Maximus, *Liber Ambiguorum* 7, quoted in Russell, *The Doctrine of Deification,* 275.

other and share attributes without loss of the integrity of each nature. The union "expresses the most excellent communication according to the exchange of properties which naturally belong to each nature of the unique Christ and Son."[74] Human beings are deified by their interpenetration with God, which is initiated and energized by the downward movement of divine love and grace. God's love calls forth a free response of human love for God and does not overwhelm or replace the human will. The Confessor explains, "So the human being is made God, and God is called and appears as a human being [in us], because of the one and undeviating wish (in accordance with the will) and movement of both."[75] The deified human soul finds itself transported out of itself into perfect harmony with the divine movement and "dwells entirely in God alone in a loving ecstasy, and has rendered itself by mystical theology totally immobile in God."[76] The immobility of the deified human soul does not extinguish it. Instead, the soul finds its natural activity wholly fulfilled and elevated in God's activity:

> A seal conforms to the stamp against which it was pressed. . . . [I]t lays hold of God's power or rather it becomes God by divinization and delights more in the displacement of those things perceived to be naturally its own. Through the abundant grace of the Spirit it will be shown that God alone is at work, and in all things there will be only one activity, that of God and those worthy of kinship with God. God will be *all in all* wholly penetrating all who are his in a way that is appropriate to each.[77]

Postlude

The history of the theology of deification did not end with Maximus, but it was not until the fourteenth century that it became the focus of theological controversy in the debate between Gregory Palamas (1296–1359) and Barlaam (1290–1348). The discussion centered on how to protect divine transcendence in God's relation to creation. Palamas solved the problem by retrieving the patristic distinction between God's *essence*, which remains unknown and

74. Maximus, *Opuscula theological et polemica* 20, quoted in Vishnevshaya, "Divinization as Perichoretic Embrace," 132.

75. Maximus, *Epistulae* 2, quoted in Vishnevshaya, "Divinization as Perichoretic Embrace," 141.

76. Maximus, *Capita theologiae et oeconomiae* 1.39, quoted in Vishnevshaya, "Divinization as Perichoretic Embrace," 135.

77. Maximus, *Liber Ambiguorum* 7, quoted in Vishnevshaya, "Divinization as Perichoretic Embrace," 141. Emphasis original.

unshared, and God's *energies* in which God relates to the world. The energies, though not the divine essence, are nevertheless divine and uncreated. The communication of God's uncreated energies, *not* his essence, is the basis of deification. Barlaam argued that this theory compromises God's transcendence. In 1368, nine years after his death, Gregory was canonized, giving him a posthumous victory.[78] In the late twentieth and twenty-first centuries there has been a steady increase of interest in the doctrine of deification among Western theologians. Not only are Western theologians studying the Greek fathers, they are also examining the soteriology of such Western theologians as Augustine, Anselm, Luther, Calvin, and Wesley for their thinking on deification. But that is a story for someone else to tell.[79]

Conclusions

What can we conclude from this survey of the patristic theology of deification? More to the point, how does this survey advance the aims of this book? First, we have seen that Christian deification does not mean becoming God in essence or ceasing to be human by nature. No writer we examined argued for that, and most were careful to distance themselves from this idea.

Second, deification is the process whereby a human being comes to participate in certain divine qualities—immortality, incorruptibility, holiness, glory, and others—by grace in so far as possible. Some writers emphasize the sacraments as a means of deification while others emphasize contemplation or ascetic practice. Most combine all three.

Third, patristic thought on deification is derived from reflection on God's saving acts accomplished in Jesus Christ: the union (without confusion) of God and humanity in the incarnation, divine love displayed in the incarnation and the cross, and the glorification of humanity accomplished in the resurrection of Christ. As I pointed out above, Athanasius points to this truth by pairing nearly every mention of deification with such New Testament concepts as adoption, renewal, sanctification, grace, metamorphosis, enlightenment, being made alive, and salvation.

Fourth, perhaps patristic writers' use of the language of deification can be explained by the need to comment on such biblical texts as Psalm 82:6 or 2 Peter 1:4, or from the influence of the Platonist idea of the ascent of the

78. For a short history of the controversy with its prehistory and aftermath, see Russell, *Doctrine of Deification*, 297–320.

79. See the chapters on these figures in Christensen and Wittung (eds.), *Partakers of the Divine Nature*. The seventeen-page bibliography in that book lists many recent works on deification written by and about Western theologians.

soul, or from the need to defend the deity of the Son and the Spirit, or the desire to preserve the true union of God and humanity accomplished in the incarnation. All of these factors played a part in motivating one thinker or another to speak of Christian salvation as deification.

But why use the language of deification, of "being made God" or "becoming gods," at all when it is not meant to be taken at face value and, so, must be qualified? In my view, a basic intuition, unarticulated but fundamental, drives this rhetoric, that is, *that the salvation accomplished in Jesus Christ and promised to those who embrace it, is far greater than any alternative imaginable.* To say that we can become sons of God and a new creation, that we are made holy, receive incorruption and immortality, share in God's glory and grace, and achieve transcendence and enlightenment sounds glorious indeed compared to our present state. But the multiplicity of these images underlines their partial nature and diffuses our focus, and a long list lacks the shock value a single hyperbole can give. The greatness of God transcends all we can think or imagine, and we have learned to think of God as perfect and infinite in every way. Hence, to assert that through union with Christ we will "become God" will for an instant allow us to transcend all the finite and particular images of salvation placed in our minds by the many images contained in the New Testament. The salvation that awaits us is far greater than we can imagine.

12

Preaching Christ as Savior

Now we return to the challenge I designed this book to meet: how can theology assist the church in helping people living today understand the message of salvation through Jesus Christ in a way that is true to the original gospel, resonates with their experience, and strikes them as good news? This book as a whole is my answer to this question. In this chapter, I want to summarize this answer crisply and make a few suggestions to anyone wishing to share the Christian message of salvation. As I understand it, the task of theology is to communicate the original Christian message to the present age without omission, addition, or distortion. To accomplish this task, theologians must listen intently both to the Bible and to the heartbeat of the age. They must live in multiple worlds and speak many languages. A theologian must be historian, exegete, and philosopher. We need the heart of a poet, the mind of a logician, and the soul of a mystic. No one possesses all these qualities to the degree this charge demands. Above all, therefore, a theologian must be humble, prayerful, and faithful. This book contains the imperfect results of my efforts to understand the biblical message of salvation *and* the minds and hearts of our contemporaries, so that my readers and I may help them experience "the glorious riches of this mystery, which is Christ in you, the hope of glory" (Col 1:27).

The Message of Salvation

The Human Condition

The Christian message of salvation includes analysis of the negative condition from which we need saving, a vision of redeemed human life, and a means by which this transition can be accomplished. As far as we can discover from self-examination, the paradox of humanity's simultaneous wretchedness and greatness finds resolution only in death. Desire can never be satisfied. The gap between what we ought to be and what we are remains unbridgeable. Within the limits of our bodies and the time we are allotted we can never experience all the good we desire or discover all the truth we long to know. The greatness of our possibilities highlights the wretchedness of our actual condition, and our wretchedness infects our greatness with a mood of despair. Even without the benefit of the biblical doctrine of sin and death, we suspect that only a God can save us.

When we turn to the biblical picture of human wretchedness and greatness, we find that instead of falsifying our self-knowledge it deepens and augments it and sets it in relation to God and our God-ordained destiny. The biblical categories of sin, death, and the devil incorporate the universal human problems of contingency and anxiety, embodiment and confinement, desire and discontent, ignorance and vulnerability, guilt and shame, death and meaninglessness, and every other form of limitation and unhappiness we experience. The Christian view of salvation becomes understandable only within this expanded vision of the paradox of our wretchedness and greatness.

Salvation and the Savior

Is there a resolution to the paradox of the human condition? Is there hope for escape from wretchedness into realized greatness? Surely, everyone would agree that such a resolution would deserve the name "salvation." And whatever power brought it about would be worthy of the title "savior." Alas, from within the human sphere salvation cannot arise. Science and technology cannot perform this service because they, too, are human and need a savior. Government simply magnifies human nature for good or ill. It cannot escape its own gravitational field, so it cannot lift us from earth to heaven. Art and music can distract us briefly from our problems, but they cannot rescue us from despair. Nothing merely human can save us from the endemic human condition. As far as we can tell, everything ends in mean-inglessness and oblivion.

Into this darkness and despair, the Christian church proclaims a mes-sage of light and hope. What human beings despair of doing, God has done. In the birth, life, teaching, death, and resurrection of Jesus Christ, God has rewritten the sad history of sin and death. As the son of Abraham and David, Jesus rewrites Israel's story, makes a new covenant, and renews the people of God. As the son of Adam, Jesus corrects the history of disobedi-ence and idolatry and through his faithful service reverses the sin of Adam to become a new beginning for the human family. Through his death and resurrection Jesus leaves behind the sphere where sin, death, and the devil reign. In faith, obedience, and love he faced our enemies, suffered their fury, and conquered them. He escaped human wretchedness and realized the possibilities for human greatness. From this place, he is able to rescue us from these wretched powers and endow us with greatness, glory, incorrupt-ibility, and immortality. No power in heaven or on earth can stop him from doing what his love compels him to do.

Communicating the Good News

Things Not to Say

First, if you want to communicate the good news of salvation to your neigh-bors, understand that you do not have to ask them to confess that they are such horrible sinners that they "are prone to hate God and their neighbors,"[1] or that they wish to commit "Deicide."[2] Our listeners can admit that they "fall short of the glory of God" (Rom 3:23) and that they have done wrong, incurred guilt, and need God's forgiveness. But no one can believe that they hate God to the core of their being. As I pointed out in my critique of the evangelical penal substitution view, this demand arises from carelessly equating the character of sin, absolutely considered, with our intentions. Hu-man beings act in sinful ways, but they are not by nature sin itself. Sin is our enemy, a cruel master bent on our destruction. It lies and deceives. In con-fessing our sins, we admit that in our stupidity and weakness we cooperate with our enemies and that we do not have the strength to free ourselves from their grip. In hearing the gospel, people can actually come to this realization

---

1. *The Heidelberg Catechism* 5, Schaff, *CC* 3:311. I changed the original singular to the plural to make it fit my sentence structure.

2. Quenstedt, *Theologia didactico-polemica sive systema theologicum,* quoted in Franks, *The Work of Christ,* 416.

and cry out in all sincerity, "God, have mercy on me, a sinner" (Luke 18:13). So, do not tell them that they hate God.

Second, if you want people to receive the gospel of Christ as good news, do not ask them to believe that God's eternal justice makes it necessary for him to punish every sin with an infinite punishment. Do not try to defend Jonathan Edwards's description of God's attitude toward us:

> It will follow, that it is requisite that God should punish all sin with infinite punishment; because all sin, as it is against God, is infinitely heinous, and has infinite demerit, is justly infinitely hateful to him, and so stirs up infinite abhorrence and indignation in him.[3]

No amount of mental gymnastics can twist the mind into this shape. People will always wonder, even if they are afraid to ask, *why* God must punish sin so that he can forgive it. What kind of forgiveness is that? Post-Reformation Protestant scholastic theologians and all who follow them tie themselves into knots trying to explain away this obvious contradiction.[4] They argue that "to forgive" need not always mean to reconcile without exacting retribution or making satisfaction. God can forgive and reconcile sinners without exacting satisfaction *from them* because God receives it from Jesus. God shows his love by offering his Son as our substitute and displays his retributive justice by punishing the innocent Jesus for our sins. Despite their heroic efforts, however, they cannot escape the contradiction. Clearly, if someone else pays my debt I am no longer under obligation. But it would not be correct to say that my debt was *forgiven.* At the end of complicated arguments to the contrary, we are still left with the disturbing thought that God cannot really forgive sin.[5] Forgiveness is like love. It is either completely free or it is not forgiveness at all. As I argued when discussing the evangelical penal substitution theory, the primal source of this contradiction is a distorted definition of divine justice as "giving everyone their due." Theologians' thoughtless incorporation of this defective definition of divine justice into the doctrine of atonement produces tensions, paradoxes, and deformities throughout the doctrine. So, if you want to share the good news about salvation, do not

---

3. Edwards, "Concerning the Necessity," 565. Notice the obvious equivocation in Edwards between "sin" and the "sinner." Edwards lets us conclude that because "*sin*" is hateful to God *sinners* are hateful to God, an obvious non sequitur.

4. See the argument made in Anselm, *Why God Became Man*, 86. Francis Turretin makes a similar argument in many places. See *IET* 14.10.17:422.

5. In Craig, *The Atonement*, we find illustrated in abundance the principle that arguments do not get better just by adding more steps.

place God's willingness to forgive under the shadow of a divine obligation to execute retributive justice on every sin.

Third, if you want our contemporaries to hear the good news, do not ask them to believe that God's "great love" (Eph 2:4; 1 John 3:1) for them was manifested in God's action of pouring out his infinite wrath and exacting his retributive justice on the innocent Jesus. However valiantly such evangelical theologians as Turretin, Edwards, Hodge, Packer, and Craig attempt to lighten the image and distract from the sight, many of our contemporaries see in this portrayal a dark, irrational side to God. Behind God's smiling face they see a brooding, unforgiving nature. Of course, this type of critique of penal substitution has been in many writers exaggerated to the point of caricature.[6] Yet it is hard to erase the thought that, in this telling of the story, Jesus represents the loving side of God and the Father the vengeful side. Jesus steps between God and us and saves us from God. In my view, this is a great distortion of the biblical picture of the God and Father of our Lord Jesus Christ. *God* is not the enemy. Sin, death, and the devil are the enemies. God is the *savior*. And Jesus embodies perfectly God's loving and just character and carries out the Father's saving plan in complete continuity with the Father. God did not pour out his wrath on Jesus. In Jesus, God embraced human nature and walked with us through life, temptation, suffering, shame, and death to save us from our enemies and bring us to glory. And this is the demonstration of God's great love (Eph 2:4; 1 John 3:1). Preach this message.

Keep It Simple

In teaching the history of the doctrine of the atonement in the university and the church and in explaining the many theories that have been proposed, I have discovered that very few believers draw comfort from any of them. Nor do outsiders come to faith because of them. They find assurance in believing that Jesus died for their sins and that his death demonstrates God's love for them. But they do not need theories that explain the connection between God's forgiveness and Jesus's suffering and death. When they hear these theories presented in detail they receive them at best as curiosities that do little to increase their awareness of divine forgiveness. They may experience the opposite effect and react like the fellow who complained, "I would not have doubted God's existence if you had not tried to prove it." In the course of meditating on the subject of the atonement day and night in the

---

6. For examples, see many of the essays in Brown and Bohn, *Christianity, Patriarchy, and Child Abuse.*

five years I worked on this book, I kept asking myself a series of questions: Why do I believe that I am forgiven? Why do I believe that God loves me and extends grace to me? Why do I believe that I am free from the power of sin, death, and the devil? At some point, I realized that my confidence in God's forgiveness does not derive from the power of traditional theories of atonement to make these truths clear to me. Each theory points in the direction of the truth, but each is also troublingly obscure in some way. I realized that I believe that God loves me, I am forgiven, God is my Father, and I am his beloved child *because Jesus said so.* I believe that Jesus told the truth in all sincerity because he sealed his word with his blood. Why accept Jesus's sincere word as the truth about God's forgiveness? Because God raised him from the dead, thereby validating his witness and vindicating his character. Perhaps there are more reasons to believe in divine forgiveness, more profound explanations of the atonement, and more nuanced treatments of the justice and mercy of God. However, when my best reasoning fails to bring peace to my heart, I cling to Jesus's words: "Do not be afraid; you are worth more than many sparrows!" (Luke 12:7). Jesus gave his life in witness to this truth, and God witnessed to Jesus's veracity by raising him from the dead. Nothing I have said in this book can add to or detract from the certainty of this truth grounded as it is in the resurrection of Jesus. At best, I hope to help readers explore its more obvious presuppositions and implications and therein find greater joy in its beauty. So, *keep it simple,* and let believers draw comfort from Jesus's words. Treat Jesus's witness to God's grace as a solid foundation on which to build a more intelligent faith rather than as scaffolding to be removed after theological maturity has been achieved.

Tell the Story of Jesus

I believe that people living today, churched or unchurched, can understand the Christian gospel of salvation I have presented in this book as very good news: wounded hearts healed, sin forgiven, slaves freed, the devil cast out, and the dead raised. Hopes realized, joy made perfect, and possibilities made actual. If anything, to modern ears the message sounds too good to be true, a fairy tale where everyone gets a happy ending. And they would be right to doubt, were it not for Jesus. Jesus of Nazareth is not a fairy-tale character, an unattainable moral ideal, or a myth. He is one of us, born of Mary during the reign of Augustus Caesar and crucified in Judea under Pontius Pilate as a blasphemer and a rebel. He entered our condition of wretchedness and greatness. He loved, he hungered and thirsted, he worked, he suffered, he bled, and he died. But God raised him from the dead and declared him to be savior and Lord. In Jesus, our humanity has been united to God, glorified, and made immortal. The Christian message of salvation proclaims that what God did for Jesus our brother he will do for us through Jesus our savior. The church should incessantly tell Jesus's story as the story of salvation, the story of how God deals with our wretchedness and brings us to a glorious destiny. It should proclaim to everyone that Jesus's story is the true human story. It is Adam's story retold, Israel's story rewritten, and our story baptized and reborn. If you want to communicate the Christian message of salvation to our age, I will say it again, *tell the story of Jesus.*

Bibliography

Abel, Frantisek. "'Death as the Last Enemy': Interpretation of Death in the Context of Paul's Theology." *CV* 58 (2016) 19–54.

Anderson, Ray. "On Being Human: The Spiritual Saga of a Creaturely Soul." In *Whatever Happened to the Soul? Scientific and Theological Portraits of Human Nature*, edited by Warren S. Brown et al., 175–94. Minneapolis: Fortress, 1998.

Anselm, *Saint Anselm: Basic Writings*. 2nd ed. Translated by S. N. Deane. LaSalle, IL: Open Court, 1968.

Aristotle. *The Basic Writings of Aristotle*. Edited by Richard McKeon. New York: Random House, 1941.

Athanasius. *First Letter to Sarapion*. In *The Letters of Saint Athanasius Concerning the Holy Spirit*, translated by C. R. B. Shapland, 58–149. London: Epworth, 1951.

———. *On the Incarnation of the Word*. Translated by a religious of C.S.M.V. Crestwood, NY: Saint Vladimir's Seminary Press, 2003.

Augustine. *Saint Augustine Confessions*. Translated by Henry Chadwick. New York: Oxford University Press, 1991.

Aulén, Gustaf. *Christus Victor: An Historical Study of the Three Main Types of the Idea of Atonement*. Translated by A. G. Herbert. London: SPCK, 1965.

Bailey, Daniel P. "Jesus as the Mercy Seat: The Semantics and Theology of Paul's Use of Hilastērion in Romans 3:25." *Tyndale Bulletin* 51.1 (2000) 155–58.

Baker, Mark D., and Joel B. Green. *Recovering the Scandal of the Cross: Atonement in New Testament and Contemporary Contexts*. 2nd ed. Downers Grove, IL: Intervarsity, 2011.

Barth, Karl. *Church Dogmatics*. 4 vols. Translated by Geoffrey W. Bromiley and T. F. Torrance. Edinburgh: T. & T. Clark, 1936–69.

Bavinck, Herman. *Reformed Dogmatics*. 4 vols. Translated by John Vriend. Grand Rapids: Baker Academic, 2003–8.

Behr, John. "Irenaeus of Lyon." In *T&T Clark Companion to Atonement*, edited by Adam J. Johnson, 569–75. London: Bloomsbury T. & T. Clark, 2017.

Berkhof, Hendrikus. *Christian Faith: Introduction to the Study of the Faith*. Rev. ed. Translated by Sierd Woudstra. Grand Rapids: Eerdmans, 1986.

Berkhof, Louis. *Systematic Theology*. 1938. Reprint, Louisville: GLH, 2017.

Berkouwer, G. C. *Sin*. Translated by Philip C. Holtrop. Studies in Dogmatics, vol. 11. Grand Rapids: Eerdmans, 1971.

Billings, J. Todd. "John Calvin: United to God through Christ?" In *Partakers of the Divine Nature: The History and Development of Deification in the Christian Traditions*, edited by Michael J. Christensen and Jeffery A. Wittung, 200–218. Grand Rapids: Baker Academic, 2008.

Blackwell, Ben C. *Christosis: Engaging Paul's Soteriology with His Patristic Interpreters*. Grand Rapids: Eerdmans, 2016.

Borg, Marcus. "Executed by Rome, Vindicated by God." In *Stricken by God? Nonviolent Identification and the Victory of Christ*, edited by Brad Jersak and Michael Hardin, 150–63. Grand Rapids: Eerdmans, 2007.

————. *Speaking Christian: Why Christian Words Have Lost Their Meaning and Power—and How They Can Be Restored*. New York: HarperOne, 2011.

Bouteneff, Peter C. *Beginnings: Ancient Christian Readings of the Biblical Creation Narratives*. Grand Rapids: Baker Academic, 2008.

Brown, Colin, ed. *New International Dictionary of New Testament Theology*. 4 vols. Grand Rapids: Zondervan, 1986.

Brown, Derek R. *The God of this Age: Satan and Letters of Paul the Apostle*. Tübingen: Mohr Siebeck, 2015.

Brown, Joanne Carlson, and Carole R. Bohn, eds. *Christianity, Patriarchy, and Child Abuse: A Feminist Critique*. New York: Pilgrim, 1989.

Calvin, John. *Institutes of the Christian Religion*. 2 vols. Edited by John T. McNeill. Translated by Ford Lewis Battles. Philadelphia: Westminster, 1960.

Catechism of the Catholic Church. Washington, DC: United States Catholic Conference, 1994.

Chalke, Steven, and Alan Mann. *The Lost Message of Jesus*. Grand Rapids: Zondervan, 2003.

Clements, Keith W., ed. *Friedrich Schleiermacher: Pioneer of Modern Theology*. Minneapolis: Fortress, 1991.

Cohn, Hans W. *Existential Thought and Therapeutic Practice: An Introduction to Existential Psychotherapy*. London: Sage, 1997.

Copleston, Frederick. *A History of Philosophy*. 9 vols. New York: Image Doubleday, 1994.

Cortez, Marc. *Resourcing Theological Anthropology*. Grand Rapids: Zondervan, 2017.

Cottingham, John. "Varieties of Retribution." *PQ* 29 (1979) 238–46.

Cottrell, Jack. *The Faith Once Delivered: Bible Doctrine for Today*. Joplin: College, 2002.

Craig, William Lane. *The Atonement*. New York: Cambridge University Press, 2018.

Crisp, Oliver. "Penal Non-Substitution." *JTS* 59 (2008) 140–68.

Cyril of Alexandria. *Commentary on John*. Edited by Joel C. Elowsky. Translated by David R. Maxwell. Downers Grove, IL: Intervarsity, 2013.

————. *Five Tomes against Nestorius*. Oxford: Parker and Rivingtons, 1881.

Dabney, Lyle D. "Schleiermacher, Friedrich Daniel Ernst." In *Biographical Dictionary of Christian Theologians*, edited by Patrick W. Carey and Joseph T. Lienhard, 450–54. Peabody, MA: Hendrickson, 2002.

Deurzen, Emmy van. *Paradox and Passion in Psychotherapy: An Existential Approach to Therapy and Counselling*. Chichester, UK: John Wiley, 1998.

Dillon, John. *The Middle Platonists: 80 B.C. to 220 A.D.* Ithaca, NY: Cornell University Press, 1996.

Dodd, C. H. *The Epistle of Paul to the Romans.* London: Hodder and Stroughton, 1932.

———. *The Johannine Epistles.* London: Hodder and Stroughton, 1946.

Dostoevsky, Fyodor. *The Brothers Karamazov: A Norton Critical Edition.* 2nd ed. Translated by Constance Garnett, edited by Susan McReynolds Oddo. New York: Norton, 2011.

Edwards, Jonathan. *The Works of Jonathan Edwards.* 2 vols. 1834. Reprint, Peabody, MA: Hendrickson, 1998.

Emonet, Pierre-Marie. *The Greatest Marvel of Nature: An Introduction to the Philosophy of the Human Person.* Translated by Robert R. Barr. New York: Crossroad, 2000.

Ensor, Peter. "Clement of Alexandria and Penal Substitutionary Atonement." *EQ* 85 (2013) 19–35.

———. "Justin Martyr and Penal Substitutionary Atonement." *EQ* 83 (2011) 217–32.

———. "Penal Substitutionary Atonement in the Later Ante-Nicene Period." *EQ* 87 (2015) 331–46.

———. "Tertullian and Penal Substitutionary Atonement." *EQ* 86 (2014) 130–42.

Erickson, Millard. *Christian Theology.* 3rd ed. Grand Rapids: Baker Academic, 2013.

Fee, Gordon D. *Pauline Christology: An Exegetical Theological Study.* Peabody, MA: Hendrickson, 2007.

Festinger, Leon. *A Theory of Cognitive Dissonance.* Stanford: Stanford University Press, 1957.

Festinger, Leon, et al. *When Prophecy Fails.* Minneapolis: University of Minnesota Press, 1956.

Finlan, Stephen. "Can We Speak of Theosis in Paul?" In *Partakers of the Divine Nature: The History and Development of Deification in the Christian Traditions,* edited by Michael J. Christensen and Jeffery A. Wittung, 68–80. Grand Rapids: Baker Academic, 2007.

Forbes, Chris. "Pauline Demonology and/or Cosmology? Principalities, Powers, and the Elements of the World in their Hellenistic Context." *JSNT* 85 (2002) 51–73.

Franks, Robert S. *The Work of Christ: A Historical Study of Christian Doctrine.* 2nd ed. New York: Thomas Nelson, 1962.

Fredrickson, David. "God, Christ, and All Things in 1 Corinthians 15:28." *WW* 18 (1998) 254–63.

Galli, Mark. "It Doesn't Get Any More Personal: Why Evangelicals Give Pride of Place to Penal Substitutionary Understandings of the Cross." *Christianity Today,* January 11, 2018. https://www.christianitytoday.com/ct/2018/january-web-only/penal-substitutionary-atonement-it-doesnt-get-more-personal.html.

Gaster, Theodore H. "Sacrifices and Offerings, OT," In *The Interpreters Dictionary of the Bible,* vol 4, edited by George A. Buttrick, 147–59. Nashville: Abingdon, 1962.

Gaventa, Beverly Roberts. *Our Mother Saint Paul.* Louisville: Westminster John Knox, 2007.

Geisler, Norman L. "Satan, Reality of." In *Baker Encyclopedia of Christian Apologetics,* edited by Norman L. Geisler, 683–84. Grand Rapids: Baker, 1999.

Gorman, Michael J. *Inhabiting the Cruciform God: Kenosis, Justification, and Theosis in Paul's Narrative Soteriology.* Grand Rapids: Eerdmans, 2009.

Green, Joel. "The Kaleidoscopic View." In *The Nature of the Atonement: Four Views,* edited by James Beilby and Paul R. Eddy, 157–85. Downers Grove, IL: Intervarsity, 2006.

Gregory of Nyssa. *Address on Religious Instruction.* In *Christology of the Later Fathers,* edited by Edward R. Hardy, 268–325. Philadelphia: Westminster John Knox, 1954.

———. "On 'Then Also the Son Himself Will Be Subjected to the One Who Subjected All Things to Him.'" In *One Path for All: Gregory of Nyssa on the Christian Life and Human Destiny,* translated by Rowan A. Greer, assisted by J. Warren Smith, 118-32. Eugene, OR: Cascade, 2015.

Grensted, Laurence W. *A Short History of the Doctrine of the Atonement.* London: Longmans, 1920.

Grillmeier. Aloys. *Christ in the Christian Tradition.* Translated by John Bowden. 2nd ed. The Apostolic Age to Chalcedon (451), vol. 1. Atlanta: John Knox, 1975.

Gross, Jules. *Divinization of the Christian according to the Greek Fathers.* Translated by Paul Onica. Anaheim: C & A, 2002.

Grudem, Wayne. *Systematic Theology.* Grand Rapids: Zondervan, 1994.

Gunton, Colin. *The Actuality of Atonement: A Study of Metaphor, Rationality and the Christian Tradition.* Grand Rapids: Eerdmans, 1989.

———. *The Triune Creator: A Historical and Systematic Study.* Grand Rapids: Eerdmans, 1998.

Hansen, Walter G. "Rhetorical Criticism." In *Dictionary of Paul and His Letters,* edited by Gerald. F. Hawthorne and Ralph P. Martin, 822–26. Downers Grove, IL: Intervarsity, 1993.

Harnack, Adolf von. *What Is Christianity?* Translated by Thomas Bailey Saunders. Philadelphia: Fortress, 1986.

Hays, Richard B. *The Faith of Jesus: The Narrative Structure of Galatians 3:1—4:11.* 2nd ed. Grand Rapids: Eerdmans, 2002.

Heppe, Heinrich. *Reformed Dogmatics.* Revised and edited by Ernst Bizer. Translated by G. T. Thomson. 1950. Reprint, London: Wakeman Great Reprints, n.d.

Highfield, Ron. *Barth and Rahner in Dialogue: Toward an Ecumenical Understanding of Sin and Evil.* New York: Peter Lang, 1989.

———. *The Faithful Creator: Affirming Creation and Providence in an Age of Anxiety.* Downers Grove, IL: Intervarsity, 2015.

———. "The Freedom to Say 'No'? Karl Rahner's Doctrine of Sin." *TS* 56 (1995) 485–505.

———. *Great Is the Lord: Theology for the Praise of God.* Grand Rapids: Eerdmans, 2008.

Hodge, Archibald Alexander. *The Atonement.* Philadelphia: Presbyterian Board of Publication, 1867.

———. *Outlines of Theology.* New York: Robert Carter and Brothers, 1860.

Hodge, Charles. *Systematic Theology.* 3 vols. 1872–73. Reprint, Grand Rapids: Eerdmans, 1981.

Holland, Glenn S. "'Delivery, Delivery, Delivery,' Accounting for Performance in the Rhetoric of Paul's Letters." In *Paul and Ancient Rhetoric: Theory and Practice in Its Hellenistic Context,* edited by Stanley E. Porter and Bryan R. Dyer, 119–40. New York: Cambridge University Press, 2016.

Holmes, Stephen R. "Penal Substitution." In *T&T Clark Companion to Atonement,* edited by Adam J. Johnson, 295–314. London: Bloomsbury T. & T. Clark, 2017.

Hornblower, Simon, and Antony Spawforth, eds. *The Oxford Classical Dictionary.* 3rd ed. Oxford: Oxford University Press, 1996.

Horton, Michael. *The Christian Faith: A Systematic Theology for Pilgrims on the Way.* Grand Rapids: Zondervan, 2011.

Jeffrey, Steve, et al. *Pierced for Our Transgressions.* Wheaton, IL: Crossway, 2007.

Jewett, Robert. *Romans: A Commentary.* Minneapolis: Fortress, 2007.

Johnson, Robert, and Adam Cureton. "Kant's Moral Philosophy." In *Stanford Encyclopedia of Philosophy.* Stanford University, 1997. Latest revision, July 7, 2016. https://plato.stanford.edu/entries/kant-moral/.

Jonsson, Gunnlaugur A. *The Image of God: Genesis 1:26—2:3 in a Century of Old Testament Research.* Translated by Michael S. Cheney. Stockholm: Almqvist & Wiksel, 1988.

Kant, Immanuel. *Critique of Practical Reason.* Translated by Thomas Kingsmill Abbott. Mineola, NY: Dover, 2004.

————. *Metaphysics of Morals.* Revised by Lara Denis, translated by Mary Gregor. Cambridge: Cambridge University Press, 2017.

Kasper, Walter. *Jesus the Christ.* Translated by V. Green. New York: Paulist, 1976.

Kelsey, David H. *Eccentric Existence: A Theological Anthropology.* 2 vols. Louisville: Westminster John Knox, 2009.

Kennedy, George A. *New Testament Interpretation through Rhetorical Criticism.* Chapel Hill, NC: University of North Carolina Press, 1984.

Kharlamov, Vladimir. "Rhetorical Application of Theosis in Greek Patristic Theology." In *Partakers of the Divine Nature: The History and Development of Deification in the Christian Traditions,* edited by Michael J. Christensen and Jeffery A. Wittung, 115–31. Grand Rapids: Baker Academic, 2008.

Kierkegaard, Søren. *Sickness unto Death.* Edited and translated by Howard V. and Edna H. Hong. Princeton: Princeton University Press, 1980.

————. *Works of Love.* Translated by Howard V. and Edna H. Hong. New York: Harper, 2009.

Kittel, Gerhard, and Gerhard Friedrich, eds. *Theological Dictionary of the New Testament.* 10 vols. Translated by Geoffrey W. Bromiley. Grand Rapids: Eerdmans, 1964–76.

Kreeft, Peter. *Christianity for Modern Pagans: Pascal's Pensées.* San Francisco: Ignatius, 1991.

Küng, Hans. *Eternal Life? Life After Death as a Medical, Philosophical, and Theological Problem.* Translated by Edward Quinn. Garden City, NY: Doubleday, 1984.

Lacroix, Jean. *Maurice Blondel: An Introduction to the Man and His Philosophy.* New York: Sheed and Ward, 1968.

Lawson, John. *The Biblical Theology of Saint Irenaeus.* Eugene, OR: Wipf & Stock, 2006.

Lee, Sang Meyng. *The Cosmic Drama of Salvation: A Study of Paul's Undisputed Writings from Anthropological and Cosmological Perspectives.* Tübingen: Mohr Siebeck, 2010.

Letham, Robert. *The Work of Christ.* Downers Grove, IL: Intervarsity, 1993.

Licona, Michael R. *The Resurrection of Jesus: A New Historiographical Approach.* Downers Grove, IL: Intervarsity, 2010.

Litwa, M. David. "2 Corinthians 3:18 and Its Implications for *Theosis.*" *JTI* 2 (2008) 117–33.

————. "Transformation through a Mirror: Moses in 2 Cor. 3.18." *JSNT* 34 (2012) 286–97.

———. *We Are Being Transformed: Deification in Paul's Soteriology.* Berlin: de Gruyter, 2012.

Livingston, James C. *Modern Christian Thought.* 2 vols. 2nd ed. Upper Saddle River, NJ: Prentice Hall, 1997.

MacDonald, Gregory. *The Evangelical Universalist.* 2nd ed. Eugene, OR: Cascade, 2012.

Macquarrie, John. *Existentialism.* Harmondsworth, UK: Penguin, 1972.

Marx, Karl. "Economic and Philosophic Manuscripts of 1844." In *Marx-Engles Reader*, edited by Robert C. Tucker, 2nd ed., 66–126. New York: Norton, 1978.

McDermott, Brian O. *Word Become Flesh: Dimensions of Christology.* Collegeville, MN: Liturgical, 1993.

McDonald, H. D. *The Atonement of the Death of Christ in Faith, Revelation, and History.* Grand Rapids: Baker, 1985.

McGuckin, John Anthony. "The Strategic Adaptation of Deification in the Cappadocians." In *Partakers of the Divine Nature: The History and Development of Deification in the Christian Traditions,* edited by Michael J. Christensen and Jeffery A. Wittung, 96–114. Grand Rapids: Baker Academic, 2017.

McLachlan, James Morse. *The Desire to be God: Freedom and the Other in Sartre and Berdyaev.* New York: Lang, 1992.

McLeod, Frederick G. *The Image of God in the Antiochene Tradition.* Washington, DC: Catholic University Press of America, 1999.

Middleton, J. Richard. *The Liberating Image: The Imago Dei in Genesis 1.* Grand Rapids: Brazos, 2005.

Milgrom, Jacob. *Leviticus 1–16: A New Translation with Introduction and Commentary.* Anchor Bible. New York: Doubleday, 1991.

Minns, Denis. *Ireneaus: An Introduction.* London: T. & T. Clark, 2010.

Mitchell, Margaret Mary. *Paul and the Rhetoric of Reconciliation: An Exegetical Investigation of the Language and Composition of 1 Corinthians.* Louisville: Westminster John Knox, 1993.

Molnar, Paul D. "Karl Rahner and Thomas F. Torrance: God's Self-Communication in Christ with Special Emphasis on Interpreting Christ's Resurrection." In *Divine Freedom and the Doctrine of the Immanent Trinity,* 167–96. Edinburgh: T. & T. Clark, 2002.

Morris, Leon. *The Apostolic Preaching of the Cross.* London: Tyndale, 1955.

Mullen, John Douglas. *Kierkegaard's Philosophy: Self-Deception and Cowardice in the Present Age.* New York: New American Library, 1981.

Nichol, Roger. "C. H. Dodd and the Doctrine of Propitiation." *WTJ* 17 (1955) 117–57.

Olbricht, Thomas H. "The Foundations of the Ethos in Paul and in the Classical Rhetoricians." In *Rhetoric, Ethic, and Moral Persuasion in Biblical Discourse: Essays from the 2002 Heidelberg Conference,* edited by Thomas H. Olbricht and Anders Eriksson, 138–59. London: T. & T. Clark, 2005.

Ortis, Jared, ed. *Deification in the Latin Patristic Tradition.* Washington, DC: Catholic University of America Press, 2019.

Osborn, Eric. *Irenaeus of Lyon.* Cambridge: Cambridge University Press, 2001.

Packer, J. I., and Mark Dever. *In My Place Condemned He Stood: Celebrating the Glory of the Atonement.* Wheaton, IL: Crossway, 2007.

Pannenberg, Wolfhart. *Anthropology in Theological Perspective.* Translated by Matthew J. O'Connell. Philadelphia: Westminster, 1985.

————. *Jesus—God and Man*. 2nd ed. Translated by Lewis L. Wilkins and Duane A. Priebe. Philadelphia: Westminster, 1977.

————. "On Historical and Theological Method." In *Basic Questions in Theology*, vol. 1, translated by George H. Kehm, 137–81. Reprint, 1970. Philadelphia: Westminster, 1983.

————. *Systematic Theology*. 3 vols. Translated by Geoffrey W. Bromiley. Grand Rapids: Eerdmans, 1994.

Pascal, Blaise. *Pensées*. Translated by A. J. Krailsheimer. London: Penguin, 1966.

Pelikan, Jaroslav. *Christianity and Classical Culture*. New Haven: Yale University Press, 1993.

Prenter, Regin, *Creation and Redemption*. Translated by Theodor I. Jensen. Philadelphia: Fortress, 1967.

Pritchard, James B., ed. *Ancient Near Eastern Texts Relating to the Old Testament*. 3rd ed. Princeton: Princeton University Press, 1969.

Rahner, Karl. "Guilt, Responsibility, and Punishment within the View of Catholic Theology." In *Theological Investigations*, vol. 6, *Concerning Vatican Council II*, translated by Karl-H and Boniface Kruger, 197–217. New York: Crossroad, 1982.

————. "Sin II: Punishment of Sin." In *Encyclopedia of Theology: The Concise Sacramentum Mundi*, edited by Karl Rahner, 1586–88. New York: Crossroad, 1975.

Risner, Rainer. *Paul's Early Period: Chronology, Mission, Theology*. Translated by Doug Stott. Grand Rapids: Eerdmans, 1998.

Ritschl, Albrecht. *The Christian Doctrine of Justification and Reconciliation: The Positive Development of Doctrine*. Translated by H. R. Mackintosh and A. B. Macaulay. Edinburgh: T. & T. Clark, 1900.

————. "Instruction in the Christian Religion." In *Albrecht Ritschl: Three Essays*, translated by Philip Hefner, 221–91. Minneapolis: Fortress, 1972.

Roberts, Alexander, and James Donaldson, eds. *Ante-Nicene Fathers*. 1885–87. 10 vols. Reprint, Grand Rapids: Eerdmans, 1988.

Rupp, George. *Culture Protestantism: German Liberal Theology at the Turn of the Twentieth Century*. Missoula: Scholars, 1977.

Russell, Norman. "A Common Christian Tradition: Deification in the Greek and Latin Fathers." In *Deification in the Latin Patristic Tradition*, edited by Jared Ortis, 272–94. Washington, DC: Catholic University of America Press, 2019.

————. *The Doctrine of Deification in the Greek Patristic Tradition*. Oxford: Oxford University Press, 2004.

Rutledge, Fleming. *The Crucifixion: Understanding the Death of Jesus Christ*. Grand Rapids: Eerdmans, 2015.

Sartre, Jean-Paul. *Being and Nothingness*. Translated by Hazel E. Barns. New York: Citadel, 1969.

Schaff, Philip, ed. *Creeds of Christendom*. 3 vols. 6th ed. 1931. Reprint, Grand Rapids, Baker, 1990.

————. *Nicene-Post Nicene Fathers*. Series 2. 1890–99. 14 vols. Reprint, Grand Rapids: Eerdmans, 1988.

Schillebeeckx, Edward. *Jesus: An Experiment in Christology*. New York: Seabury, 1979.

Schleiermacher, Friedrich. *The Christian Faith*. Edited by H. R. Mackintosh and J. S. Stewart. Philadelphia: Fortress, 1976.

————. *On Religion: Speeches to Its Cultured Despisers.* Edited by Richard Crouter. Cambridge: Cambridge University Press, 1996.

Schmid, Heinrich. *Doctrinal Theology of the Evangelical Lutheran Church.* Translated by Charles A. Hay and Henry Jacobs. 1899. Reprint, Minneapolis: Augsburg, 1961.

Schmiechen, Peter. *Saving Power: Theories of Atonement and Forms of the Church.* Grand Rapids: Eerdmans, 2005.

Schürer, Emil. *The History of the Jewish People in the Age of Jesus Christ.* 2 vols. Revised and edited by Geza Vermes and Fergus Millar. Edinburgh: T. & T. Clark, 1973.

Scott, Charles A. Anderson. *Christianity according to St Paul.* 1927. Reprint, Cambridge: Cambridge University Press, 1961.

Sedley, David. *Creationism and Its Critics in Antiquity.* Berkeley: University of California Press, 2007.

————. "The Ideal of Godlikeness." In *Plato 2: Ethics, Politics, Religion, and the Soul,* edited by Gail Fine, 309–28. Oxford: Oxford University Press, 1999.

Seeberg, Reinhold. *Text-Book of the History of Doctrines.* 2 vols. Translated by Charles Hay. Grand Rapids: Baker, 1977.

Selby, Gary S. *Not with Wisdom of Words.* Grand Rapids: Eerdmans, 2016.

————. "Paul the Seer: The Rhetorical Persona in 1 Corinthians 2:1–16." In *The Rhetorical Analysis of Scripture; Essays from the 1995 London Conference,* edited by Stanley E. Porter and Thomas H. Olbricht, 351–73. Sheffield, UK: Sheffield Academic, 1997.

Shedd, William. *Dogmatic Theology.* 3 vols. New York: Scribner's Sons, 1891.

Southern Baptist Convention 2017 Resolutions. http://www.sbcannualmeeting.net / sbc17/resolution?ID=2278.

Starr, James. "Does 2 Peter 1:4 Speak of Deification?" In *Partakers of the Divine Nature: The History and Development of Deification in the Christian Traditions,* edited by Michael J. Christensen and Jeffery A. Wittung, 81–92. Grand Rapids: Baker Academic, 2007.

Storm, Anthony D. "The Concept of Anxiety." http://sorenkierkegaard.org/concept-of-anxiety.html.

Tidball, Derek, et al., eds. *The Atonement Debate: Papers from the London Symposium on the Theology of Atonement.* Grand Rapids: Zondervan, 2008.

Tobin, Thomas H. *Paul's Rhetoric in Its Context: The Argument of Romans.* Grand Rapids: Baker Academic, 2005.

Tolstoy, Leo. *A Confession.* Translated by Aylmer Maude. Mineola, NY: Dover, 2005.

Torrance, Thomas F. *Space, Time and Resurrection.* Edinburgh: T. & T. Clark, 1998.

Trinkaus, Charles. *In Our Image and Likeness: Humanity and Divinity in Italian Humanist Thought.* 2 vols. Notre Dame, IN: University of Notre Dame Press, 1995.

Tucker, Robert. *Philosophy and Myth in Karl Marx.* Cambridge: Cambridge University Press, 1961.

Turretin, Francis. *Institutes of Elenctic Theology.* 3 vols. Edited by James T. Dennison, Jr., translated by George Musgrave Giger. Phillipsburg, NJ: Presbyterian and Reformed, 1992.

Van Kooten, George H. *Paul's Anthropology in Context: The Image of God, Assimilation to God and the Tripartite Man in Ancient Judaism, Ancient Philosophy and Early Christianity.* Wissenschaftliche Untersuchungen zum Neuen Testament 232. Tübingen: Mohr Siebeck, 2012.

Vishnevshaya, Elana. "Divinization as Perichoretic Embrace in Maximus the Confessor." In *Partakers of the Divine Nature: The History and Development of Deification in the Christian Traditions*, edited by Michael J. Christensen and Jeffery A. Wittung, 132–45. Grand Rapids: Baker Academic, 2017.

Walen, Alic. "Retributive Justice." In *Stanford Encyclopedia of Philosophy*. Stanford University, 1997–. Article published June 18, 2014. https://plato.stanford.edu/archives/win2016/entries/justice-retributive/.

Wallace, P. J. "Charles Hodge." In *Biographical Dictionary of Evangelicals*, edited by Timothy Larsen, 303–7. Downers Grove, IL: Intervarsity, 2003.

Walsh, David. *After Ideology: Recovering the Spiritual Foundations of Freedom.* Washington, DC: Catholic University Press of America, 1995.

Weber, Otto. *Foundations of Dogmatics*. 2 vols. Translated by Darrell L. Gruder. Grand Rapids: Eerdmans, 1983.

Webster, John. "The Dignity of Creatures." In *The Love of God and Human Dignity: Essays in Honor of George Newlands*, edited by Paul Middleton, 19–33. London: T. & T. Clark, 2007.

Weinandy, Thomas. *Jesus The Christ.* No loc: Ex Fontibus, 2017.

Welch, Claude. *Protestant Thought in the Nineteenth Century.* 2 vols. New Haven: Yale University Press, 1985.

Westermann, Claus. *Creation.* Translated by John J. Scullion. Philadelphia: Fortress, 1974.

———. *Genesis 1–11: A Commentary.* Translated by John J. Scullion. Minneapolis: Augsburg, 1984.

Williams, Garry J. "Jonathan Edwards." In *T&T Clark Companion to Atonement*, edited by Adam J. Johnson, 467–71. London: Bloomsbury T. & T. Clark, 2017.

Wink, Walter. *Naming the Powers: The Language of Power in the New Testament.* Philadelphia: Fortress, 1984.

Witherington III, Ben. *New Testament Rhetoric: An Introductory Guide to the Art of Persuasion in and of the New Testament.* Eugene, OR: Cascade, 2009.

Wright, N. T. *The Day the Revolution Began: Reconsidering the Meaning of Jesus's Crucifixion.* San Francisco: HarperOne, 2016.

———. *Evil and the Justice of God.* Downers Grove, IL: Intervarsity, 2006.

———. *Jesus and the Victory of God.* Minneapolis: Fortress, 1996.

———. *The New Testament and the People of God.* Minneapolis: Fortress, 1992.

———. *Paul and the Faithfulness of God.* 2 vols. Minneapolis: Fortress, 2013.

———. *The Resurrection of the Son of God.* Minneapolis: Fortress, 2003.

———. *Surprised by Hope: Rethinking Heaven, the Resurrection, and the Mission of the Church.* New York: HarperOne, 2008.

Subject Index

Abelard, 100
Adam, Jesus as the new Adam, 149–51, 159
Address on Religious Instruction (Gregory of Nyssa), 175–76
Against Heresies (Irenaeus of Lyon), 170
"the age to come"/coming age, 67, 72, 86
Alexander the Great, 63
Anderson, Ray, 28n12
Anselm of Canterbury, 104, 105, 125n22, 182
anxiety, 13–14, 34, 47, 55, 185
Apollinarius, 176, 178
Arians, 172, 173
Aristotle, 4n3, 63, 78, 79, 117
Athanasius, 59, 154, 159, 160, 172–74, 176
atonement
    use of term, 83n2
    alternative theological framework for, 131–32
    cautions in constructing unified theory of, 145
    Christus Victor theory of, 99, 130, 152
    deification or imparting divine life theory of, 99–100
    historical theories of, 98–114
    historiography of theories of, 101–3

moral influence theory of, 100, 133–42
as one unified act, 128
penal substitution theory of, 100, 102. *See also* penal substitutionary atonement (PSA)
ransom theory of, 98–99
recapitulation theory of, 99
satisfaction theory of, 100
as solving a human problem, 131–32
as solving "divine dilemma," according to PSA defenders, 127
The Atonement (Craig), 121–24
The Atonement (Hodge), 114
Augustine of Hippo, 3, 4, 10, 40, 104, 125n21, 182

Baker, Mark, 124n19
Barlaam, 181
Barth, Karl, 27n10, 39n11, 46n23, 53n35
Basil of Caesarea, 174
Bauer, Ferdinance Christian, 101
Bavinck, Herman, 113
Beelzebub, 51
Behr, John, 157
Being and Nothingness (McLachan), 14
Berkhof, Louis, 113, 114
Berkouwer, G. C., 42–43

Scripture Index

Psalms

	48
8	32
8:3–5	29
8:3–5 KJV	30n15
14:1–3	41n16
32:5	37
73:1–14	49
82:6	164n6, 170, 171, 182

Ecclesiastes

1:2	34
7:15	49
8:11	49
8:14	49

Isaiah

10:21	149
25:8	46
40–55	86, 90, 96, 147, 149
51:4	149
52:3—53:12	90
52–53	88
53	88, 91, 100
60:3	149

Jeremiah

27	147
29:13	147
31	86, 87, 96
31:31–34	88

Ezekiel

12	147
40–48	87

Daniel

	88
7, 9, 12	96
7–9	86

9	96
12	96
12:1	88

Deuterocanonical Books

2 Maccabees

6:12–17	147
7:36–38	147

4 Maccabees

6:27–29	147

New Testament

Matthew

	65
4:1–11	51
5–7	38
5:39, 44	65
5:44	65
7:17–19	38
7:28–29	65
10:8	51
10:28	92
12:12–29	99
15:19	38
22:23–32	67
26:17–30	91

Mark

	64
1:1	64
1:5	37
1:13	51
1:15	37, 64
1:17	64
1:21–28	51
1:24	64
1:40–45	64
2:5	65
2:7, 15–17	90